John Buck Iconography

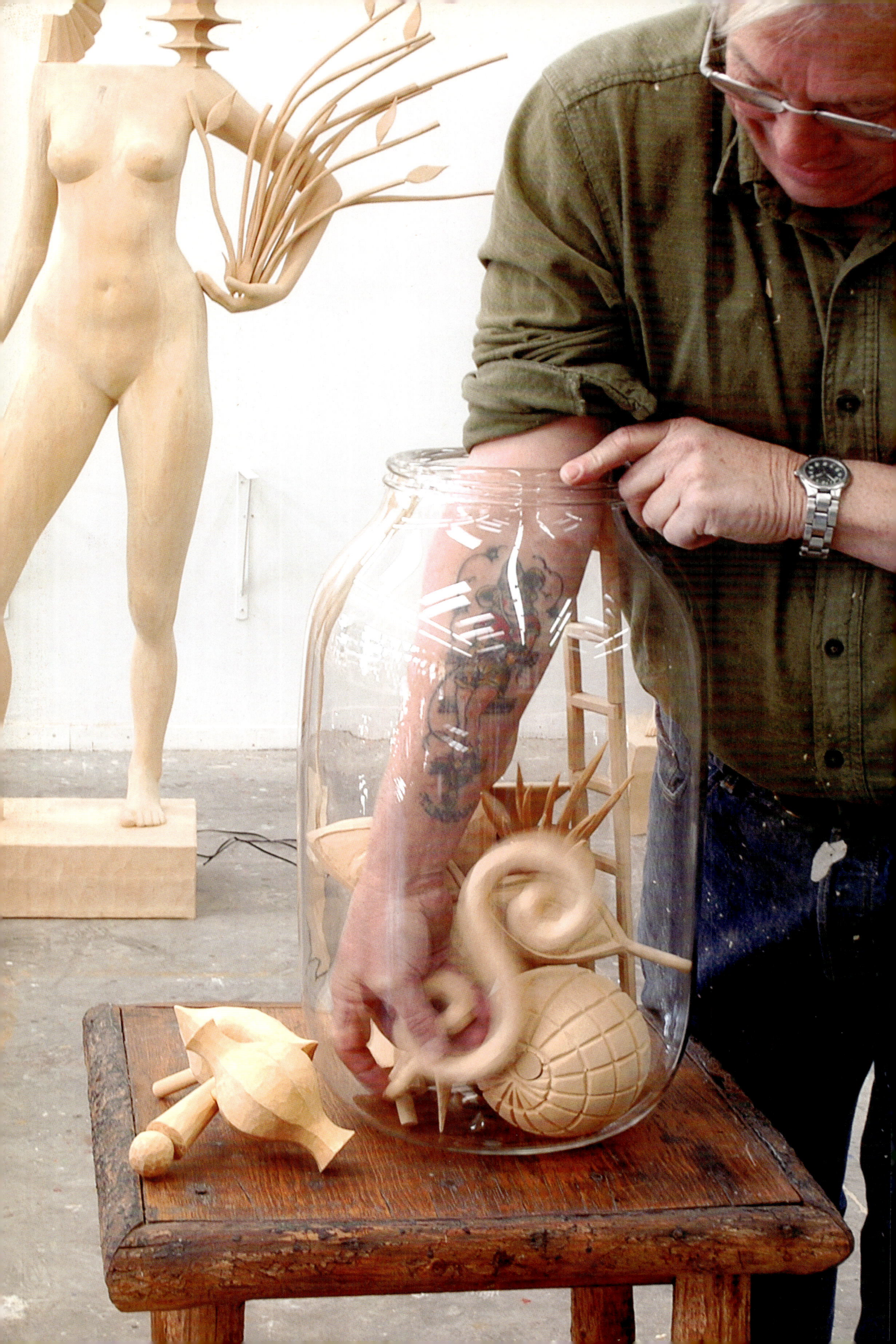

John Buck Iconography

FROM THE COLLECTIONS OF JORDAN D. SCHNITZER
AND HIS FAMILY FOUNDATION

WITH ESSAYS BY

Eleanor Heartney

John Yau

Bud Shark

Organized and curated by Ben Mitchell

NORTHWEST MUSEUM OF ARTS & CULTURE
SPOKANE, WASHINGTON

DISTRIBUTED BY
UNIVERSITY OF WASHINGTON PRESS
SEATTLE AND LONDON

This publication was produced in conjunction with the exhibition *John Buck: Iconography, From the Collections of Jordan D. Schnitzer and his Family Foundation*, organized by Ben Mitchell of the Northwest Museum of Arts & Culture, Spokane, Washington, with major support from the Jordan Schnitzer Family Foundation.

Northwest Museum of Arts & Culture, Spokane, Washington
May 17–November 16, 2008

Fort Wayne Museum of Art, Fort Wayne, Indiana
January 24–April 26, 2009

Cedar Rapids Art Museum, Cedar Rapids, Iowa
May 30–August, 16, 2009

Bellevue Arts Museum, Bellevue, Washington
November 3, 2009–February 28, 2010

Yellowstone Art Museum, Billings, Montana
April–August, 2010

Crocker Museum of Art, Sacramento, California
Fall/Winter 2010–2011

Front cover: *The Times*, 1991
Back cover: *The Inside*, 1998

Library of Congress Control Number: 2008922680

ISBN 978-0-910524-37-7

Distributed by the University of Washington Press
P.O. Box 50096, Seattle, WA 98145 U.S.A.
www.washington.edu/uwpress

Produced and designed by Phil Kovacevich
Editorial review by Sigrid Asmus
Printed in China by Palace Press International

Contents

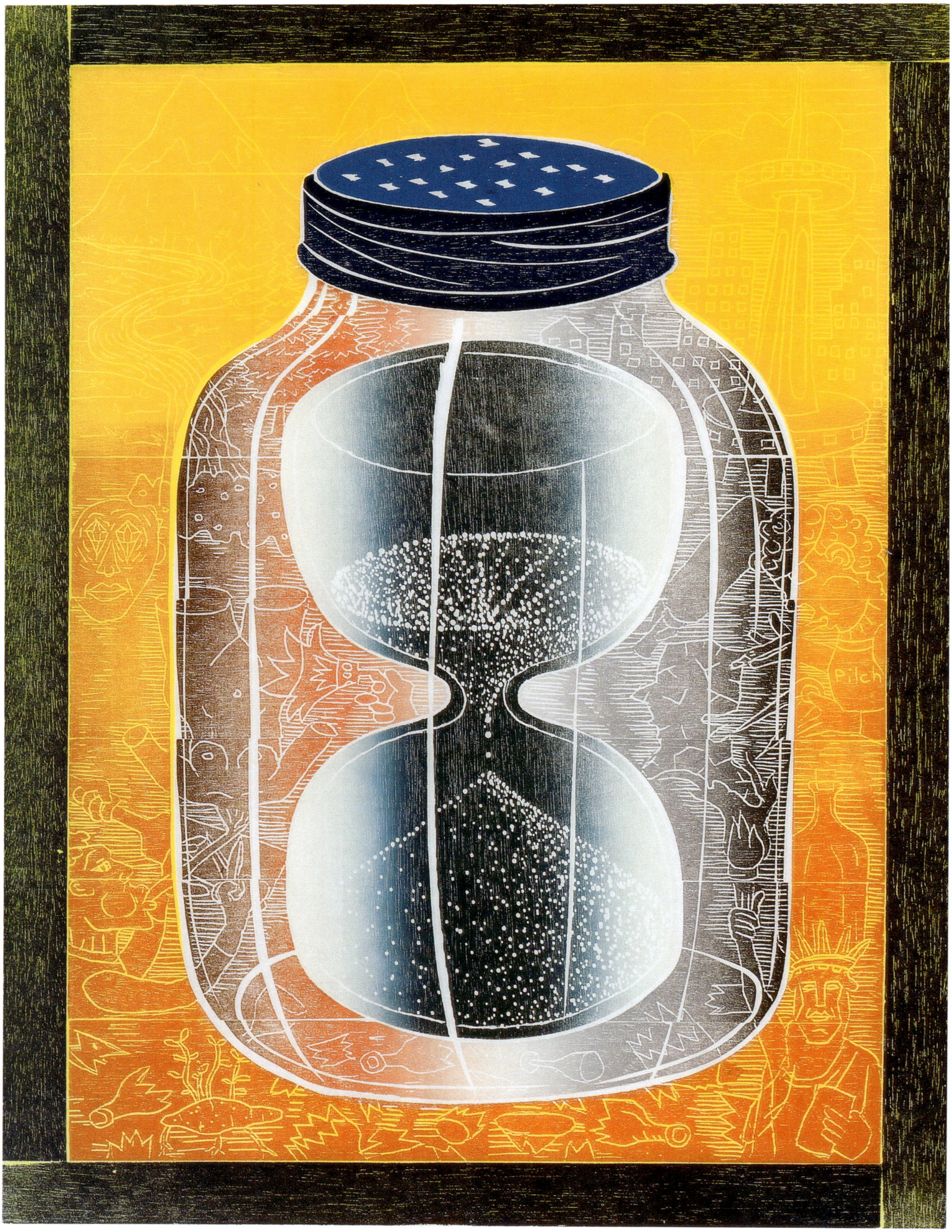

PLATE I

THE GLASS FURNACE, AP 4/4
1997
Fifteen-color woodcut
18 x 23¾ inches

Acknowledgments

This exhibition has been three years in the making, but its true beginnings extend back more than a decade ago when I first visited John Buck's studio, in Bozeman, Montana, to plan an exhibition of his work. As it happened, that project did not work out. But like so many slow-growing things, there was an inherent strength and tenacity in the idea and what has now come to fruition is this rich and dynamic overview of John Buck's marvelous work. An exhibition of this scale and depth is long overdue for John and I am honored to have been a small part of the whole. My deepest thanks to John Buck for his time and limitless patience, but even more for the originality of his insights, and for the deep gifts of his imagination that he brings to us in his art.

This exhibition would not have been possible without the vision, unbounded enthusiasm, and enormous generosity of Jordan Schnitzer. As Mr. Schnitzer's collection grows deeper and larger, so too does his commitment to sharing it with as many people as possible. Jordan Schnitzer and the Jordan Schnitzer Family Foundation provided a major grant that made possible the exhibition and tour and this beautiful exhibition catalogue, as well as significant educational outreach programs. We are deeply appreciative of this support. Additional support for the exhibition and this catalogue was generously provided by *The Spokesman-Review* (Spokane); Scot and Sue Bradley; DC Moore Gallery, New York; Gallery Paule Anglim, San Francisco; Greg Kucera Gallery, Seattle, Washington; Imago Gallery, Palm Desert, California; Robischon Gallery, Denver, Colorado; and the Zolla/Lieberman Gallery, Chicago, Illinois.

For their central and generous contributions to this publication I am privileged to thank Eleanor Heartney and John Yau, whose insights and familiarity with the scope of John Buck's achievement help us find a path toward more fully understanding the artist's beautiful work. Thanks also to master printer Bud Shark for his generous reflections on printing the artist's challenging and complex graphics.

Our gratitude also goes out to many individuals whose tireless efforts and keen professionalism made this project possible. My heartfelt thanks to Kandis Brewer

Nunn, Jordan Schnitzer Family Foundation Vice President, and Catherine Malone, Collections Manager, who with grace and endless generosity of time helped steer a large and complex project through to completion. Thanks also to Kelly Kerwick, Jordan Schnitzer Family Foundation Art Program Manager, who, though joining us in the late innings, has helped enormously. I wish to also acknowledge Dawn Ahlert, John Buck's office manager and assistant in Bozeman, Montana, and Roseanne Colachis at Shark's Ink., who, together with Catherine Malone, and with tireless patience and terrific attention to detail, helped us organize many aspects of this project, especially the Catalogue Raisonné of the artist's prints. Special thanks go out as well to Greg Kucera for his support and belief in the project.

I'm also grateful to Phil Kovacevich, who designed this beautiful book, and to Sigrid Asmus for her editorial review. It is a rare gift to work with colleagues who possess such creativity and intellectual depth.

My Northwest Museum of Arts & Culture colleagues comprise an incomparable team who make this work all the easier. There are too many to name here, but I wish to extend special thanks to Ryan Hardesty and Heidi Arbogast for their wonderful work and ongoing support.

I also wish to thank our many colleagues with whom we are sharing this exhibition: Charles A. Shepherd III, Executive Director, and Sachi Yannari-Rizzo, Curator of Collections and Exhibitions, Fort Wayne Museum of Art, Fort Wayne, Indiana; Terrence Pitts, Executive Director, and Sean Ulmer, Curator, the Cedar Rapids Art Museum, Cedar Rapids, Iowa; Michael Monroe, Executive Director, and Stefano Catalani, Curator, the Bellevue Arts Museum, Bellevue, Washington; Robyn G. Peterson, Executive Director, and Robert Manchester, Senior Curator, the Yellowstone Art Museum, Billings, Montana; and Lial Jones, Museum Director, and Scott Shields, Chief Curator, the Crocker Art Museum, Sacramento, California.

Finally, we are enormously grateful for the interest, care, support, and vision of all those who helped make this exhibition a success.

Ben Mitchell, Senior Curator of Art
Northwest Museum of Arts & Culture

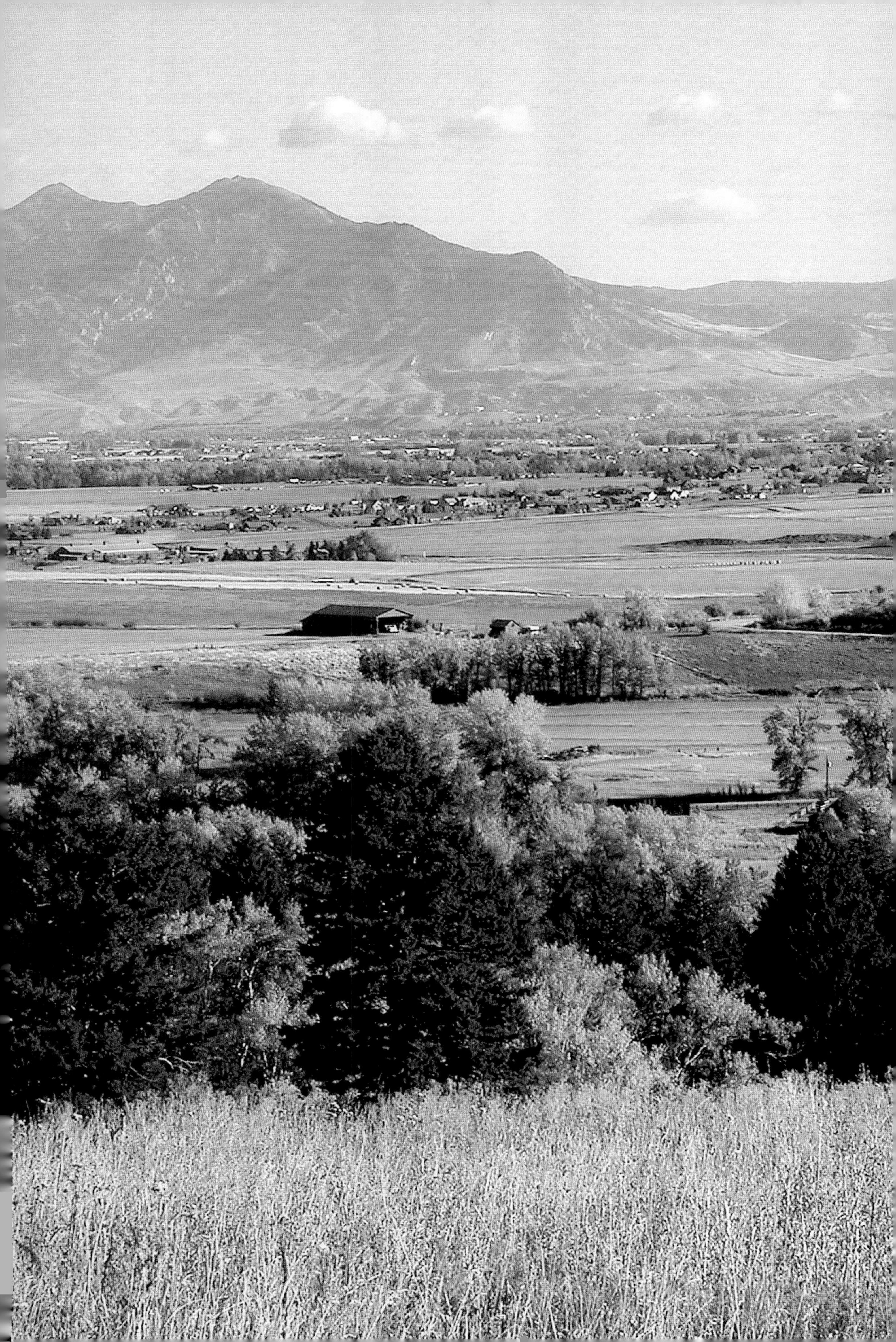

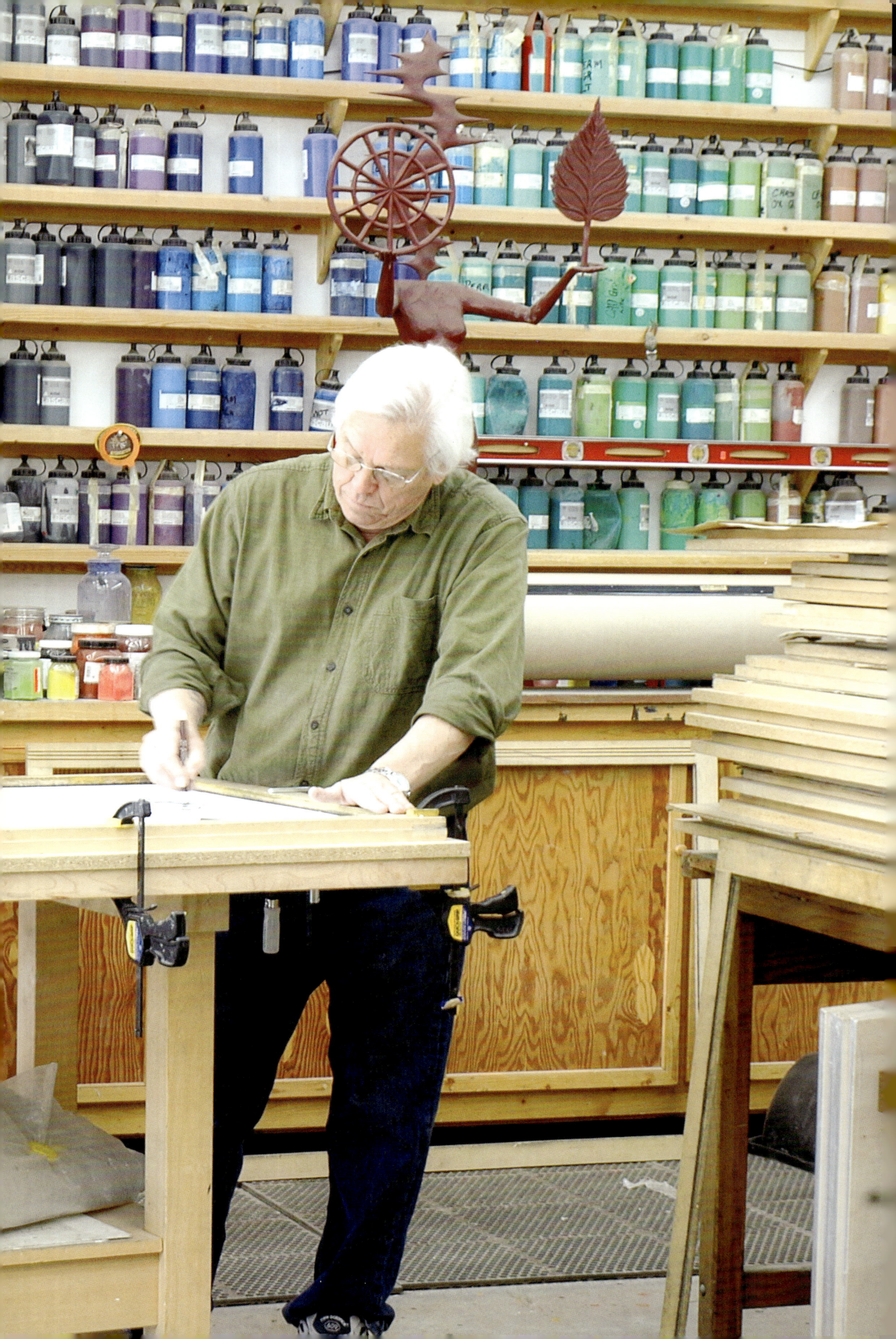

What the Fox Knows: The Art of John Buck

by Eleanor Heartney

The fox knows many things, but the hedgehog knows one big thing.
—Archilochus (7th century BCE)

John Buck is a fox. Among the things he knows are the storied history of modernist art, the narrative play of West Coast funk, the unvarnished directness of folk art, the polemical voice of the political broadside, the tools of the sculptor and the printmaker, the soft give of wood, the fragility of blown glass, and the monumentality of bronze. He also knows the contradictory nature of American politics, the majesty and vulnerability of the natural landscape, the power of symbols, and the enduring pull of national mythology. Above all he knows the danger of utopian thinking.

In *The Hedgehog and the Fox*, his famous essay on Tolstoy, Isaiah Berlin took Archilochus' distinction as a way of distinguishing between thinkers who subscribe to a single, central vision of reality and those who pursue many divergent ends and truths. While hedgehogs are able to articulate social and political systems that may galvanize groups or whole societies, they are prone to dangerous oversimplifications, which, in the worst case, can lead to fascism and tyranny. Foxes take a cautionary view. Aware of the complexity of reality, they refuse to trim its messy ends to achieve an overarching, unitary view. Instead, they are more likely to point to the fault lines that threaten to bring down ambitious intellectual and ideological edifices, and to entertain the possibility of multiple truths and contradictory beliefs.

John Buck's work reflects his fox nature. He works simultaneously in a variety of formats and he articulates ideas drawn from many disciplines. His works include monumental woodcut prints created from blocks that have been pieced together like jigsaw puzzles from pieces of carved wood; wood and cast bronze sculptures consisting of carefully balanced elements that reflect aspects of nature, society, philosophy, and art; wood relief sculptures inset with niches in which he has placed evocative or symbolic objects; and elaborate kinetic constructions that take many of the same elements and set them in motion like circus carousels or gear-crank toys.

Buck makes little distinction between media. Elements that first appear in one format easily gravitate to others, bringing with them an accumulating load of associations. Nor does Buck discriminate between elements of art and things that have drifted into his life from other sources. His home and his studio are full of marvelous objects—among them taxidermied animals, found paintings of Western scenes by untutored artists, trophy fish, cigar boxes, Native American kachinas, Japanese salt and pepper shakers, and tourist glasses emblazoned with their point of origin. Such objects often reappear in his work, set into relationship with other items to create an ever-expanding visual vocabulary. In his work, as in his life, Buck is an inveterate collector. He is not, however, an archivist. Instead, his sensibility more closely resembles those seventeenth-century amateur scientists who assembled Cabinets of Curiosities, delighting in the variety of the natural and human world without worrying about grand classificatory schemes or taxonomic organization.

Buck was born in Iowa in 1946. His father also had dreams of an art career but was forced to put them aside, and instead supported his family as a construction worker. His son was luckier. At the Kansas City Institute and School of Design he learned the basics of sculpture, focusing during his school years on welded steel and bronze casting. This was followed by a stint at the Skowhegan School of Painting and Sculpture in Maine and a Master's degree from the University of California at Davis. In California, Buck met his wife, the artist Deborah Butterfield. After school, he turned to wood carving, in part because he no longer had access to the expensive equipment required for welding and casting. Then, in 1976, Buck and Butterfield moved to Bozeman, Montana. They now live between Bozeman and Hawaii, maintaining a working horse ranch, studios, and a household that currently includes several dogs, cats, and a number of migratory geese. In the course of this journey, the Western landscape and a certain frontier ethos have seeped into Buck's consciousness, broadening and deepening his hands-on approach to art and life.

Two things unite Buck's work. One is the craftsman's intimate knowledge of wood, a material that underlies both his sculptures and prints. In both cases, his work begins with carving into wood. This is most evident in the sculptures and reliefs, which are generally created out of jelutong, a soft wood that is often used in furniture making and whose surface reveals the gouges and marks of the chisel. Even his bronze sculptures are originally fashioned from wood and retain the texture of the carved surface. Wood is also crucial to his graphic works, which are composed of separate pieces carved with a stylus and arranged within a frame. Individual elements can be lifted out and inked separately, then reassembled like pieces of a puzzle. The format of these prints consists of a large central image, surrounded by smaller, linear images that form a kind of memory bank against which the dominant image can be read. Drawing on traditional woodblock print techniques, they often retain traces of the wood grain of the blocks into which the images are incised.

The other thread running through Buck's work is a sensibility that tends toward multiplicity. His prints are characterized by layered images. The smaller linear images that set off the central form deepen and complicate the reading of the print. Colors too are carefully calibrated to bring out meanings and connections. In many of the earlier prints color is rudimentary, often confined to flat black and white and red. More recently, the palette has become complex. Central images are frequently realized in multiple colors, while a rainbow roll gives the background a gently variegated blend of hues. Buck's three-dimensional works are similarly intricate. They consist of assemblages of elements tied together by loose associations. Anchored by a human figure, they feature quatrefoils, stylized foliage, wheels, masks, columns, globes, and abstract organic forms. Both prints and sculptures resist didactic or literal readings, requiring instead a poetic understanding of the way that meaning hovers between and above chains of images.

Such heterogeneity makes Buck well-suited to explore what emerges as one of his overriding concerns—namely, the conflict between our pastoral, utopian ideals and the sad reality of conflict, urbanization, power, militarism. In certain ways, his work is quintessentially American, not only in the focus on craftsmanship and the clarity of his forms, but even more in the recourse to images and symbols that resonate through American history. Buck notes that his prints often offer a direct or indirect commentary on news events, filtered through a linear style that diffuses the content and allows for the juxtaposition of different kinds of information. By playing the central image off a mosaic of smaller images he is able to suggest the complexity and even the contradictory qualities of apparently simple symbols.

Take, for instance, *American Eagle – The Great Divide* (1993) (plate 2, p. 14). This woodcut is dominated by the familiar image of America's national symbol, the Bald Eagle. Here the bird is shown in profile, resting on a branch, a proud symbol of American independence and integrity. Behind it, smaller linear images in black and white tell a different story. One makes out a narrative about the environmental costs of the nation's omnivorous appetite for energy. A rippling highway clogged with cars weaves like a garland behind the bird, between images of factories, urban skylines, oil derricks, energy plants, nuclear cooling towers, denuded forests, and hydroelectric dams. The contradictions between the country's benign image of itself and its destructive appetites could not be clearer.

Similar contradictions abound in *Argosy* (1999) (plate 3, p. 15). Here the dominant image is a potato suspended with toothpicks in a jar of water. Like a child's science experiment, it has grown roots and sprouted. The title is an evocation of the hundred-eyed Argus of Greek mythology. In keeping with this theme, the potato is covered with tiny eyes, making it an observer of the parade of human folly that surrounds it. The background consists of a tapestry of tragicomic images. A blindfolded Mickey Mouse holding a bag of money mocks the symbol of blind Justice that he evokes. Bambi pulls a cart filled with emblems of American power, among them the Capital Building and the Washington Monument. The Statue of Liberty rises from a shopping cart pushed by the shrouded figure of death. Other characters include a skeleton on a pogo stick and several homeless people, one of whom pointedly pokes at an artist's palette. Against this complex backdrop, the glowing green of

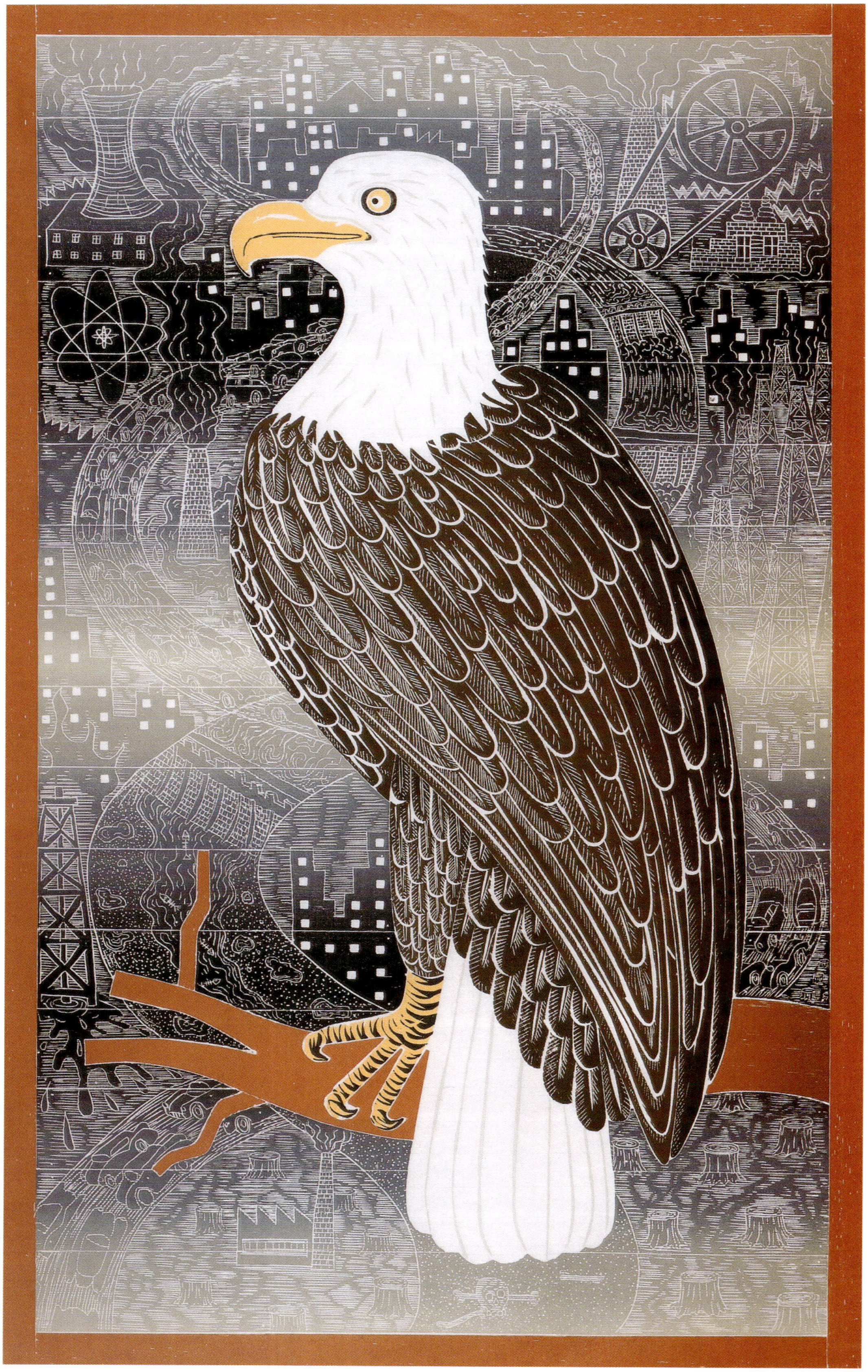

PLATE 2

American Eagle / The Great Divide, edition 10/15

1993

Eleven-color woodcut

60½ x 36½ inches

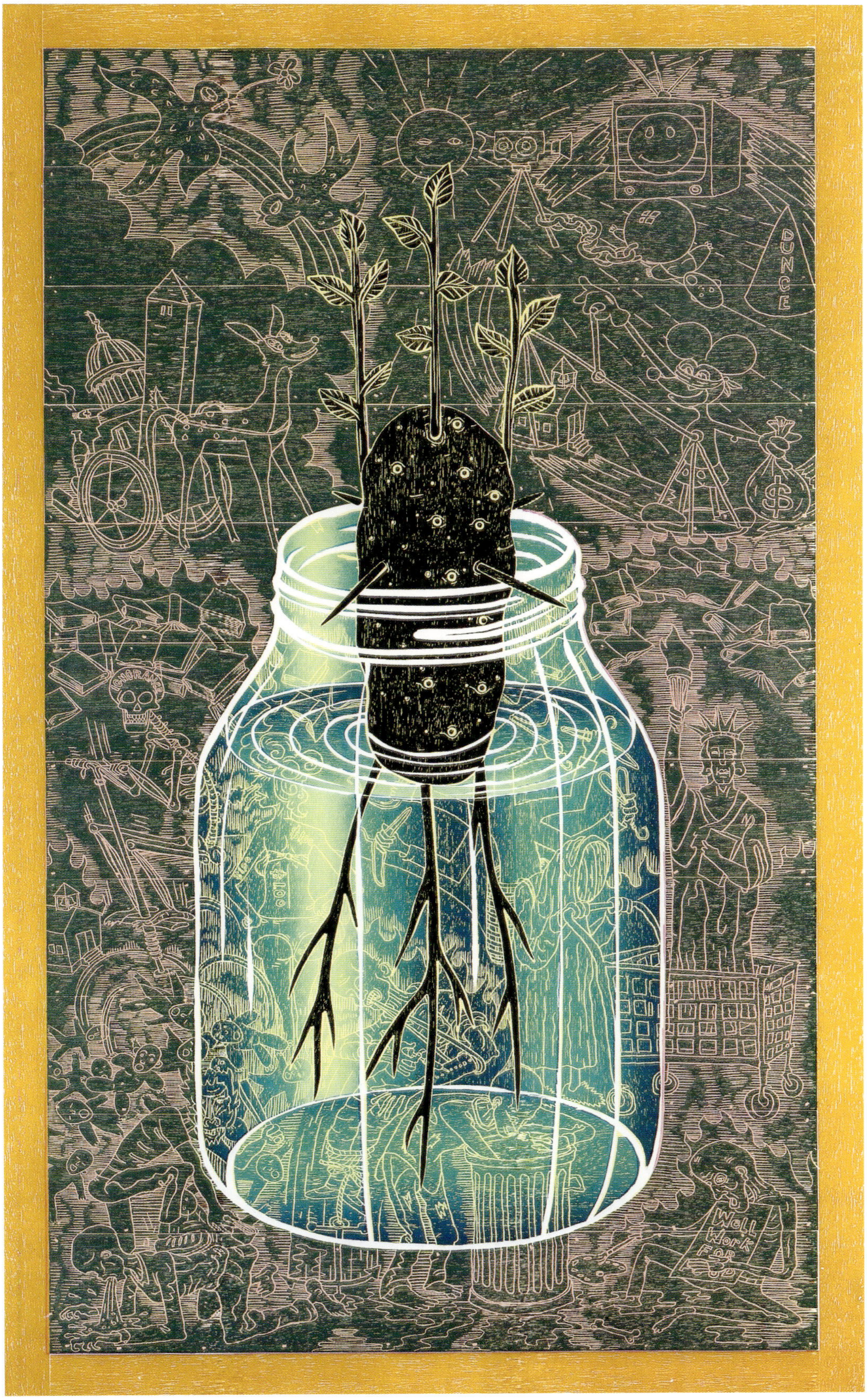

PLATE 3

ARGOSY, edition 10/15
1998 (signed 1999)
Eight-color woodcut
62½ x 37 inches

the jar in which the potato grows suggests a possible choice between the culture of life and the culture of greed, death, and destruction.

In *Trails Plowed Under* (1989) (plate 22, p. 51) images from the natural world serve as symbols of the migration of Mexican immigrants to the United States. Here a giant thistle is emblazoned in white silhouette over a slightly compressed map of South and North America. Palm trees in the lower sector give way to more problematic symbols in the upper quadrant, culminating in the upper right-hand corner with a figure who is being literally split down the middle, suggested the often cruelly divided identity of the immigrant. Laid over the North American continent is a silhouette of the Statue of Liberty, emblem of a welcoming message that no longer seems to apply to residents of the lower hemisphere.

The misuses of religion take center stage in various works. In *Phoenix Rising* (2006) (plate 4, p. 17), the central image is not in fact the phoenix, symbol of resurrection and regeneration, but rather the dodo, that now extinct bird that once populated the island of Mauritius in the Indian Ocean. Behind the dodo in intense shades of red and yellow are a filigree of images referring to civic and religious edifices—including a country church, the U.S. Capital Building, mosques, and even the Tower of Babel, a recurring symbol in Buck's works for the arrogance of power and the failure to communicate across cultures. Spilling around these emblems are swarms of people, presumably the secular and religious armies mobilized by the ideologies represented by these structures. In the context of these background images, the dodo serves as a cautionary emblem of the consequences of an ill-considered mingling of politics and religion.

As this work suggests, Buck does not confine himself to commentary on American events and problems. Many works deal with international crises and conflicts. For instance *Beruit,* of 1983, (plate 6, p. 21) was inspired by the information that Israeli soldiers occupying Lebanon were using its ancient cedars for target practice. Dominating this print is the red image of a leafless tree surrounded by the outlines of human figures and architectural, religious, and other symbols. *Crossroads,* created in 1987 (plate 18, p. 46), takes on South Africa's system of apartheid. The outline of a flame covers a field that suggests the contrasting reality of the workers confined to shantytowns outside the city and the booming metropolis their labor supported. *East/West* (1999) (plate 5, p. 19) presents a human figure within a globe surrounded by symbols of Eastern and Western culture. One glimpses here both their differences as well as the potential for coexistence. With such works, Buck opposes the American tendency toward isolationism, which seems to grow stronger in times of adversity. He decries the desire to circle the wagons, arguing instead for an engagement in the wider world.

Over the years, Buck has developed a recurring vocabulary of images whose meanings accumulate and grow from work to work. One of the most pervasive is the human figure, presented in the pared-down, radical simplicity that we have come to associate with the icon for "person" on international highway and service signs. In

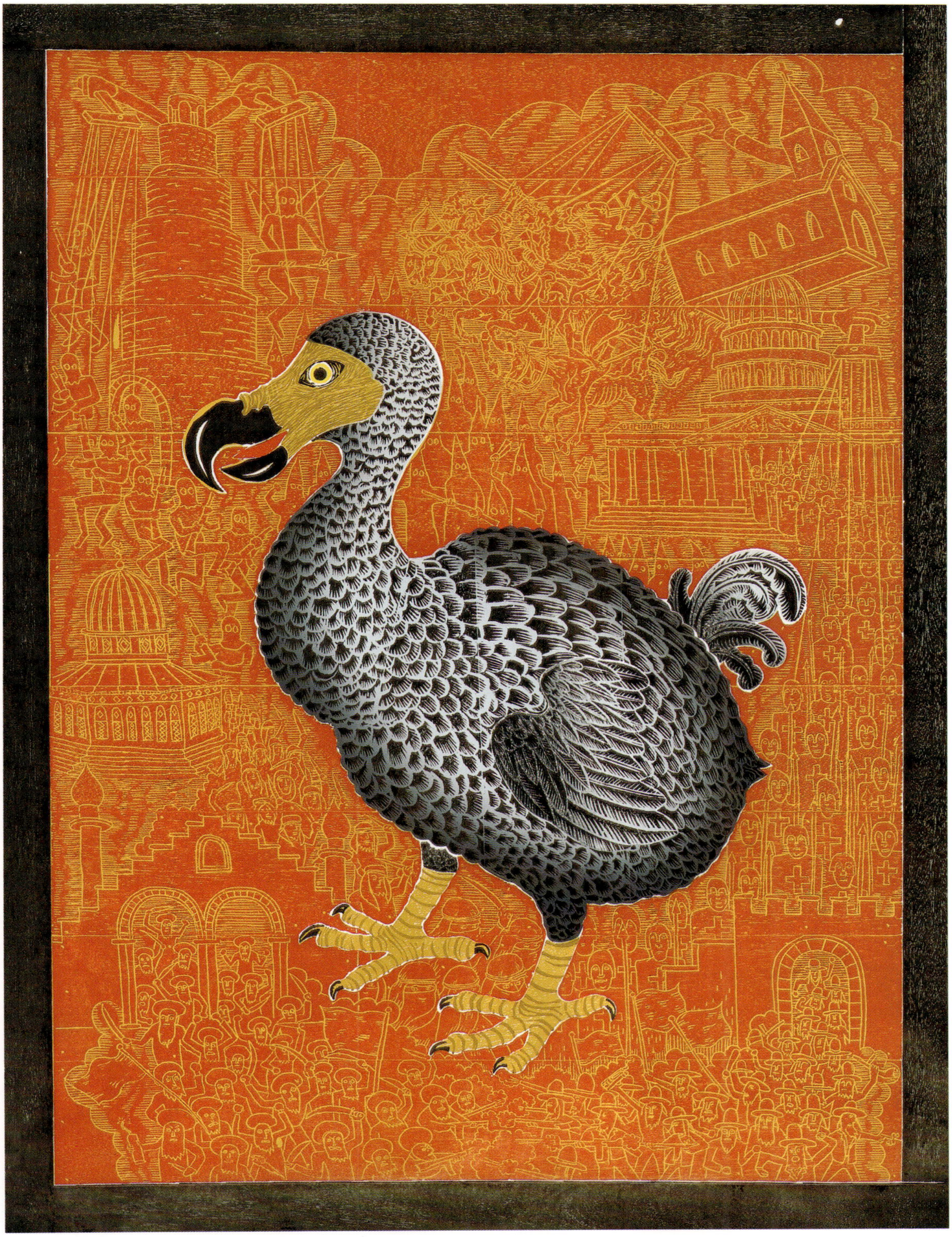

PLATE 4

Phoenix Rising, edition I/10
2006
Seven-color woodcut with pochoir
50 x 37 inches

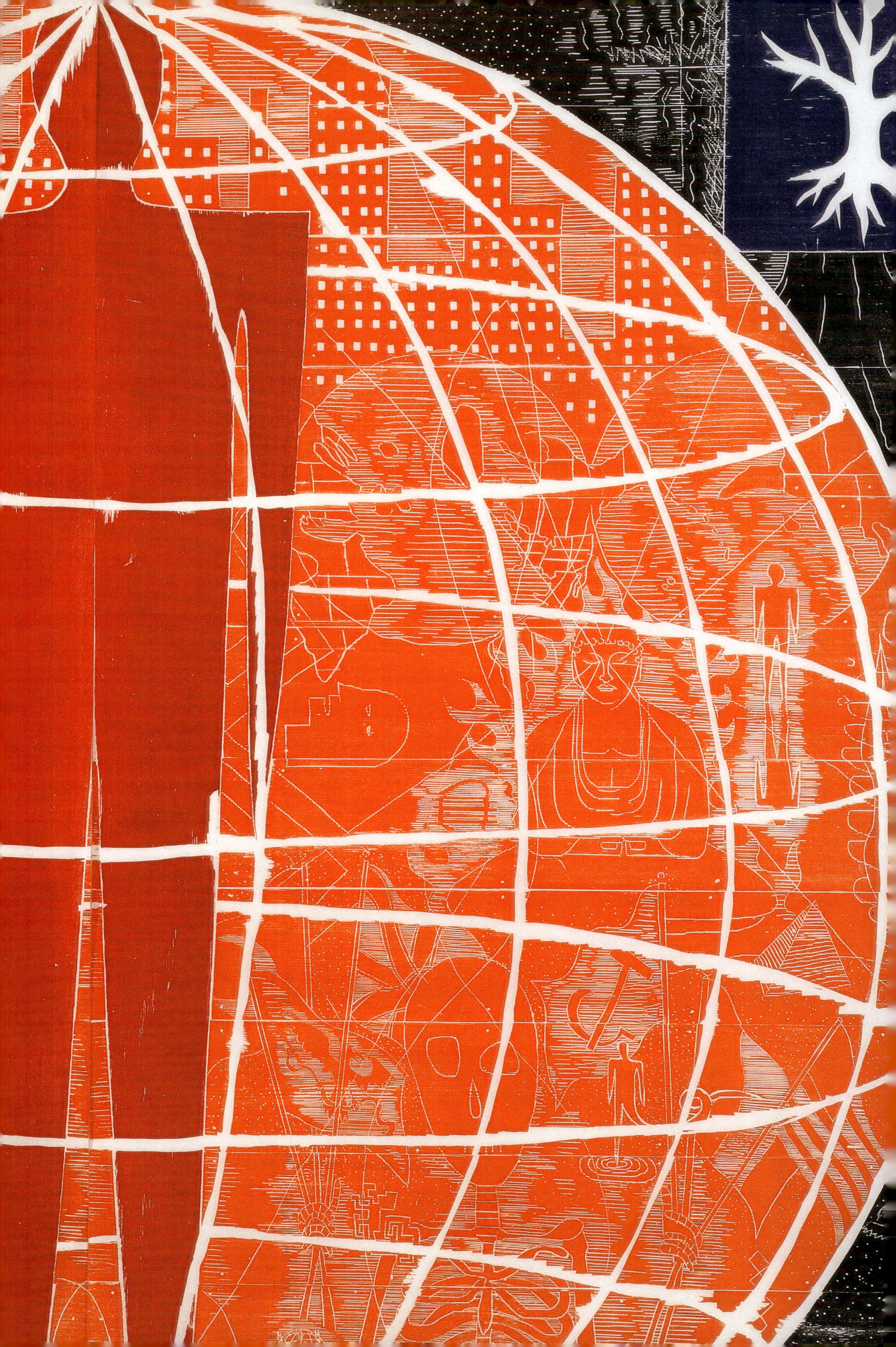

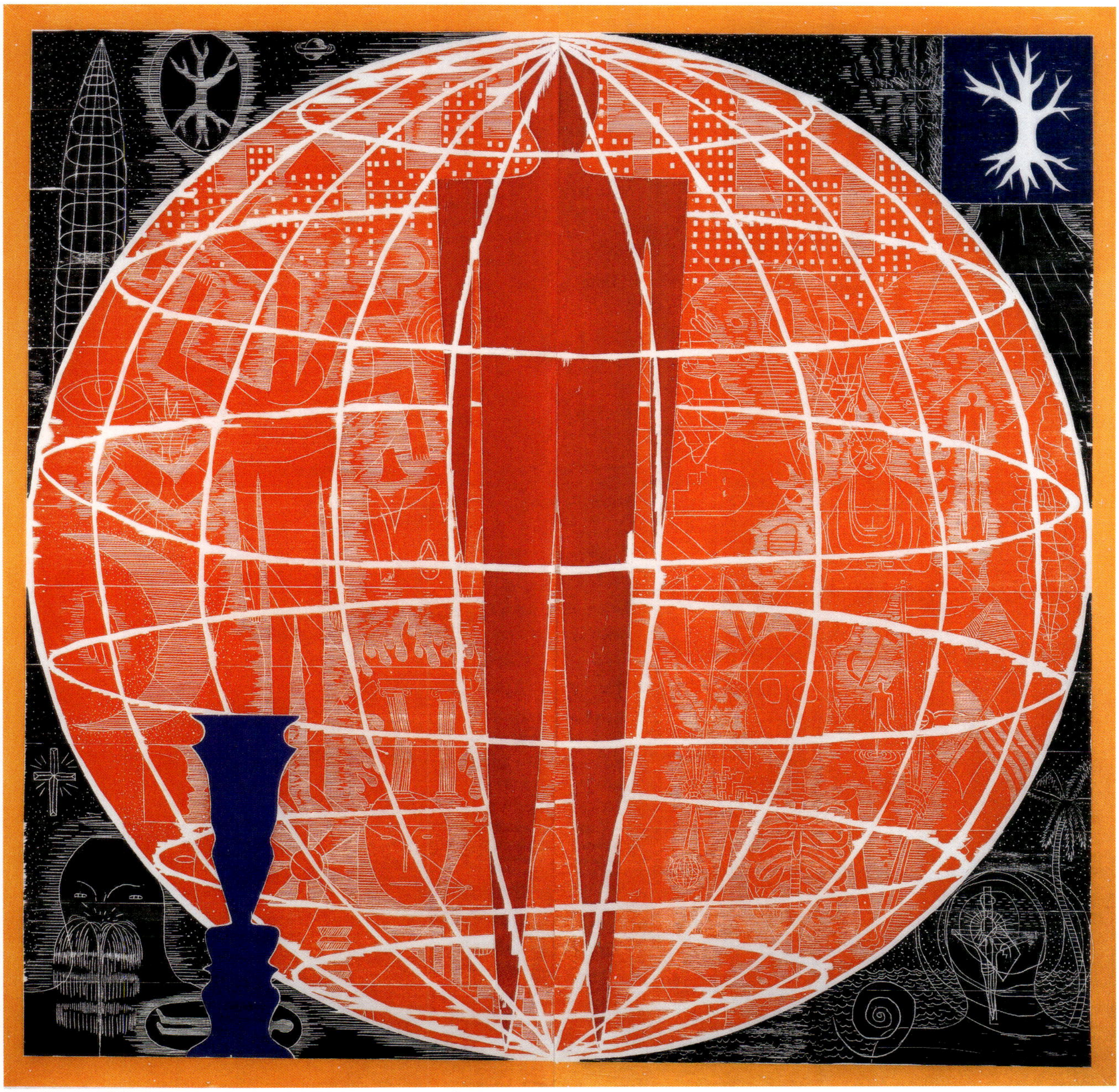

PLATE 5

East/West, edition PP 3/4
1988
Six-color woodcut
74 x 73½ inches

Buck's hands, this figure becomes a symbol of everyman (or woman) and, placed in different contexts, can speak of individualism, mass psychology, or the assertion of culture over nature. While the figure is frequently headless, suggesting an abandonment to blind will or irrationality, it is sometimes presented with symbolic substitutes for the head; for instance, the shoulders may be topped with a diminishing set of railroad tracks, a globe, a horse corral, a spiral, even at times a set of hands brandishing weapons and tools like Shiva, Hindu god of destruction. Sometimes the figure becomes an empty armature, harboring birds or other emblems of nature. Or it may become a skyscraper, an emblem of humankind's desire for mastery over the environment.

Another recurring trope is the evocation of imagery of the Mexican Day of the Dead. The works are full of dancing skeletons, grinning skulls, and figures of death that are at once comic and threatening, mocking our sense of power with a reminder that death awaits us all. Here the threat of death is not just personal but extends to our social and environmental realities. Lack of respect for larger forces and cycles of nature, Buck seems to be suggesting, may be writing the obituary for our species.

Other recurring images include urban skylines and skyscrapers, realized as blocky, geometric forms that stand in contrast to the more organic shapes of trees and plants. Flames emerge from many works, sometimes as the dominant image, sometimes in the background. They suggest both destruction and rebirth. Books refer to the storehouse of human knowledge, which can be used for good or ill. The U.S. Capital Building recurs, exploited in part, Buck notes, because of its resemblance to a gas station, with all its reminders of our gas-guzzling lifestyle. Similarly, the Washington Monument often begins to resemble a bomb or rocket, a recognition of the tie between nationalism and militarism.

Buck's woodcuts are deliberately couched in the visual language of popular art, recalling graffiti art, cartoons, and political broadsides. His sculptures also draw on popular sources, especially the simplified forms of country woodcarvers, but they also contain echoes of the abstracted forms of modernist artists like Brancusi, Giacometti, Miró, and Picasso. The sculptures are less overtly narrative than the prints. Instead, they offer assortments of symbolic objects balanced upon the headless body of male or female figures. These sculptures hark back to Buck's early work in the 1970s when he was creating freestanding figurative sculptures accompanied by props that commented on the male role. However, like his prints, Buck's sculptures have evolved into ever more complex and multilayered compositions. The headless figures, typically posed frontally on sculpture stands, have had their heads replaced by elaborate assemblages of sculpted forms that draw on the natural, man-made, and conceptual worlds. Often they hold objects in their hands, much like medieval representations of saints holding the "attributes" that relate to the nature of their martyrdom or their holy lives. Many of these same symbols can be found in Buck's prints, but here their connections are often more mysterious and ambiguous, and relate more to the ways

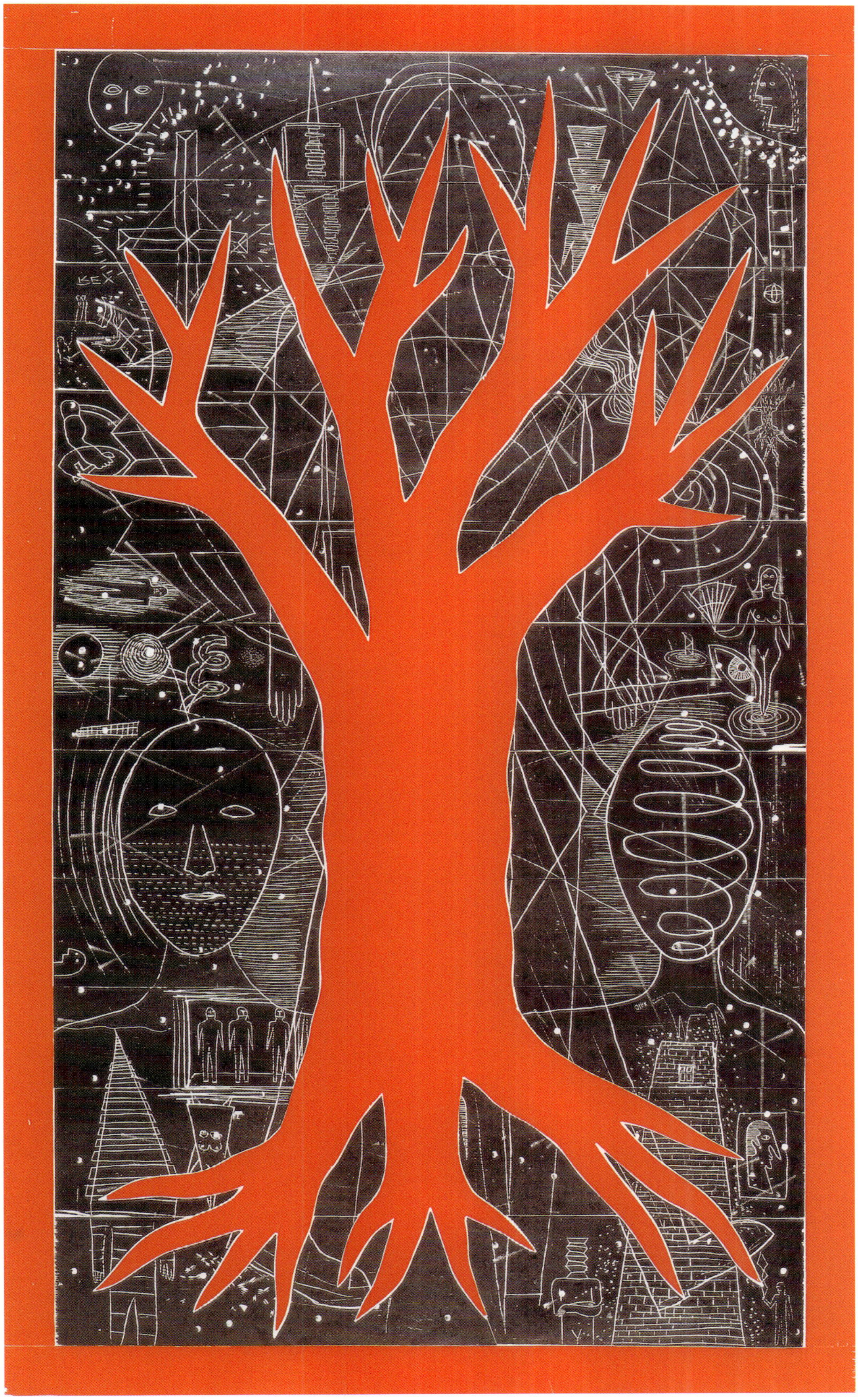

PLATE 6

BEIRUT, workshop proof edition 2/3
1983
Two color woodcut
62½ x 36 inches

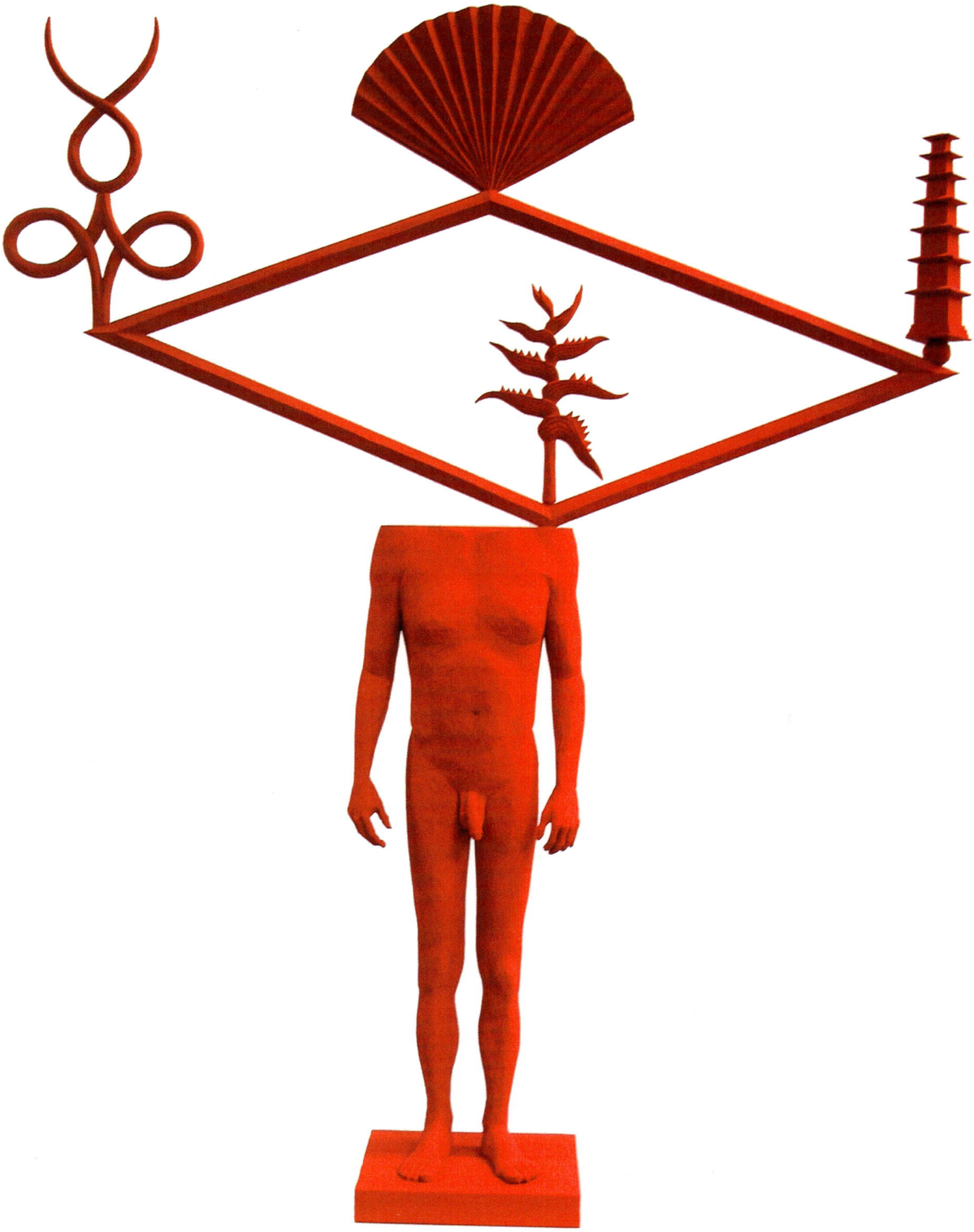

PLATE 7

Zona Rosa II
2005
Wood sculpture with acrylic paint
65 x 53 x 9 inches overall

that meaning is made than to any concrete political or social message.

For instance, *Zona Rosa II* (2005) (plate 7, p. 22) appears as a compendium of symbolic elements balanced on a slightly distorted open diamond attached to a forked stick at a male figure's headless shoulder. The elements in this red sculpture speak of the aspects of nature, culture, and gender, including a plant, a pagoda (suggestive of the East), a fan (with its connotations both of Asia and femininity), and a looping abstract form that could be a mathematical symbol or a decorative flourish. Perfectly balanced on the open diamond, they suggest the harmonious coexistance of such usual opposites as male and female, Asia and the West, and the worlds of nature and mind.

Recently Buck has begun to combine his two- and three-dimensional languages in relief works that consist of wooden boxes in which carved elements are inset in niches or within wooden grids. Like the sculptures, these are less narrative than associative, and elements are often arranged to bring out visual or conceptual rhymes. *Scrimshaw* (2004) (plate 18, p. 24), for instance, seems at least in part a meditation on the nature of Buck's activity as an artist. The title refers to carvings created by sailors to while away the time on long ship voyages. Typically the sailors carved images or letters onto whalebone or walrus tusk and then stained the carved lines with ink to make the image visible, a practice alluded to here in a square niche that contains a wooden version of a whale tooth carved with a sailing vessel next to a carved wooden knife. Other elements conjure other associations—a relief of a turkey head in a diamond-shaped niche brings to mind the fact that Benjamin Franklin wanted that bird to serve as our national symbol. An oval niche contains an extended hand holding a match, suggesting enlightenment or knowledge. A ship's wheel in a circular niche returns to the nautical theme, while other niches contain abstracted forms or references to the natural world. An ear and a nautilus shell share a certain spiral form, while a star, a butterfly, and a sleeping bat seem connected visually if not biologically. In their sturdy concreteness, these sculpted wooden objects have something of the quality of the carved and painted signs that designated a shop's nature in colonial America. Taken together, they map a string of meanings that have to do with America's natural and social history.

The maritime reference reappears in a series of glass and wood works, in which jumbles of carved elements are displayed in blown-glass jars much like larger versions of the proverbial ship in a bottle. These works grew out of Buck's residencies at Pilchuck Glass School in Stanwood, Washington, in 1997, 2002, and 2007. *The Inside* (2000) (plate 31, p. 65), for instance, encloses a tangled collection that includes carved wooden replicas of otherwise unrelated tools, creatures, and plants.

Buck's work draws on an almost bewildering array of sources, from natural history and science to popular culture, folk art, politics, and literature. But for all its multiplicity, it presents a complex yet coherent vision of the conflicted nature of American modernity. Embodied in these sculptures, reliefs, and prints is the contradiction between the rugged individualism

and love of nature that characterize the frontier mentality, on one hand, and the darker realities of our present state. Sunny optimism and the can-do spirit clash in these works with militarism, corporatism, and ecological irresponsibility. But all is not lost, Buck suggests. The individual creative mind can still imagine a better world. And of the many things the fox knows, that may be the most important one.

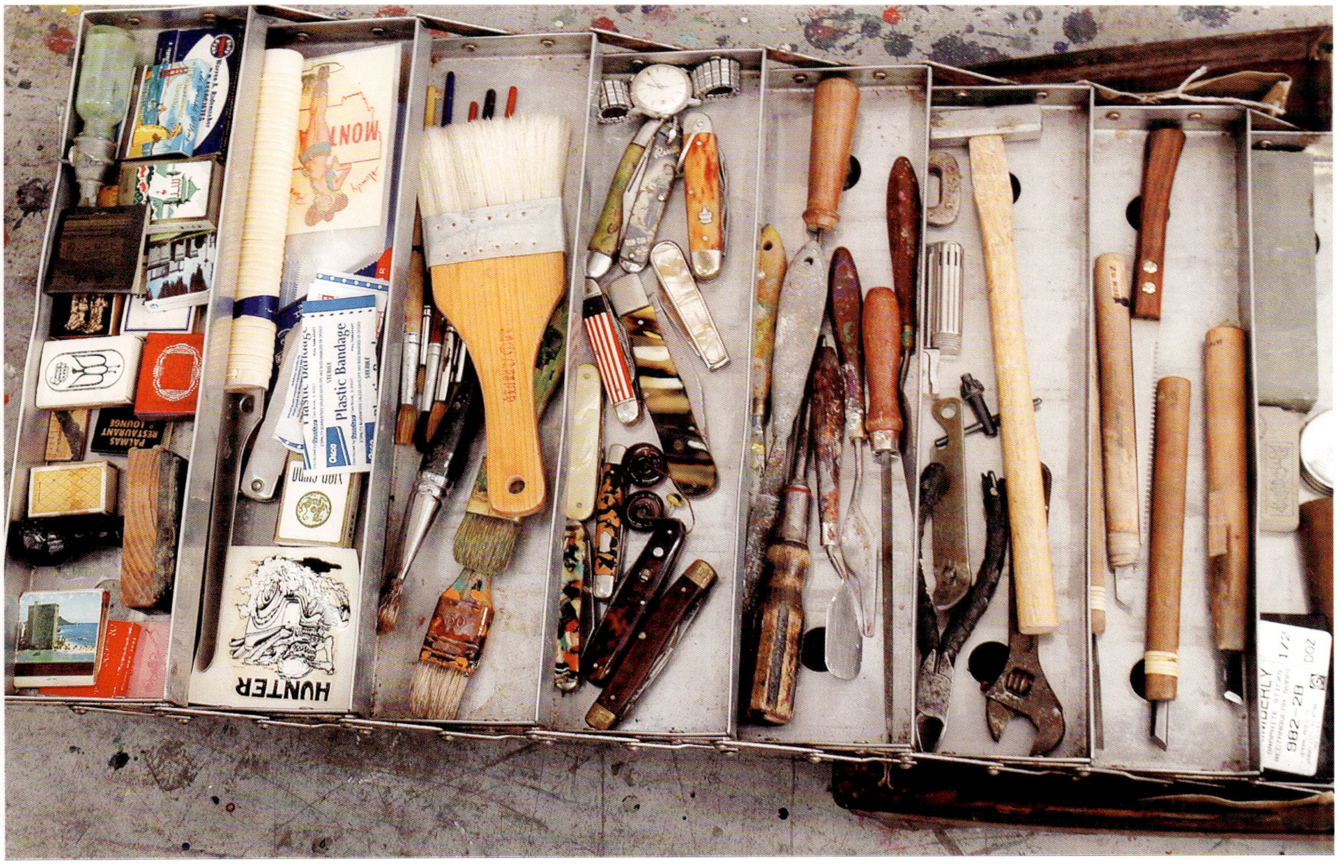

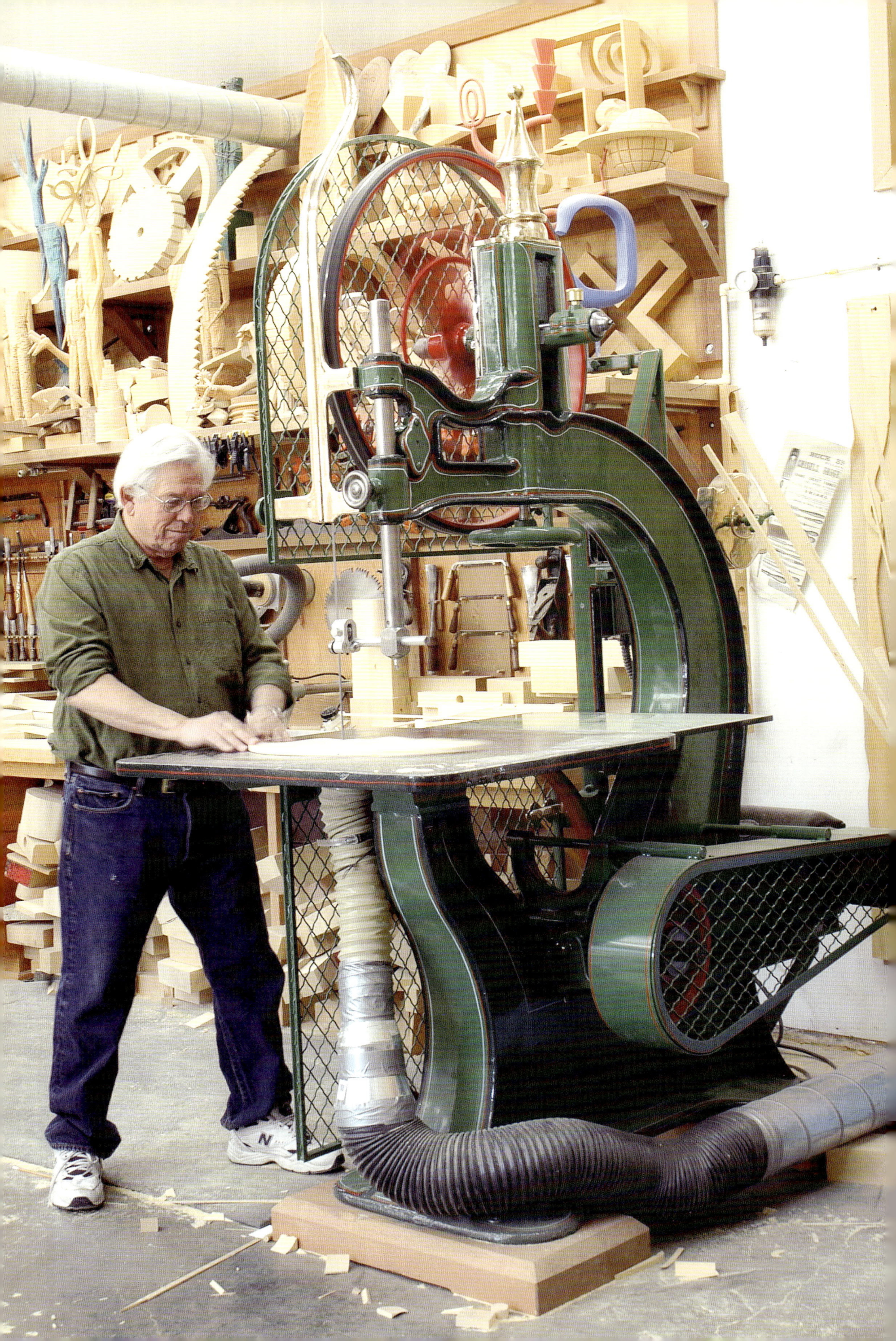

The Master of Wood

by John Yau

I.

There are a handful of obvious and important points about John Buck's art that I would like to make at the outset. The first and perhaps foremost is that he can carve a piece of wood into anything he wants, and I mean anything. The array of things that he makes and doesn't always use in his sculptures is mind-boggling. On a recent visit to his studio, I saw a large antique camera, all kinds of accurately evoked birds, many and different figures, all made of wood, which for some reason or another he hadn't incorporated into his sculpture. They, and much else, were resting on shelves lining his studio. Buck's mastery of his materials has enabled him to work with wood as a three-dimensional form that can be carved, and as a two-dimensional surface that can be incised. More recently, he has incorporated motors and pulleys into his work and has completed a number of kinetic sculptures that have many parts moving simultaneously. Wood is as central to Buck's project as steel was to David Smith's.

The second point is that Buck's woodcuts don't look like anyone else's. This isn't only because of the large scale he has been able to achieve with a medium that was used primarily in books during the Middle Ages. It is also because the artist has also expanded upon techniques found in traditional European and Japanese woodcuts, as well as made his own unique contributions to the medium. His woodblocks tend to be made up of interlocking and modular pieces, like a jigsaw puzzle. By dividing the block into modular units, Buck can incise each one differently, as well as work on a larger scale. He can also control the tonal modulation of a color in ways that are unique. In *The Eternal Flame,* of 1995 (No. 50, p. 130), he articulates a pale blue aura around the candle flame, while in *Deep End* (2000) (plate 9, p. 28), he conveys both the jar's interior and the light reflecting off its rounded, transparent surface. Yet for all his technical mastery, Buck never shows off. Everything he does is at the service of the work, its intrinsic subject matter.

In addition, the artist can use the same incised blocks to make both large, colorful prints and black-and-white rubbings. The idea for making rubbings came from a trip Buck made to China, where, in a forest, he

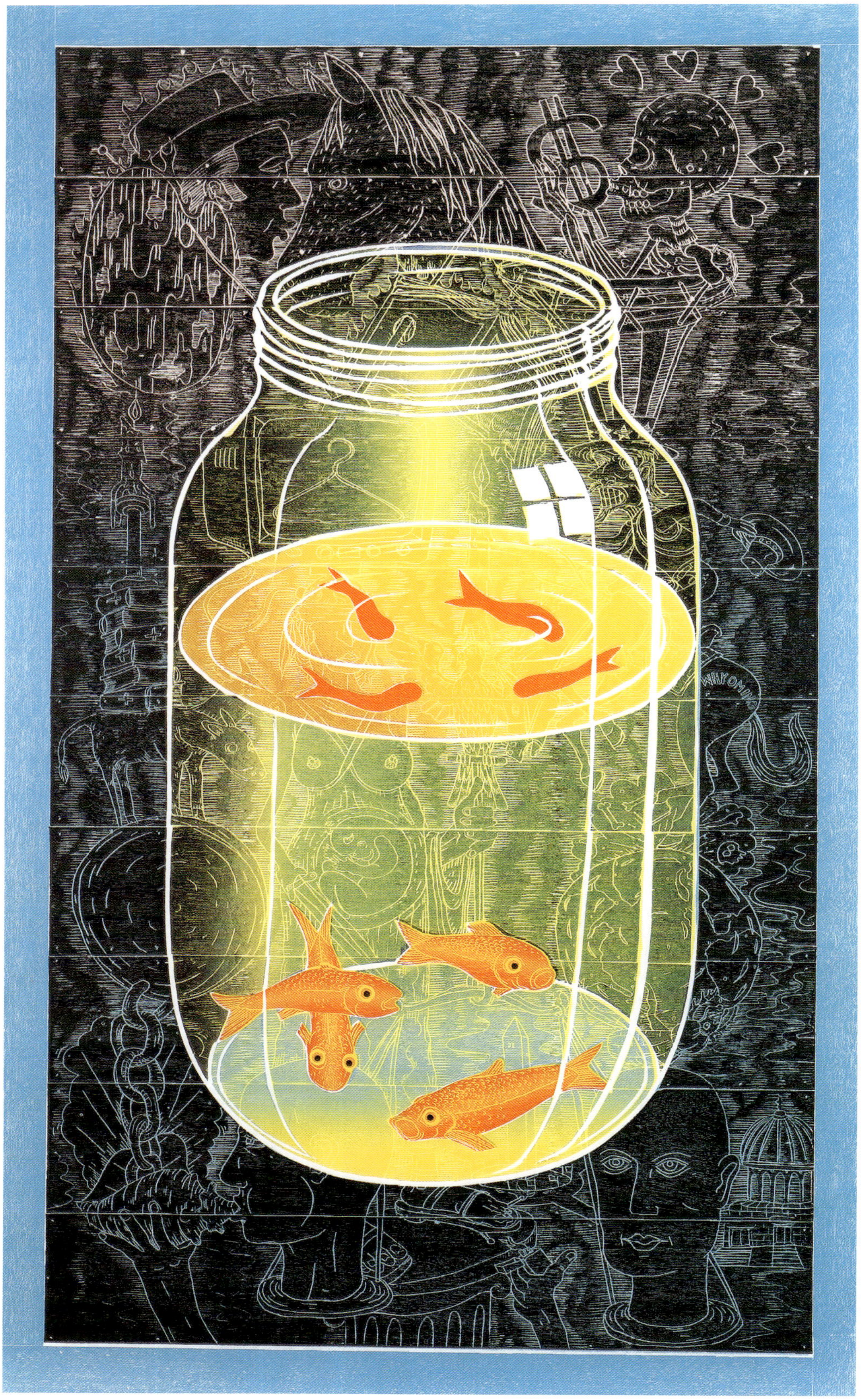

PLATE 9

The Deep End, edition 9/15
2000
Thirteen-color woodcut and chine-collé
62 x 37 inches

saw "craftsmen taking rubbings" from "gigantic stone tablets." Although they may share the same subject matter, the woodcuts and rubbings strike different emotional chords in the viewer. Also, in some cases the rubbing can precede the print, as when prints have yet to be editioned. In terms of his imagery, which is both direct and bold, Buck draws on a wide range of inspiration, including the *Calaveras* or animated skeletons of the great Mexican artist José Guadalupe Posada (1851–1913), Native American symbols, and the highly precise bird studies of John James Audubon (1785–1851), to name just a few.

The third point, which follows from the first two, is that Buck has thoroughly reinvented the medium so that one of his woodcuts, *Language of the Times*, of 1990, (plate 13, p. 35) is nearly eight feet high and more than four feet wide, and chock full of arresting images, all of which issued from the artist's hand. For this and other reasons, his woodcuts and, in a different way, his rubbings constitute an unrivaled achievement in American art. The scale of the woodcuts and rubbings is one that we are most likely to associate with large paintings, and certainly that is part of what makes them contemporary. The other reason they feel contemporary is because of their subject matter, as well as their prescience. He titled a lithograph from 1984 *Jihad* (plate 15, p. 43), long before the word entered our everyday vocabulary.

Since 1980, when Buck made his first woodcut, aptly titled *My First Print* (plate 10, p. 30), he has not only seamlessly joined technique to subject matter, but has also deepened his engagement with both. This joining further distinguishes his work from those artists who claim to have a lot to say but whose technical weaknesses end up diminishing their work. No such waning takes place with Buck's woodcuts. In fact, the techniques he has developed and mastered, which can be said to consist of incising the wood, or drawing *into it* with a sharp instrument, are matchless. From the smallest linear form to the largest, often multicolored, iconic composition, the palpable images in Buck's prints speak to each other, as well as concentrate, jolt, and shift our attention.

In *Great Falls*, 1991, (plate 11, p. 31) he bends and morphs an abstract form so that it moves from being a symbol of a human to become a waterfall and winding river, with the latter conveying a sense of great distance and a vanishing point. He has articulated a three-dimensional, transparent form, such as a jar, and then gone on to delineate the different things inside it. His ability to layer the images, so as to convey volume and depth, is incomparable. In *The Reflecting Pool* (2003) (No. 63, p. 133), he depicts five frogs poking their heads above the water, their darker green bodies bobbing below the surface, along with the objects lying on the pool's bottom, including the Tower of Babel. Everything is defined by the thickness of the line, which Buck always seems to get perfectly right. The things closer to the surface, the rippling water, for example, are made up of thicker lines, while those at the bottom of the pond are farther away and made of thinner lines. While his mastery of line is more immediately evident in the rubbings, it is also an essential aspect of the woodcuts. No matter where we turn our attention, there is something there to engage us.

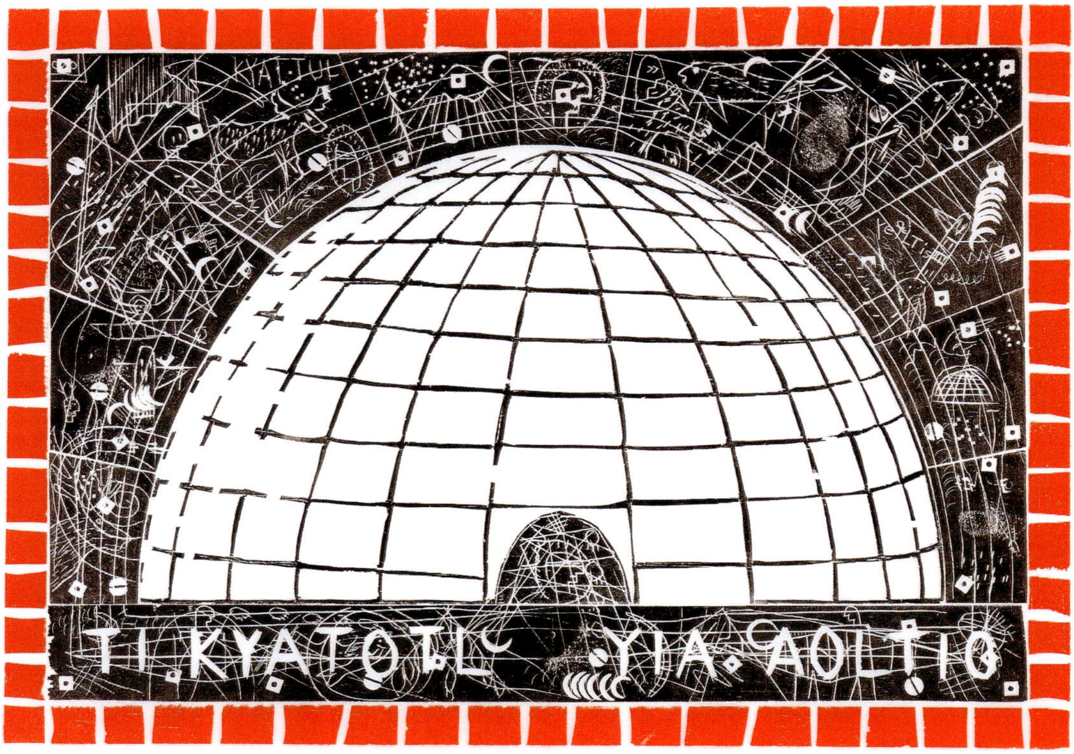

PLATE 10

My First Print, edition 6/13
1980
Three color woodcut
26 x 34 inches

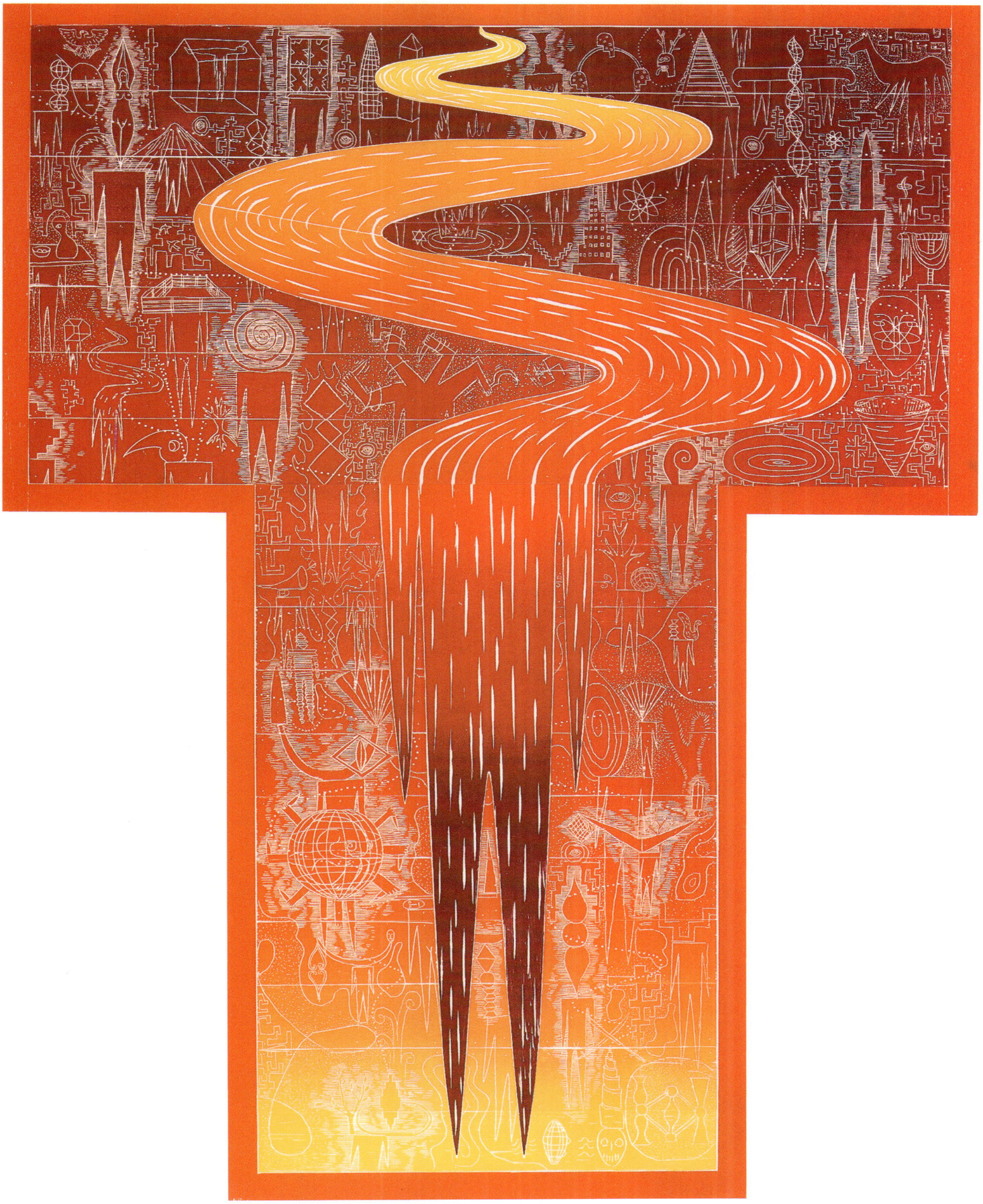

PLATE II

GREAT FALLS, edition 14/15
1991
Five-color woodcut
83¾ x 66 inches

By any measure, Buck is a contemporary master of the woodcut and of sculpture made of carved wood; and, in the case of his prints and rubbings, this means that he is a virtuoso draughtsman who has learned to draw with different kinds of sharp tools. And central to all of his devotion to craft, and in fact what makes his work so important, are his ongoing preoccupations. In his sculptures, woodcuts, and rubbings, Buck investigates both local and global issues, always in a way that eschews didacticism. His work is simultaneously a celebration and a lamentation, a song of praise and a mournful dirge. There is no simple message to his work, but there is always a deep and compassionate understanding of the difficulties of contemporary life, and an awareness of the many conflicts that impact our existence.

As an artist who lives and works in rural Montana and Hawaii, and who grew up in a family that was serious about fishing and hunting, Buck is highly conscious of the deleterious impact modern society has often had on our natural resources. At the same time, he is neither nostalgic for a supposedly simpler time nor is he an outsider commenting on how another group lives. Rather, he is the quintessential insider who examines a way of life with which he is deeply familiar. His is an art of self-reflection and rumination, of looking and looking again at the world in which we live. The intensely detailed woodcuts and rubbings make plain that, in both life and art, looking should never lead to idyll and that there is more to beauty than the picturesque. If anything, the very act of looking should make us more conscious of the fragile world we inhabit, and of the ways we interact with our material circumstances—how we use what we do. In this regard, Buck differs from many other artists with a strong social consciousness because he doesn't assume the mantle of witness or judge, but is someone who is always willing to implicate himself.

There is a diaristic impulse to Buck's woodcuts and rubbings, a need to make immediate observations and clarifications as well as to explore his changing states of feeling. However, in contrast to most diary-like work, his works on paper never feel opaquely personal, narcissistic, or closed-off. The artist depicts a complex visual world that invites long scrutiny; he wants the viewer's attention to wander through the layered reality he suggests as well as to connect one thing to another in the mind's eye. And concurrent with this impulse is the increasing intricacy, both in color and line, that has been brought to bear in the artist's work since 1980, when he made his first woodcut. In the two dozen woodcuts that Buck made between 1980 and 1988, the artist generally used two or three colors, with the exception of *Pacifica*, 1985 (No. 15, p. 121), which had four. These early woodcuts are largely graphic, and the colors are uniform throughout. In 1989, in *Green Fruit* (No. 126, p. 124), the artist made a woodcut that includes twenty-three colors. Since then, his woodcuts generally have between six and ten colors, all deep and rich in tone. And many of them—I am thinking of *Little America* (1992) (No. 37, p. 127), *The Lamp* (1994) (plate 12, p. 33), and *Crystal Lake* (2001) (plate 37, p. 74)—emit a sensual glow.

At the same time, and very near the beginning of his exploration of printmak-

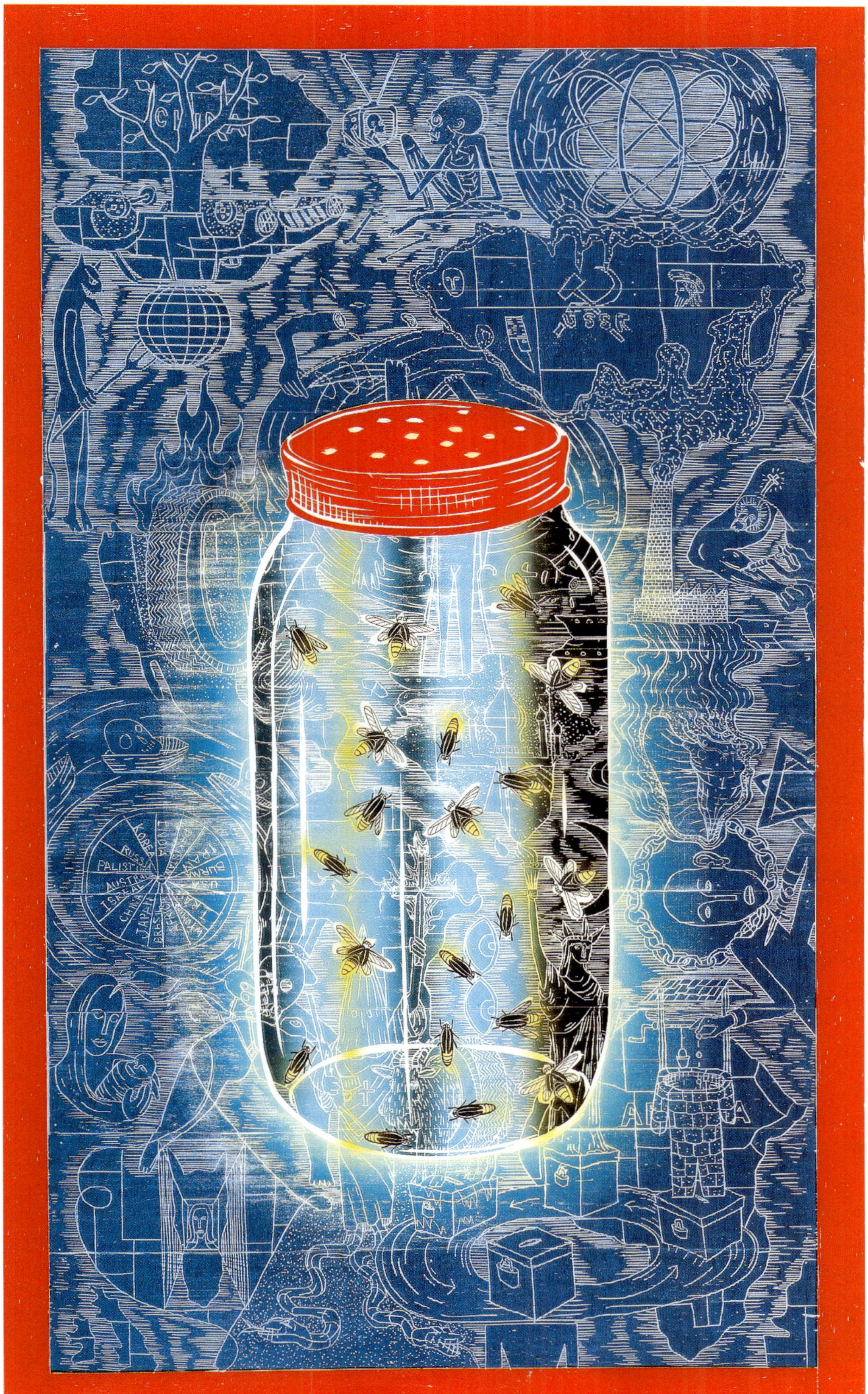

PLATE 12

THE LAMP, edition I/I Archive impression
1994
Twelve-color woodcut with rubber stamp and hand coloring
62 x 37 inches

ing, Buck found a way to implicate himself, as well as to dissolve the barriers between subjective expression and objective observation. In *Beruit,* 1983 (plate 6, p. 21), and *Big Stick,* 1984 (No. 7, p. 119), the artist's use of a red tree in the former, and a thick branch in the latter, introduces a self-reflective element into the work. In depicting a tree or branch as the largest central—and galvanizing—element in a woodcut, a medium in which the wood itself is essential, Buck connects his artistic materials to something common and essential to life, suggesting that the boundaries between the two are both porous and changing. The iconic image that Buck places in the center of many of his woodcuts is often a surrogate self-portrait, as well as a vision of a living being surrounded by the nearly chaotic and often overwhelming maelstrom of information that defines each of our days. Is it possible to process all this information and keep our attention focused on the things we have to do, ranging from the simplest chores to paying attention to the events and issues roiling our life? It is this very basic contemporary dilemma that Buck addresses in print after print. Can we keep paying attention? Can we keep looking, no matter how disturbing and unsettled the world keeps becoming before our very eyes?

In *The Language of the Times* of 1990 (plate 13, p. 35), the artist defines a grid of light and dark yellow squares in order to openly explore a question all artists face. In a world where there is no common language, how does an artist develop a visual language that is not solipsistic, literal, or burdened by its symbolism? In the print, the artist has drawn a wide range of red linear symbols, signs, and silhouettes into the squares, with some overlapping and others contained by the squares. Superimposed on this checkerboard of images is a circular black tower outlined in white. The tower alludes to the well-known biblical story of the Tower of Babel. In the story, the builders want to erect a tower that would reach to heaven. Offended by their arrogance, God causes the structure to fall by having everyone working on it begin to speak a different language, making communication of the simplest kind virtually impossible. For us, it is the realization of this same inability to communicate, and the same resulting rancor, that resides at the heart of much of Buck's work. He clearly recognizes that universal communication is an impossible ideal, but he nevertheless explores his own role as an artist.

In the top row of *The Language of the Times,* from left to right, one sees the symbol of the Yin and Yang, the silhouette of a city, a looping abstract line that suggests a butterfly, a layered abstraction that suggests both a landscape and a body, a tank rolling toward a tent, and an optical conundrum in which a vase (or negative space) is formed by two profiles facing each other. Each of these symbols exists on its own, so that it is the viewer who must connect them, making something out of them. In their separateness, they remind us of what befell the people who tried to erect the Tower of Babel. And yet, even though we speak different languages—I mean this both literally and metaphorically—and we often find it difficult to communicate with each other, the desire to do so never leaves us. Instead of coming up with a solution, which certainly would never satisfy everyone, Buck

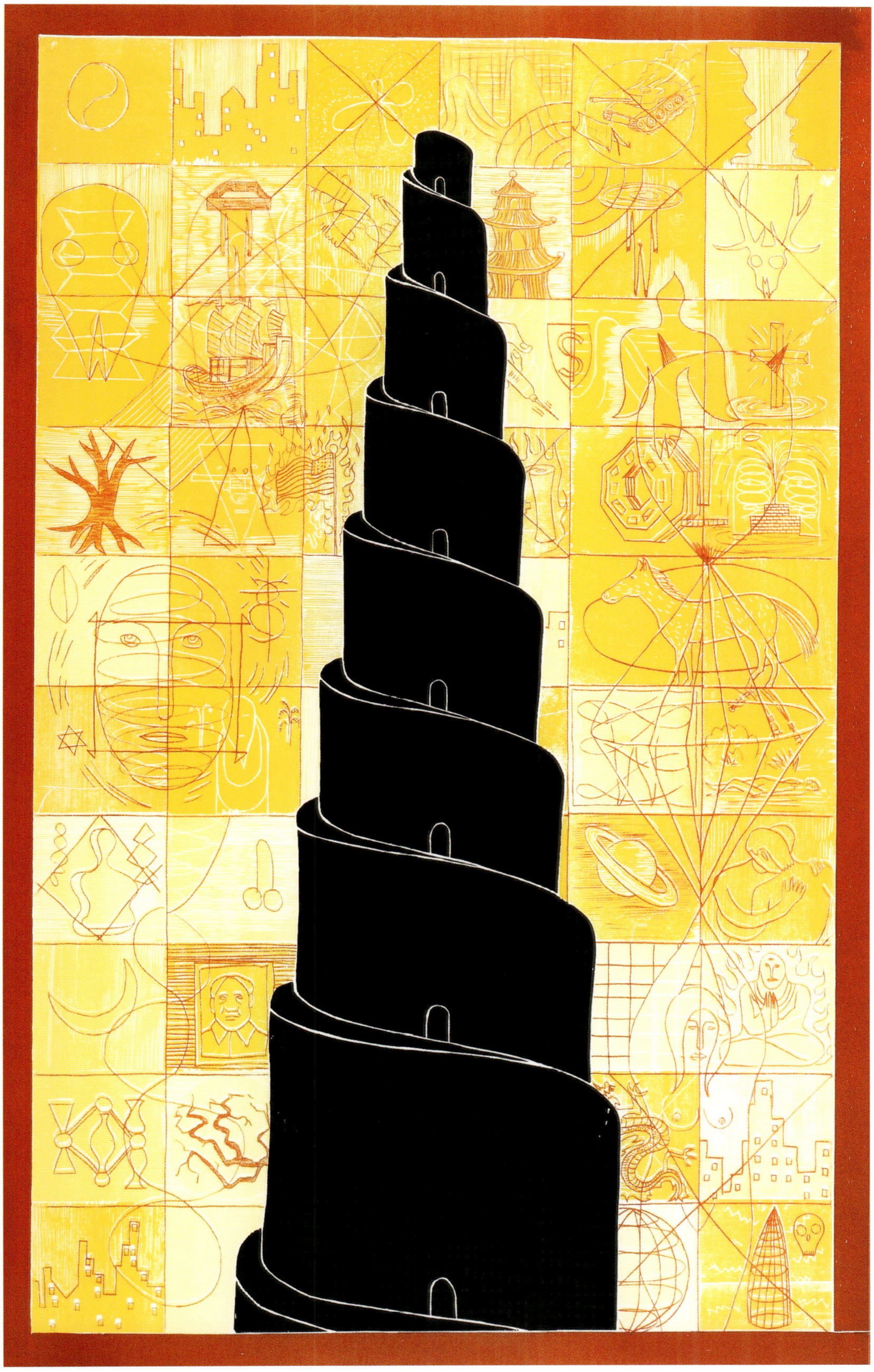

PLATE 13

The Language of the Times, edition 4/36
1990
Woodcut and drypoint
80 x 52 inches

conveys the need to negotiate the vast differences separating us. We must get beyond our own chauvinism in order to start dealing with the *Other*.

II.

The Ivory-billed woodpecker is the subject of a woodcut and a rubbing, and dominates a wall sculpture, all of them titled *The Singer Tract* and dated 2005 (plate 14 at p. 38, and plate 42 at p. 81). Many experts believe that the Ivory-billed woodpecker, one of the largest members of the woodpecker family, is extinct. However, in the first years of this century a number of sightings were recorded by trained experts, though none have ever been proven beyond a shadow of a doubt. The controversy over whether the Ivory-billed woodpecker is extinct or not has become one of the recent meanings of Buck's print. Another reason the artist may have chosen the Ivory-billed woodpecker as a subject is because of the bird's bill, which it uses to pound, wedge, and peel the bark from dead trees to find the larvae of the wood-boring beetles that are central to its diet. The ivory-colored bill is flattened at one end, like a beveled wood chisel, which, for Buck, is an essential tool. This link suggests that the artist might consider the Ivory-billed woodpecker to be a surrogate portrait, that he and this extinct or, at the very least, rare bird have something in common.

In both the woodcut and the rubbing, the woodpecker is hammering away at a rotted tree trunk rising from a swamp. Both the bird and rotted trunk are inside a sealed glass jar, which suggests that they are either specimens or that the jar is a kind of diorama. On one level, Buck seems to be commenting on the ongoing extinction of animals, which is usually caused by civilization's increasing encroachment upon natural habitats. On another level, however, the image of the woodpecker in a glass jar, hammering away at a tree, can be read as a self-deprecating self-portrait. As an artist devoted to craft, he too may be feeling as if he were on the verge of extinction, particularly in the contemporary art world, where craft—and particularly the art of carving wood—is regarded by many theorists as old-fashioned. On still another level, the image of the woodpecker can be regarded as humorous; even though he has been pronounced extinct he seems not to have gotten the news and is still hammering away. The artist's seemingly uncomplicated image isn't so simple after all.

Buck has populated the background or area around the bird and rotted tree with images, each of which provokes us to reflect upon its meaning. On one side of the woodpecker, the artist has made a linear ghost of the Statue of Liberty holding up its torch, welcoming the "tired" and the "poor," while on the other side he has made a linear image of a cowboy pushing an alligator through what looks like a sewing machine. Here again, one sees Buck's ability to make complex meanings out of accessible and in some cases familiar images. The image of the cowboy working at his machine is both funny and disturbing. Is it meant to evoke alligator pocketbooks and shoes, and how our preoccupation with fashion can include a strong disregard for the natural world? What about the Statue of Liberty? One of Buck's great strengths is the economical way in which he articulates complex

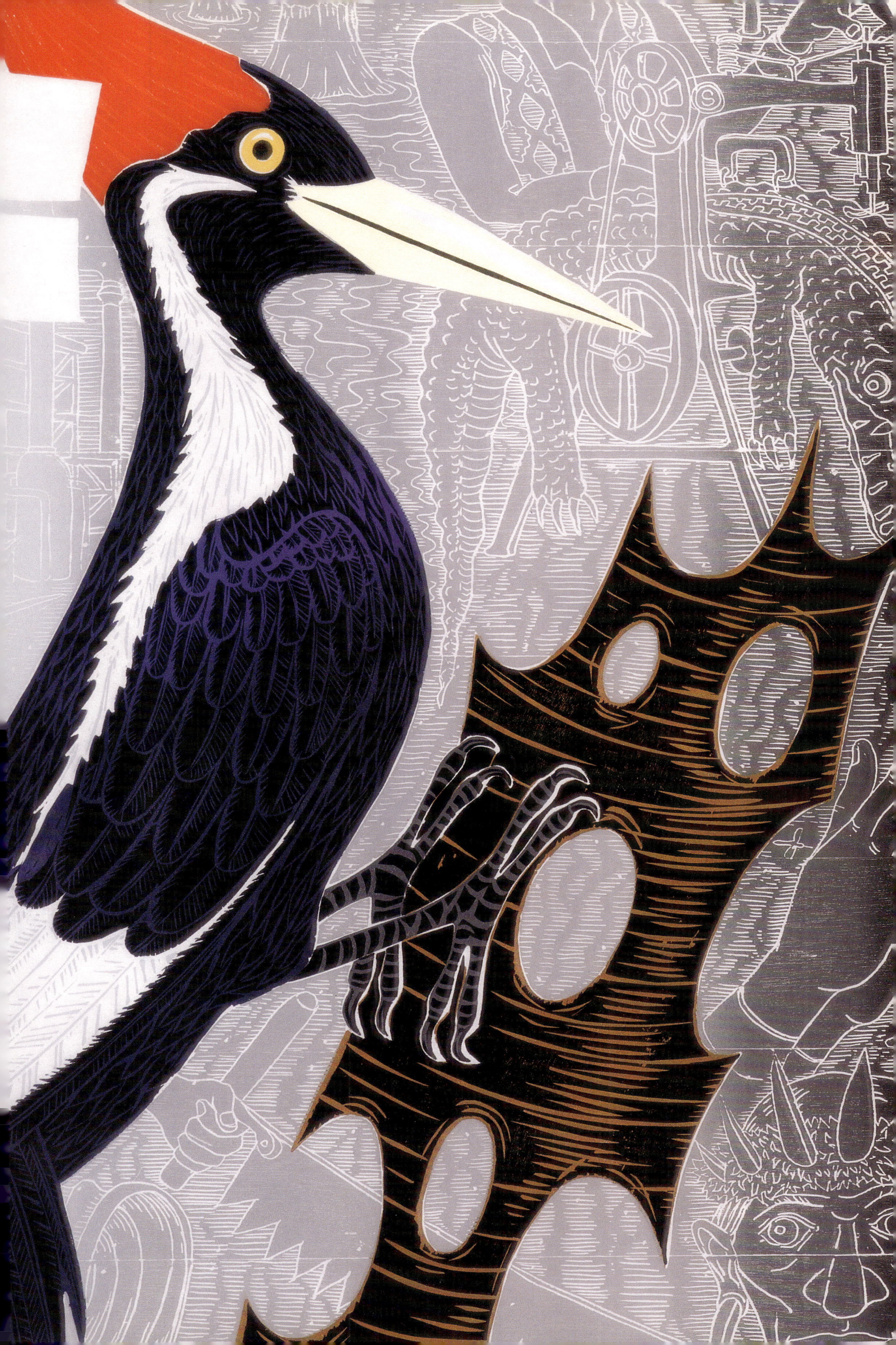

images, and how they provoke us to consider their meanings. His art ranges from the tender to the pointed, and from anger and concern to sympathy and love. The woodcuts and rubbings are both expansive and resolute. His sculptures, both the still and the kinetic, are full of countless details.

Whatever the medium, everything that Buck does requires that we slow down and take a long and careful look. And in that slow looking there are many pleasures, many visual instances where our eyes can marvel both at the whole and its details, while our minds can follow and consider the various things Buck is reflecting upon. Few artists are able to get as much into their work as he does, seemingly without effort. His ability to contain so much is a major achievement in the art of our time.

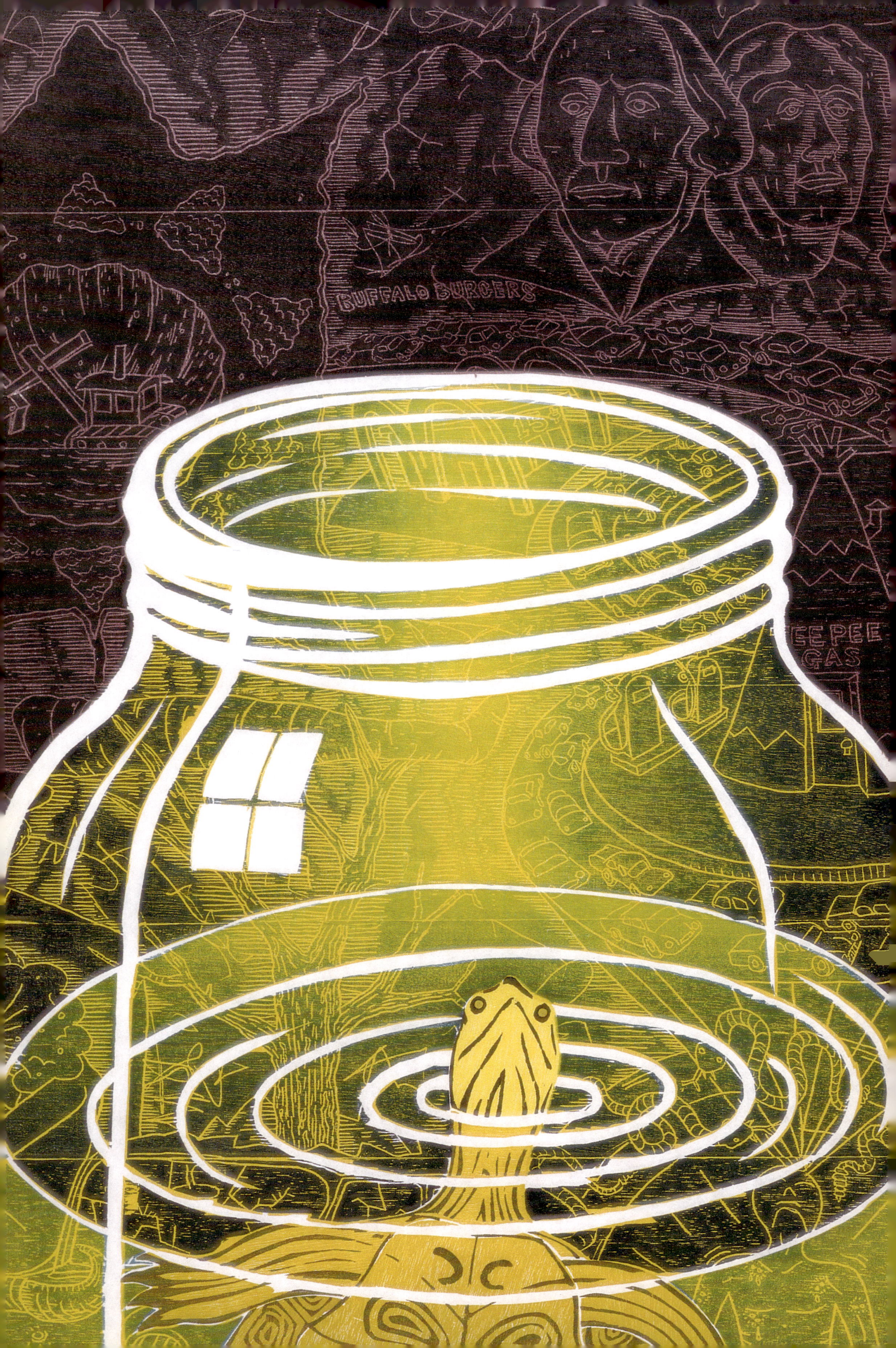
BUFFALO BURGERS
EE PEE
GAS

Portfolio

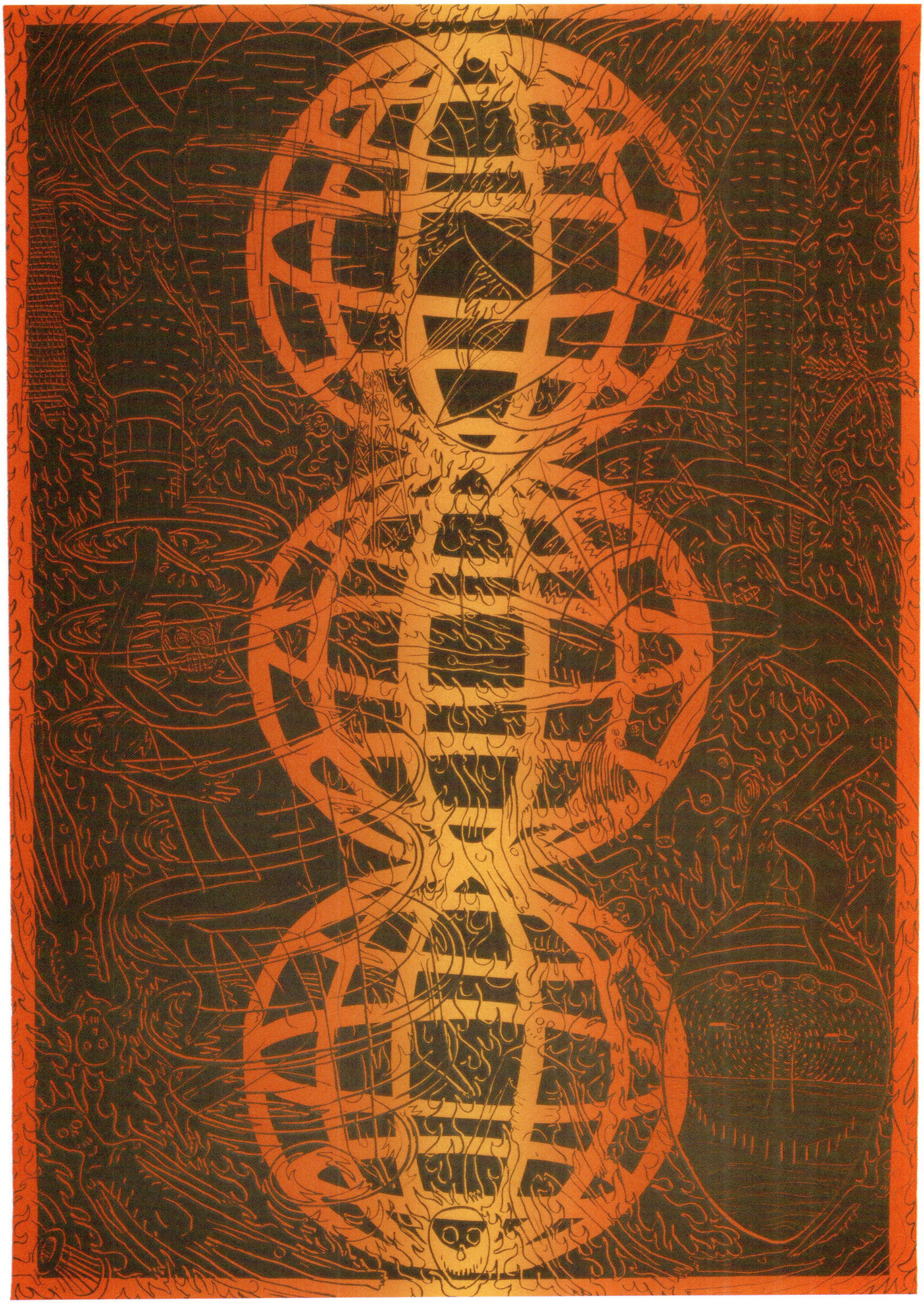

PLATE 15

JIHAD, edition 7/30
1984
Four color lithograph
44 ½ x 30 inches

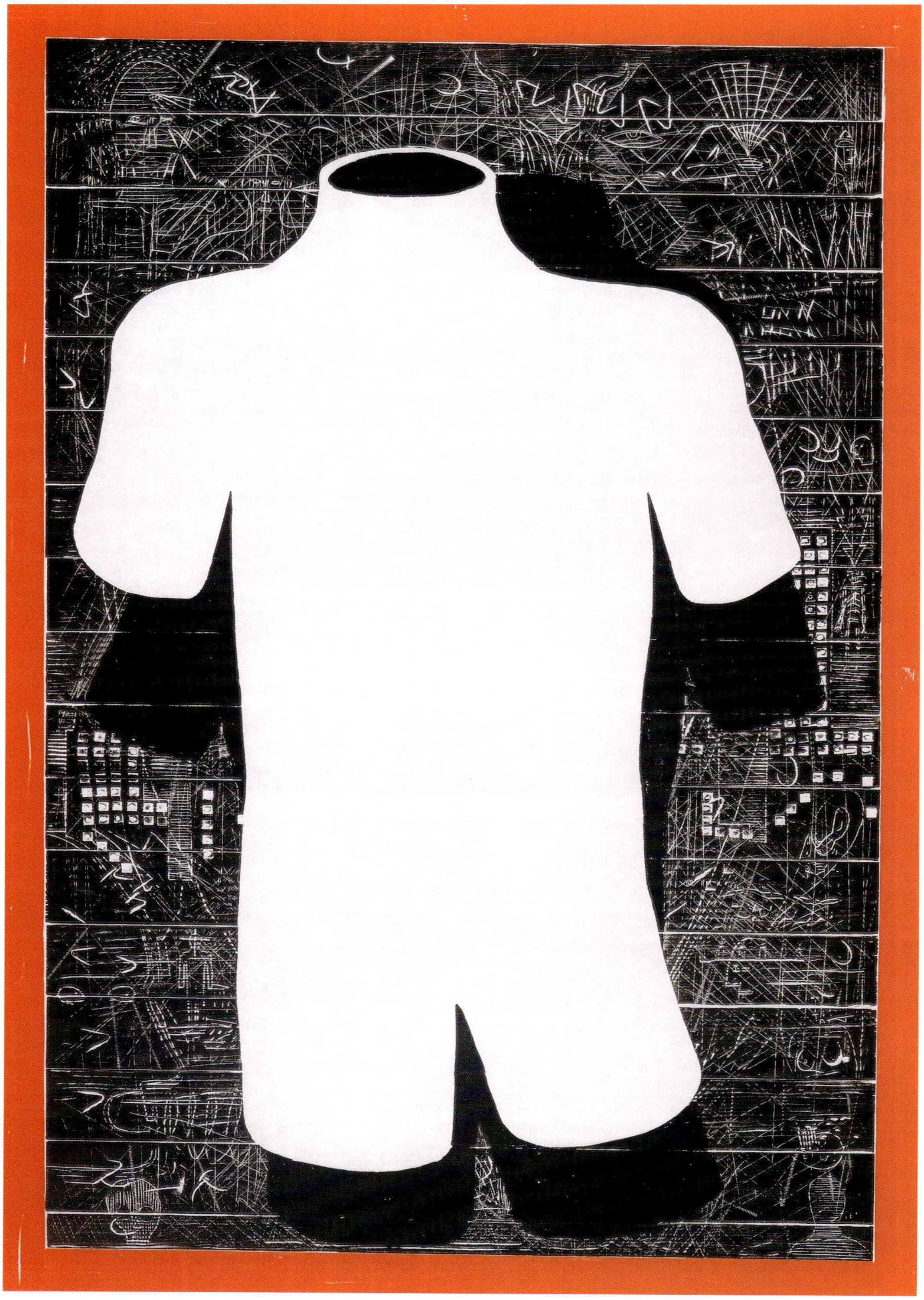

PLATE 16

Avenue of the Americas, edition RTP
1985
Two color woodcut
50 x 34 inches

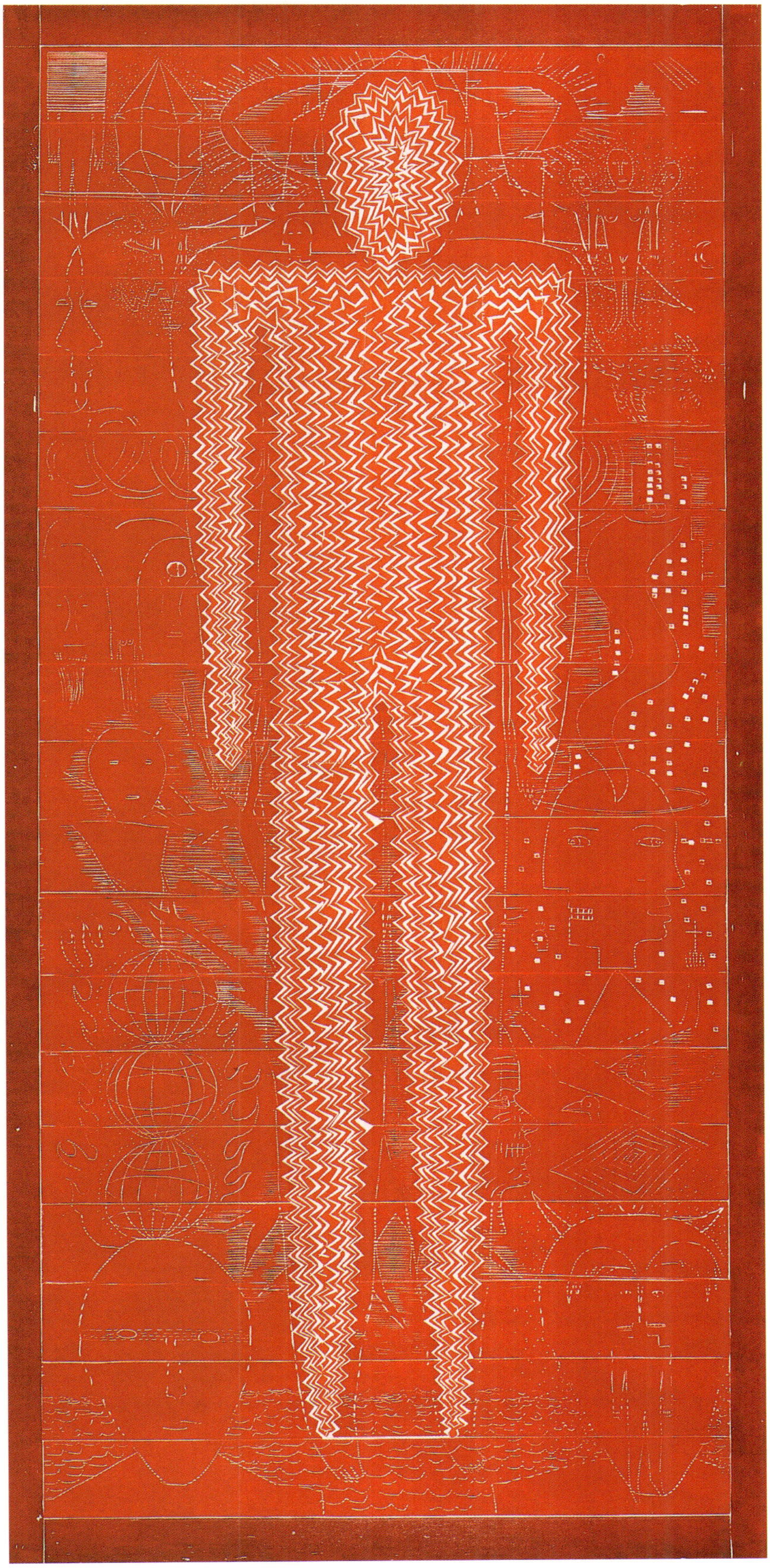

PLATE 17

Red Jesus, edition 28/30
1986
Three color woodcut
74 x 37 inches

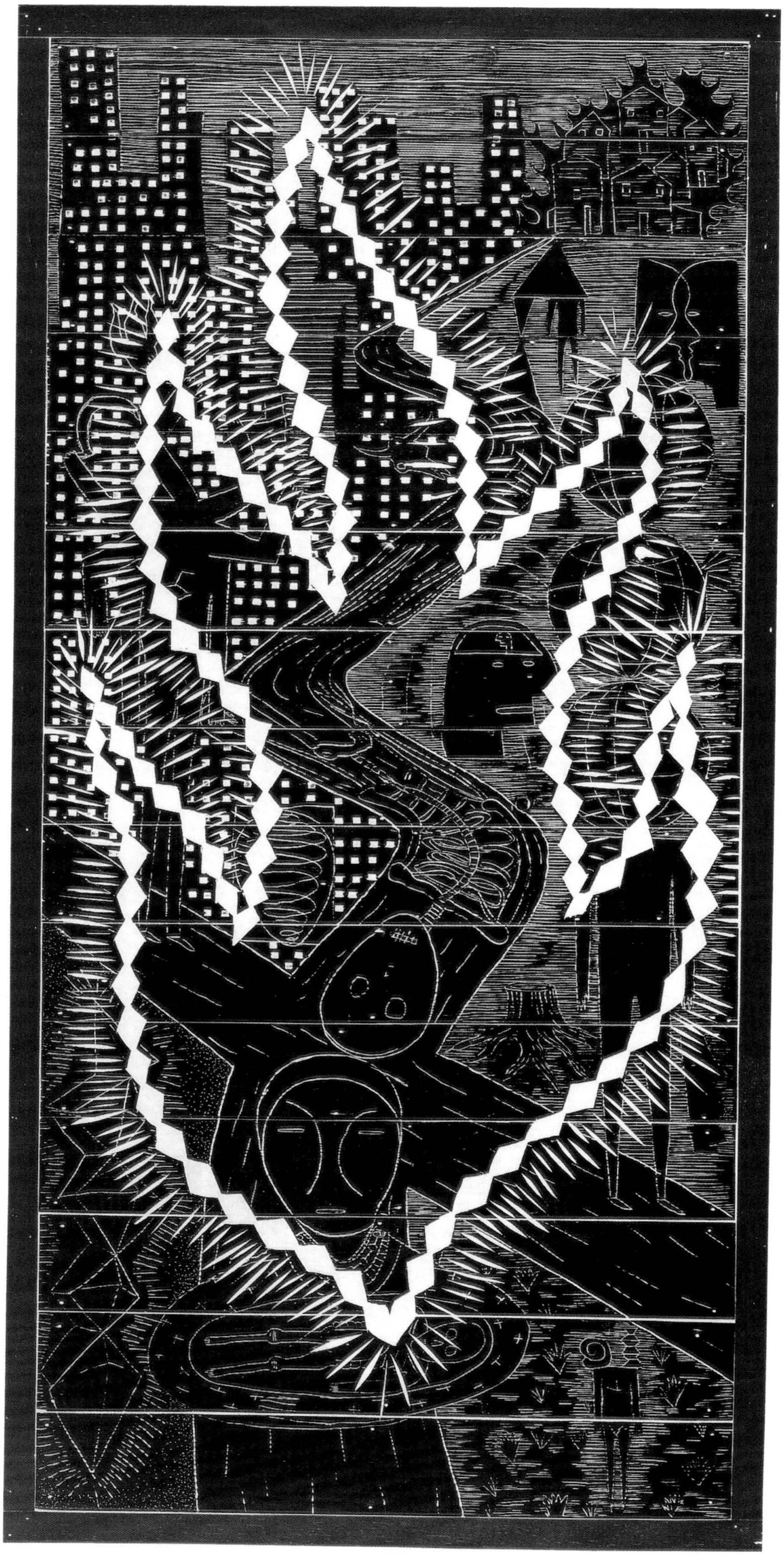

PLATE 18

Crossroads, edition 2/15
1987
Two color woodcut
74 x 37 inches

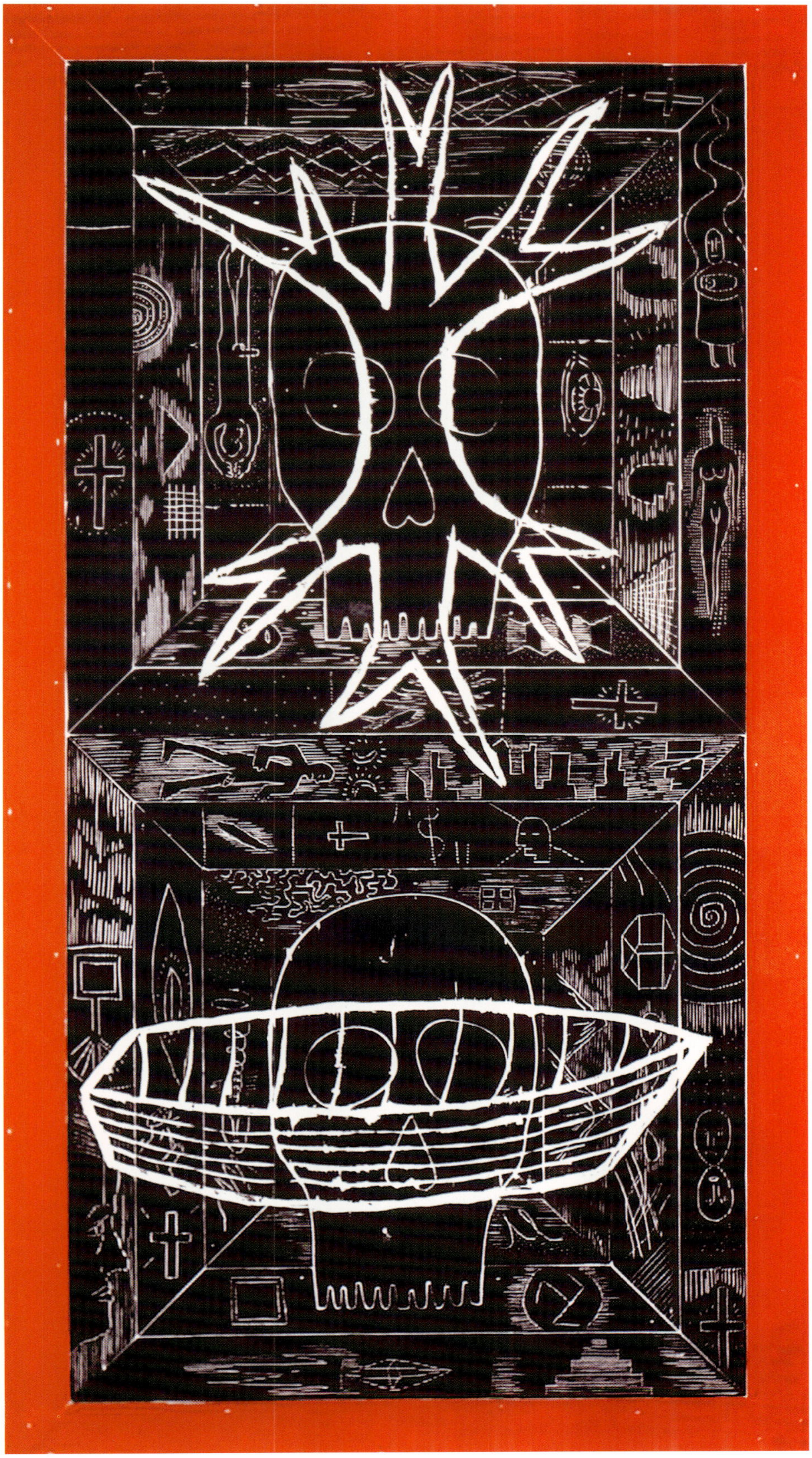

PLATE 19

The Have and the Have Nots, edition 3/14
1987
Two color woodcut
67 x 38 inches

PLATE 20

PRISONER, edition WP I
1987
Three color woodcut
74 x 37 inches

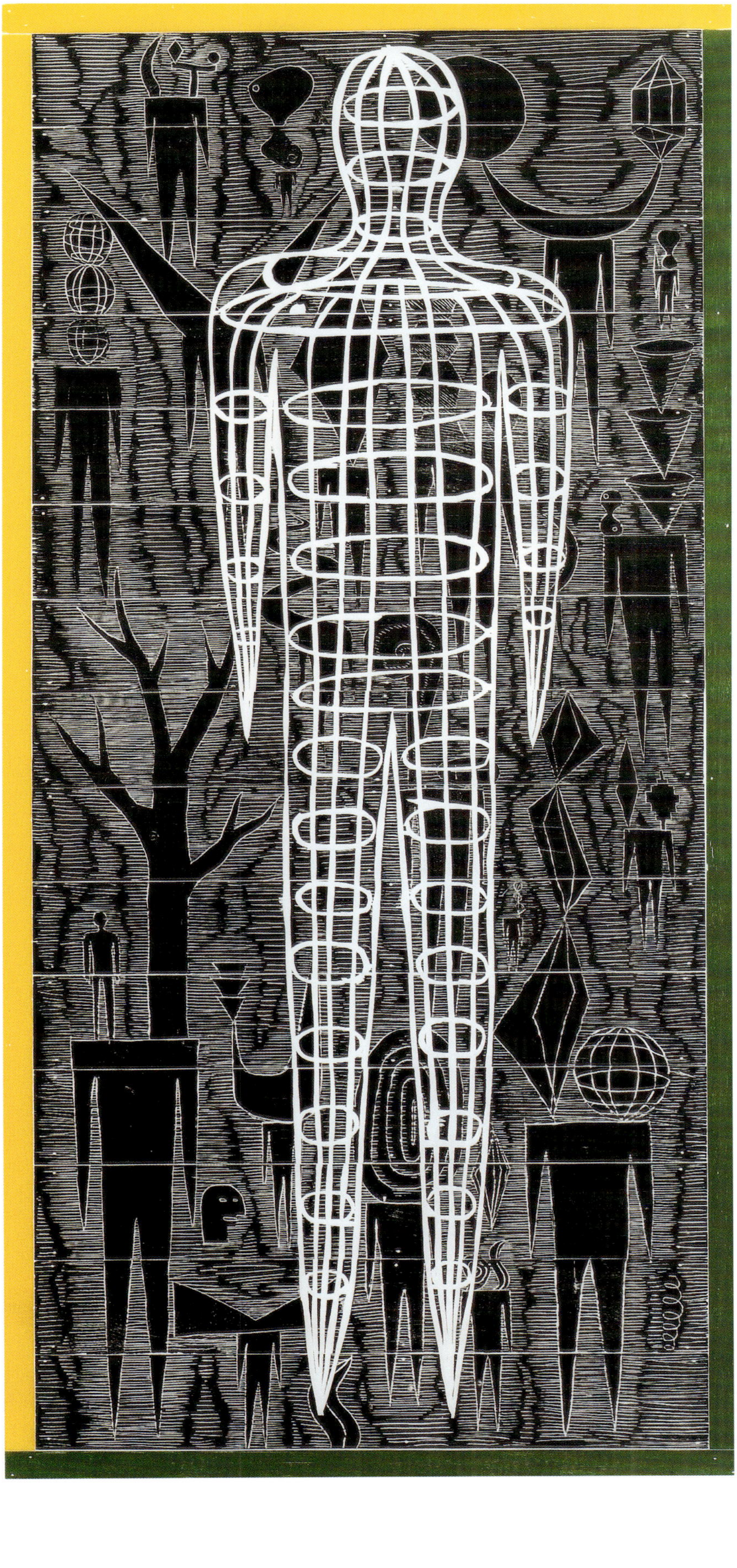

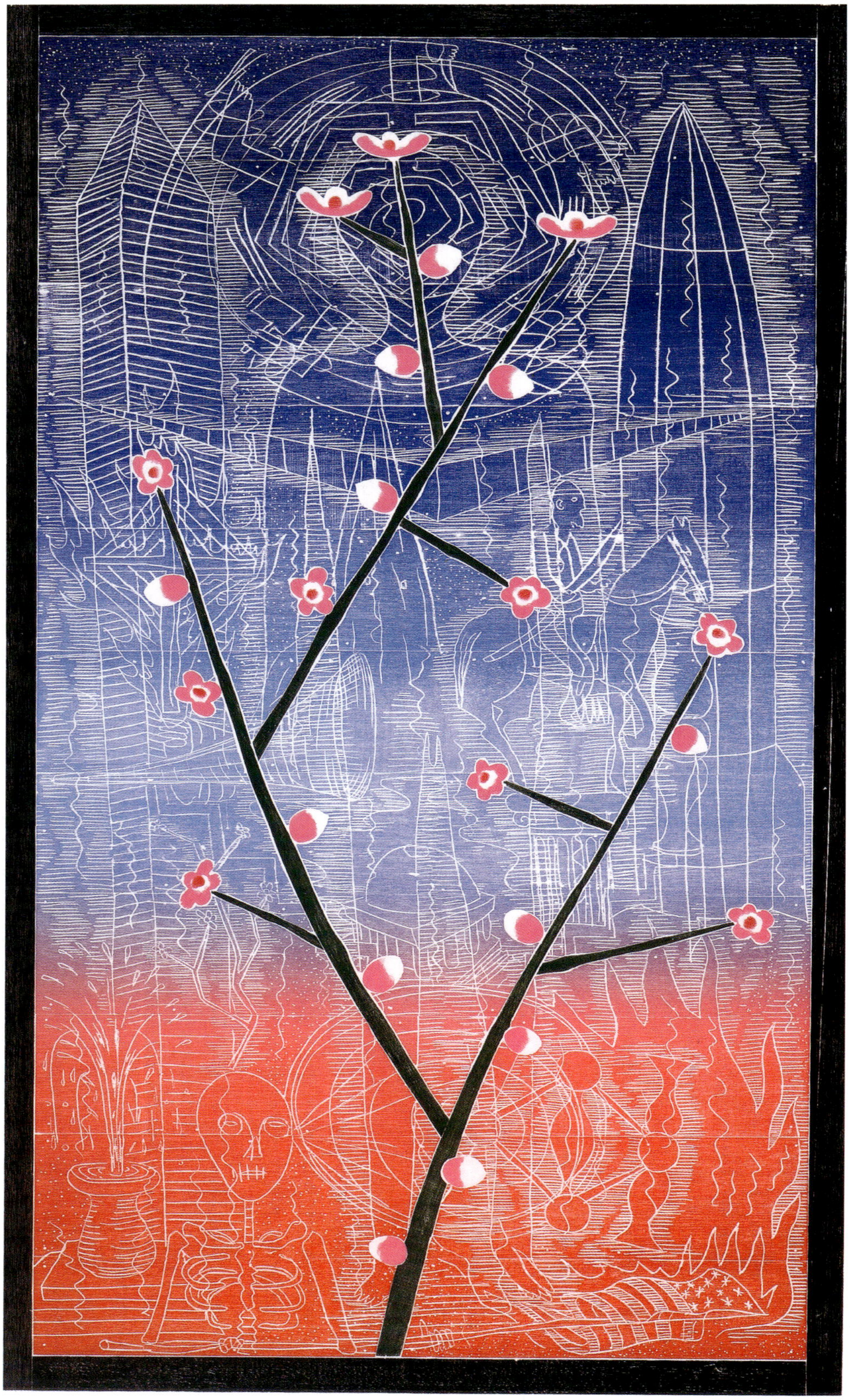

PLATE 21

Cherry Blossom Time, workshop proof edition I/I
1988
Ten-color woodcut
63½ x 37 inches

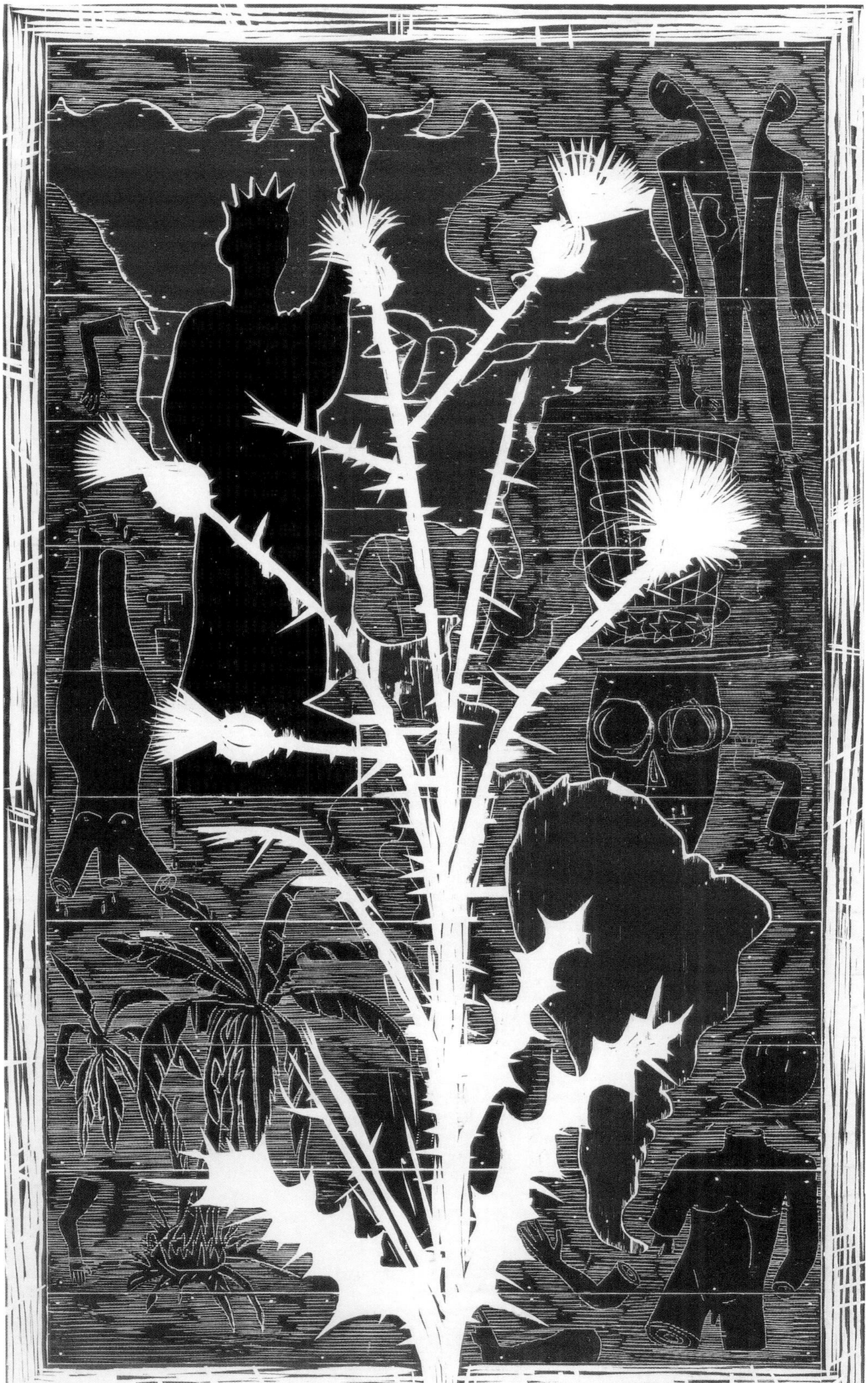

PLATE 22

TRAILS PLOWED UNDER, edition 2/15
1989
Three color woodcut
63½ x 37 inches

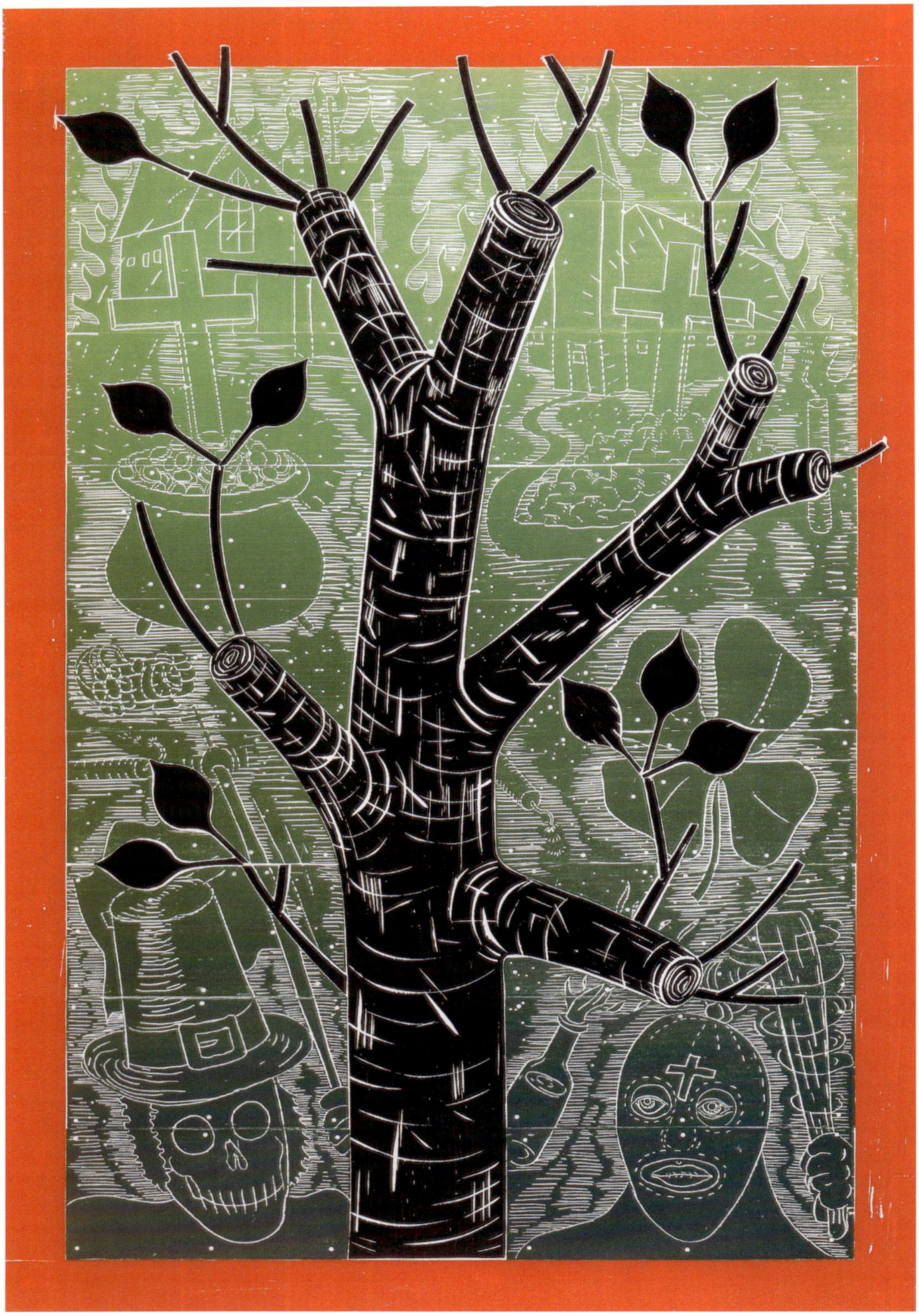

PLATE 23

The Shillelagh Tree, edition 7/15
1990
Five-color woodcut
52 x 36 inches

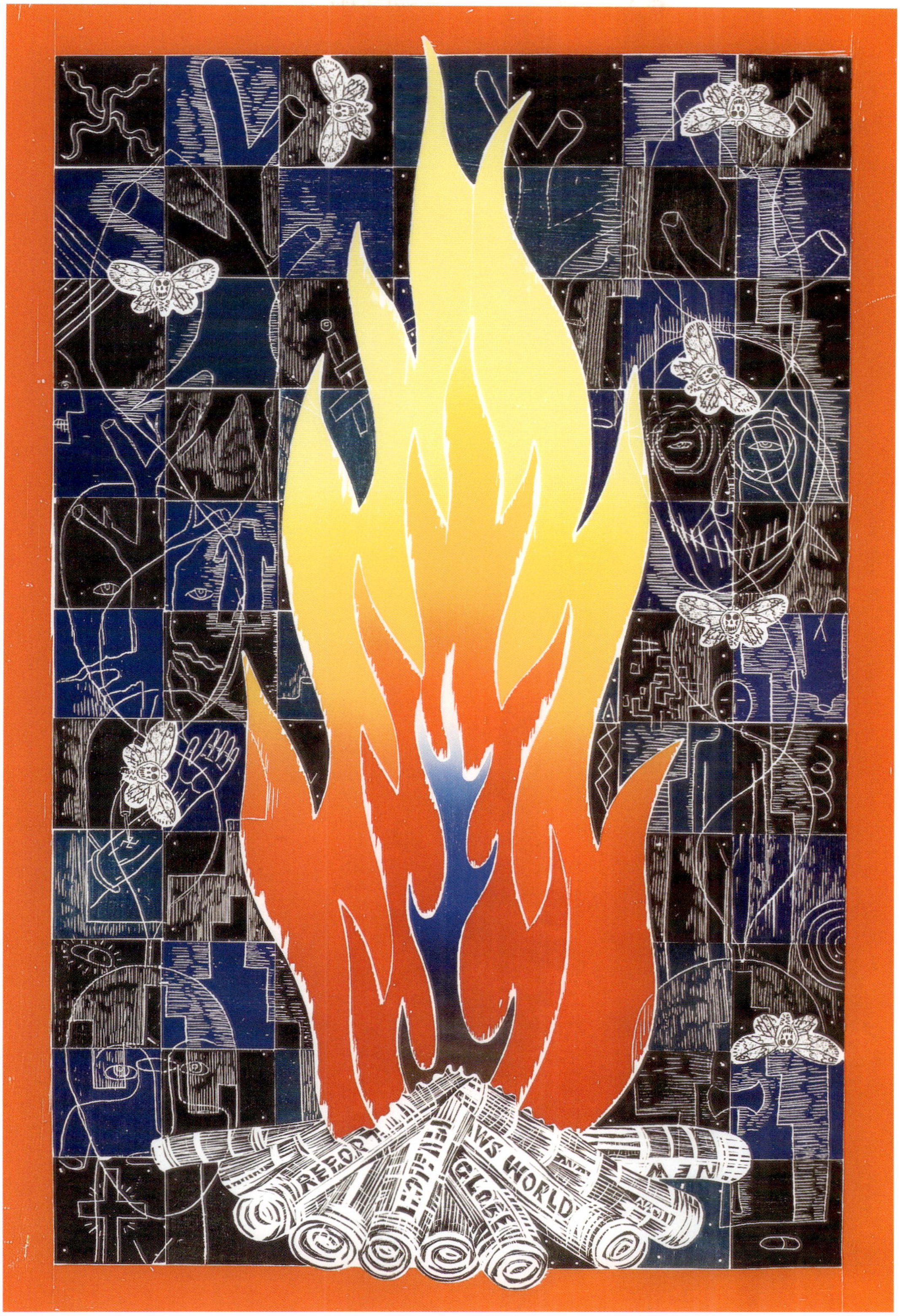

PLATE 24

The Times, edition 13/15

1991

Eleven-color woodcut

53 ½ x 36 ¼ inches

PLATE 25

A Common Tongue, edition 6/15
1992
Eight-color woodcut
62 x 36½ inches

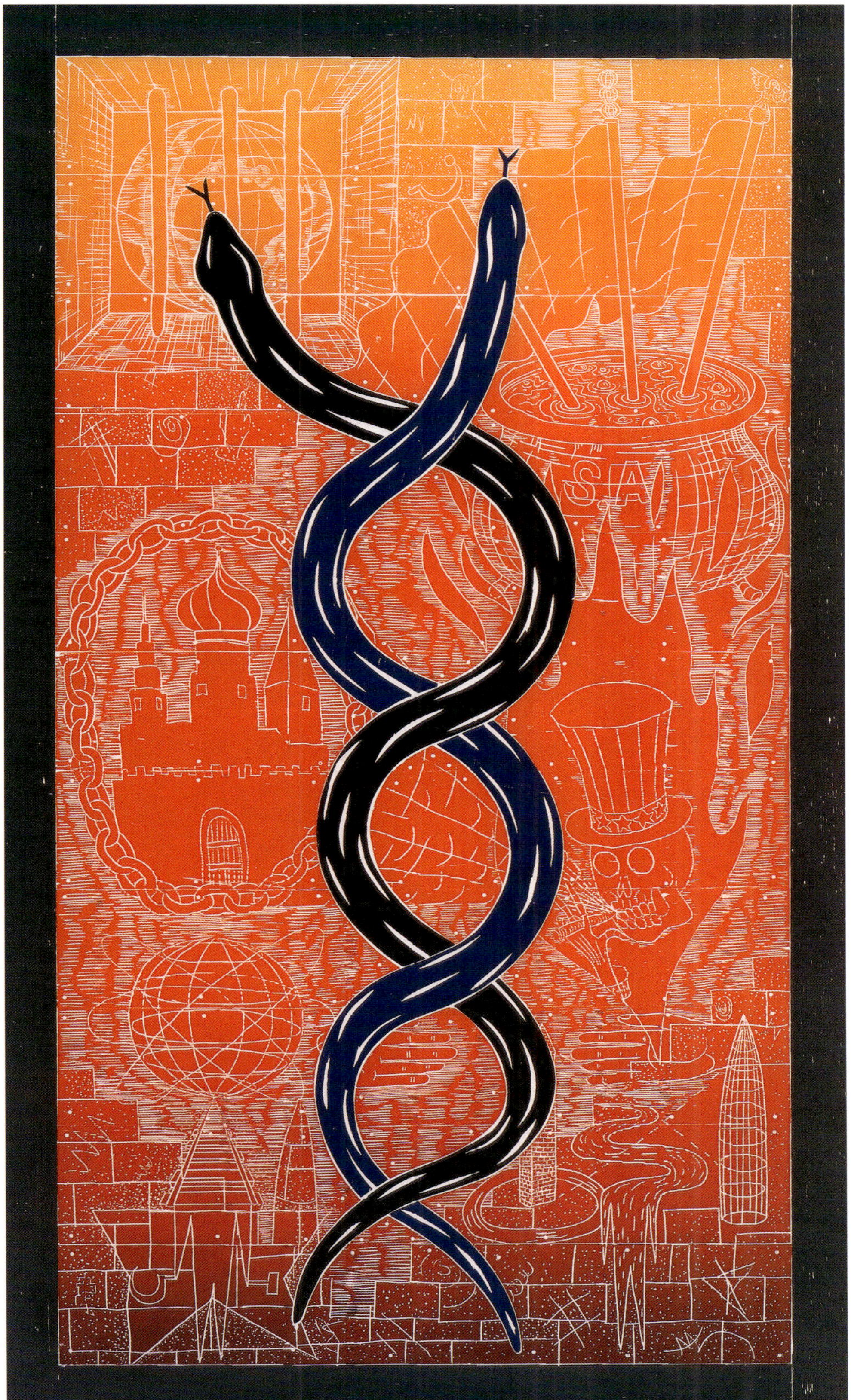
U.S.A.

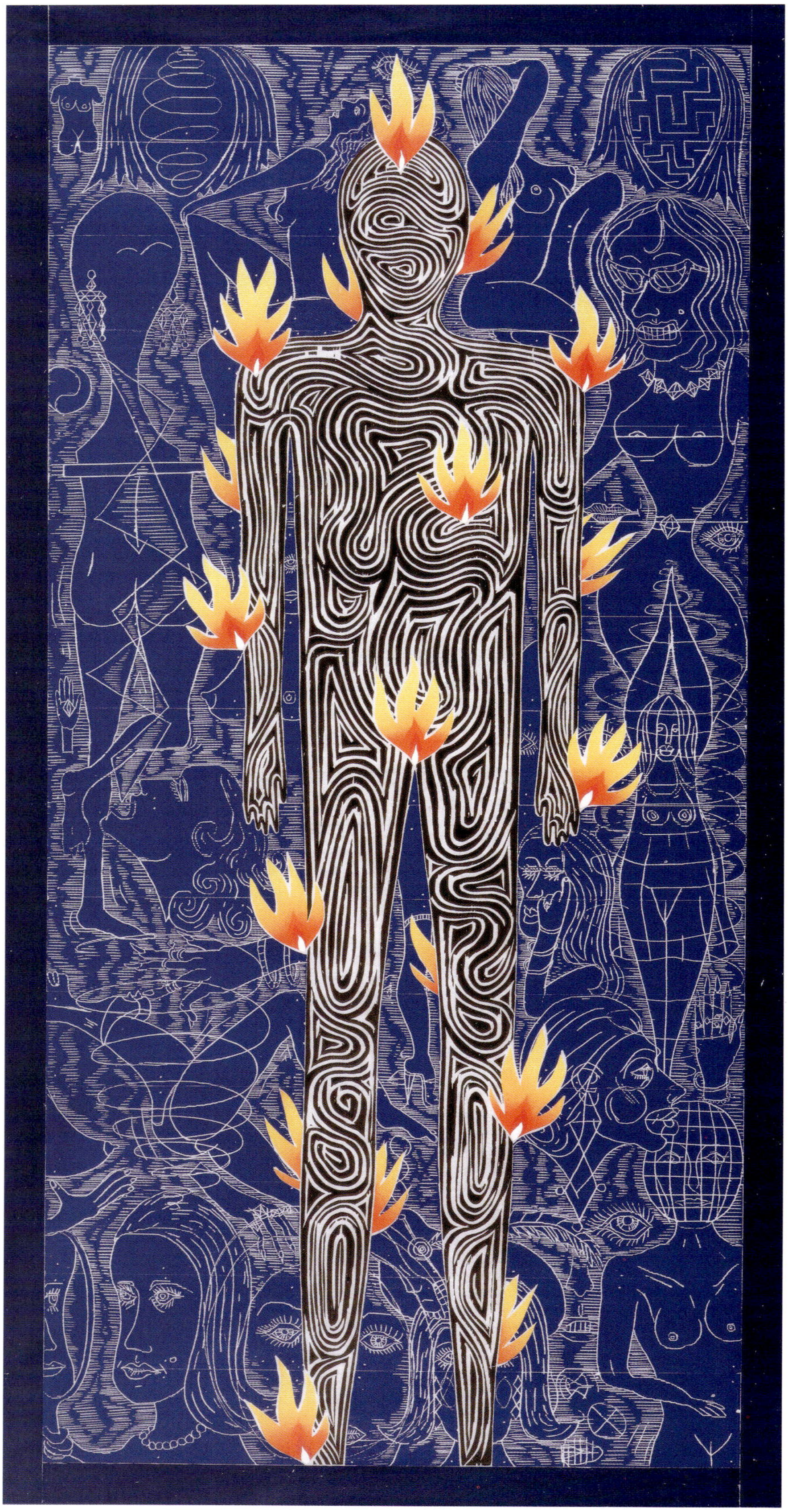

PLATE 26

Tattoo, edition 4/15
1992
Five-color woodcut, lithograph, chine-collé
74 x 37 inches

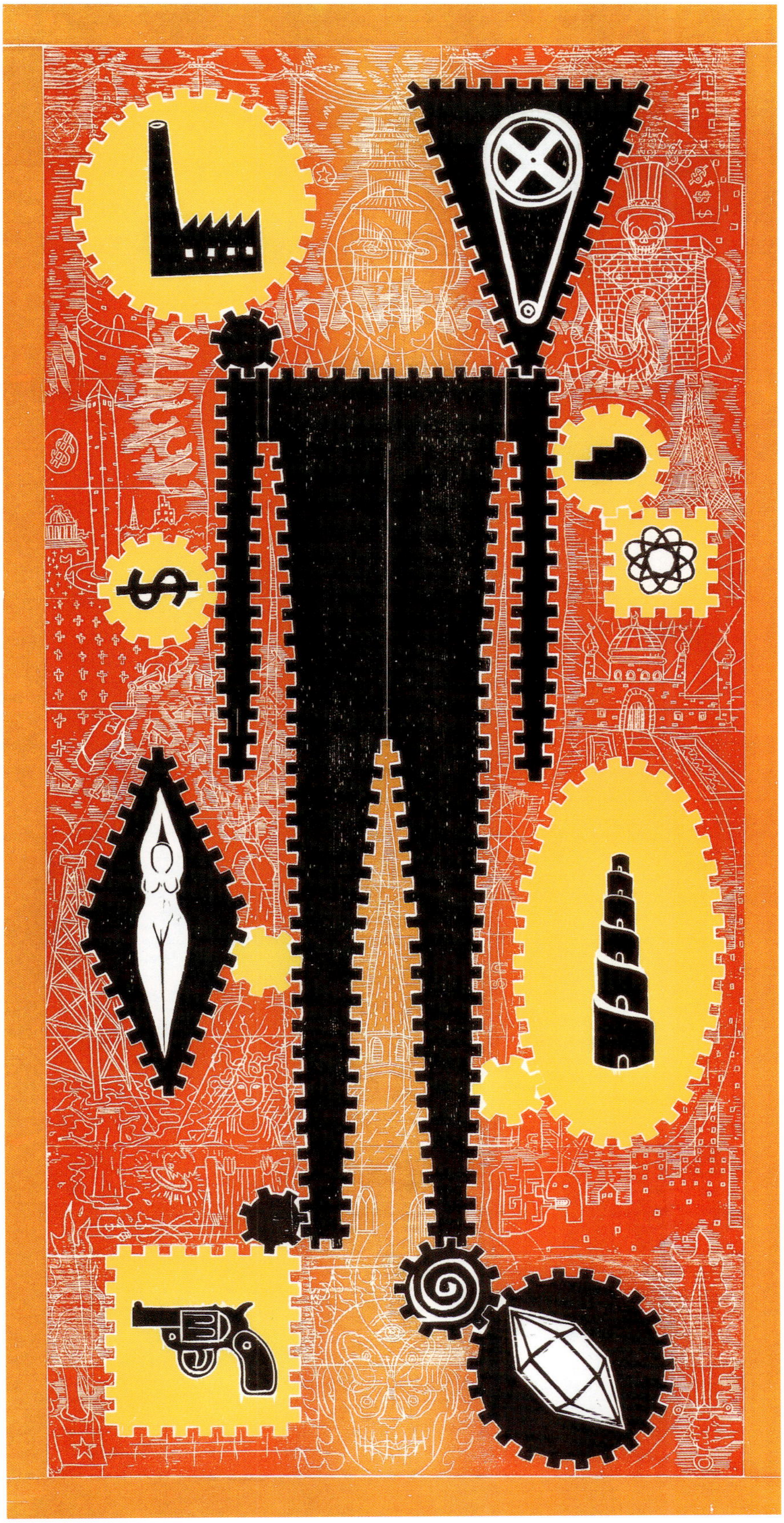

PLATE 27

The Mechanic, edition 13/15
1994
Six-color woodcut
73 x 37 inches

PLATE 28

THE COAL MINE, edition 6/15
1996
Four color woodcut
62 x 37 inches

PLATE 28

THE COAL MINE, edition 6/15
1996
Four color woodcut
62 x 37 inches

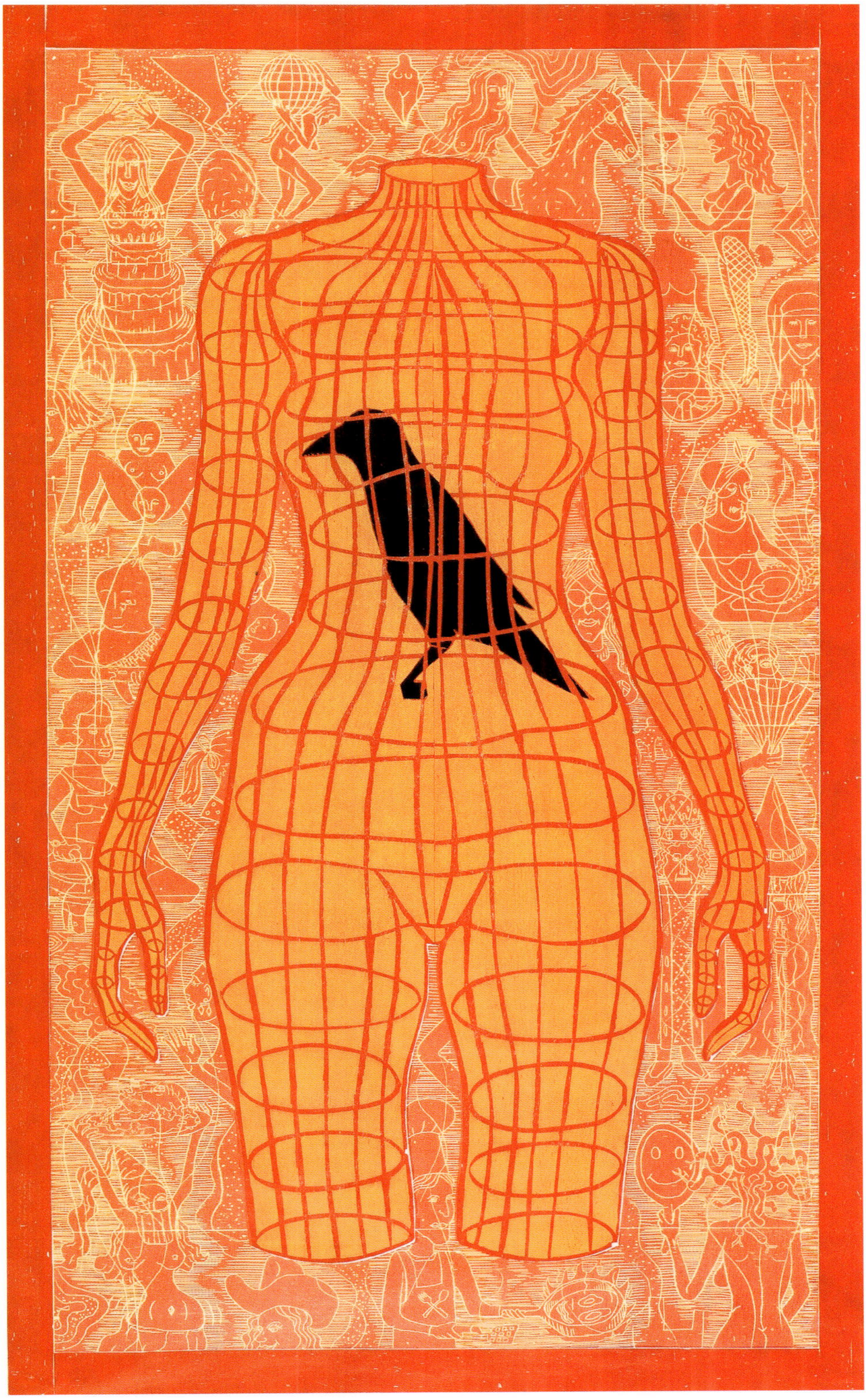

PLATE 29

NINE QUARTER CIRCLE

1996

Wood sculpture with graphite

95 x 73 x 17 inches overall

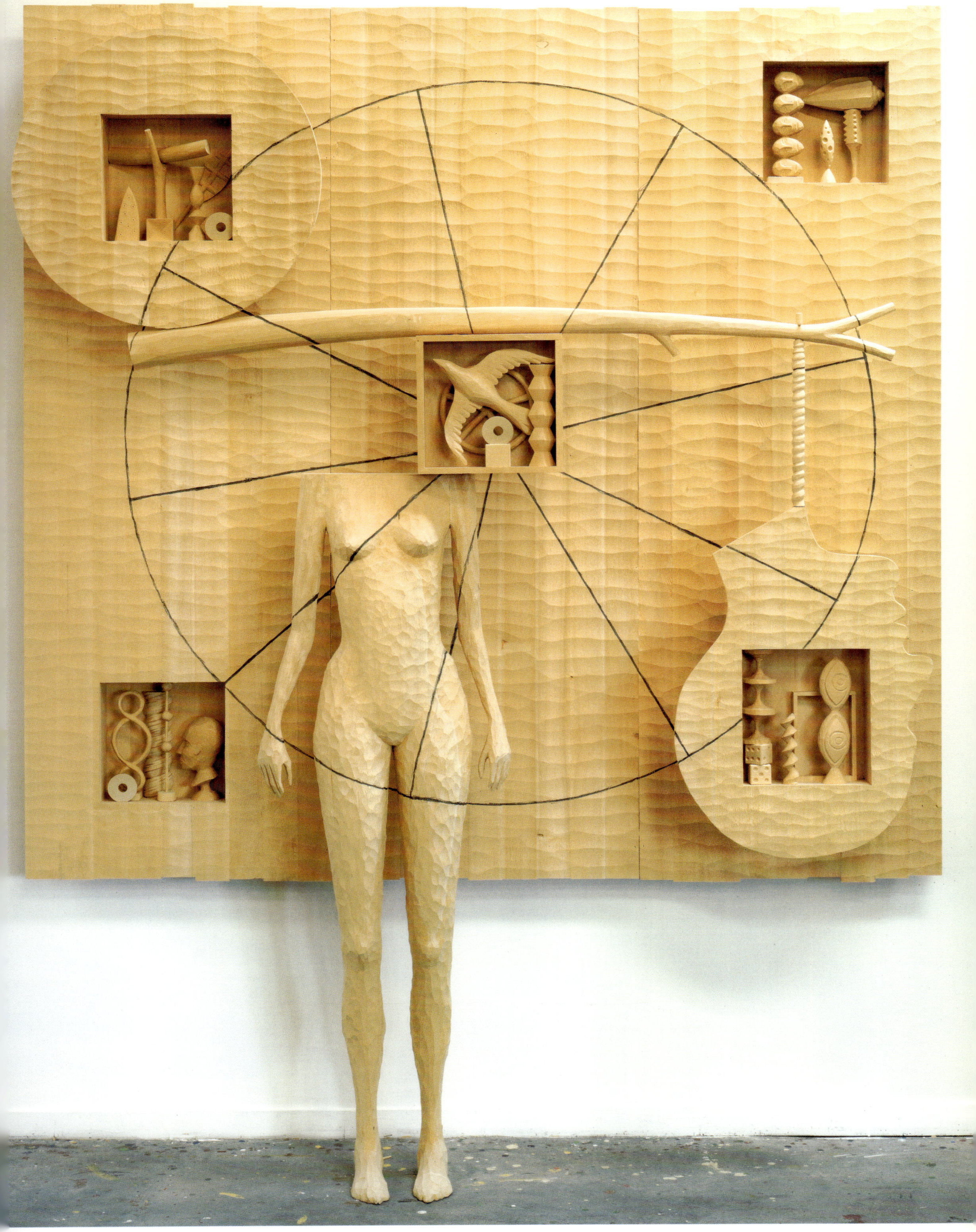

PLATE 30

FACT AND FICTION, edition 9/15
1997
Eight-color woodcut
74 x 58 inches

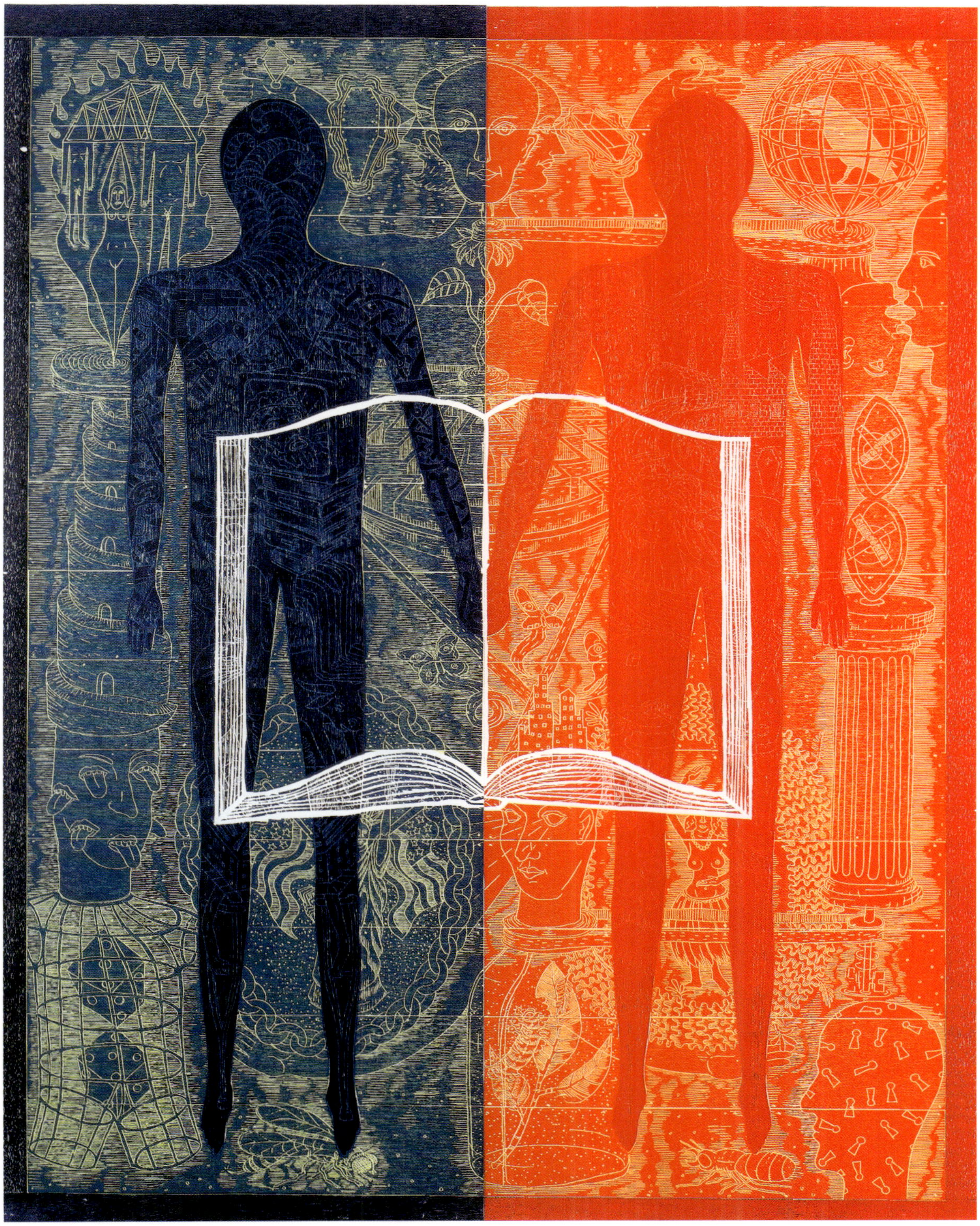

PLATE 31

THE INSIDE

1998

Blown and lampworked glass with carved wood elements

23 x 14 x 14 inches overall

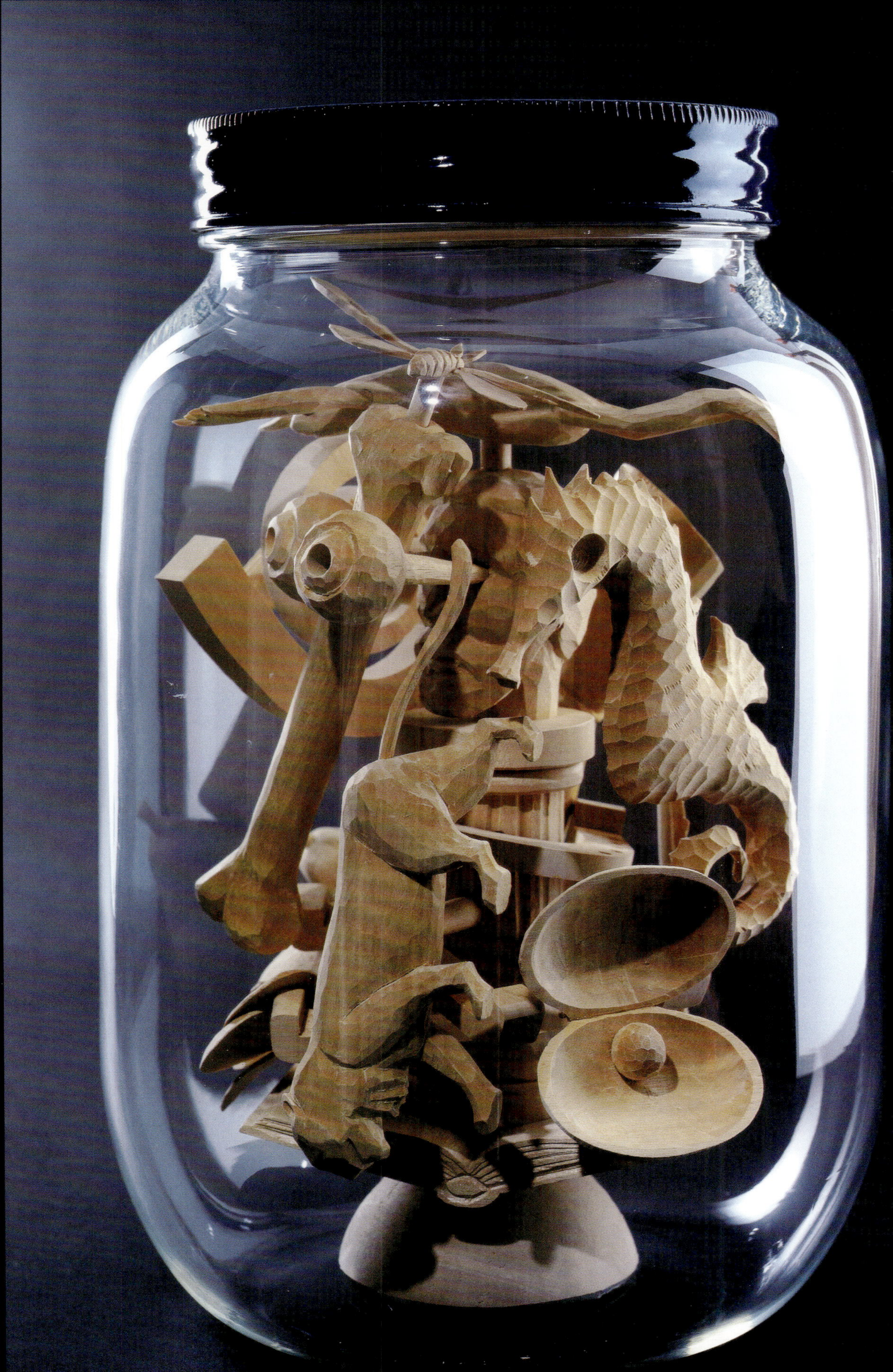

PLATE 32

Ladder, Ring, Leaf

1999

Wood with acrylic paint

38 x 16 x 4 inches overall

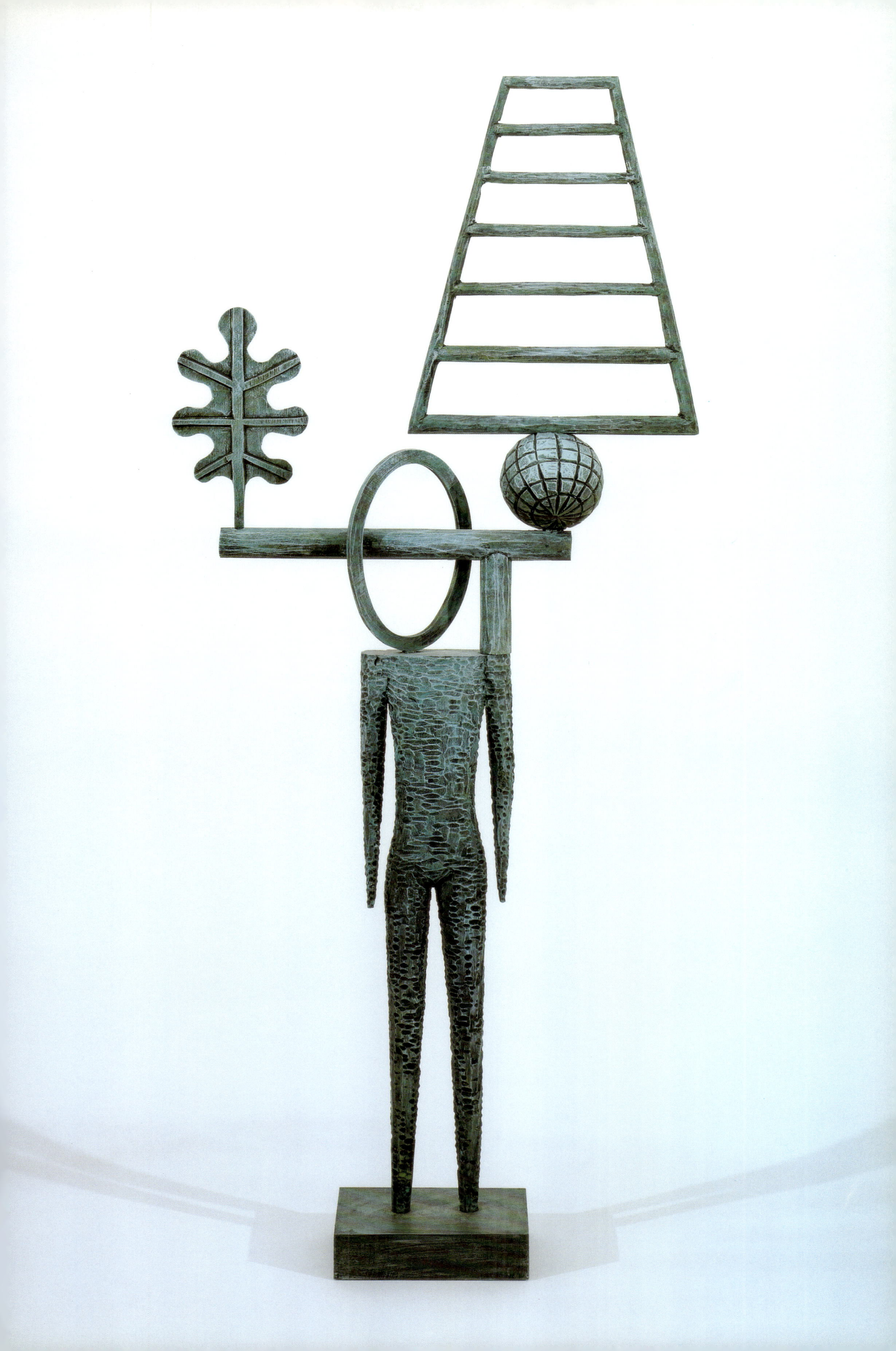

PLATE 33

HEART MOUNTAIN, WYOMING, edition 6/15
2000
Seven-color woodcut
62 x 37 inches

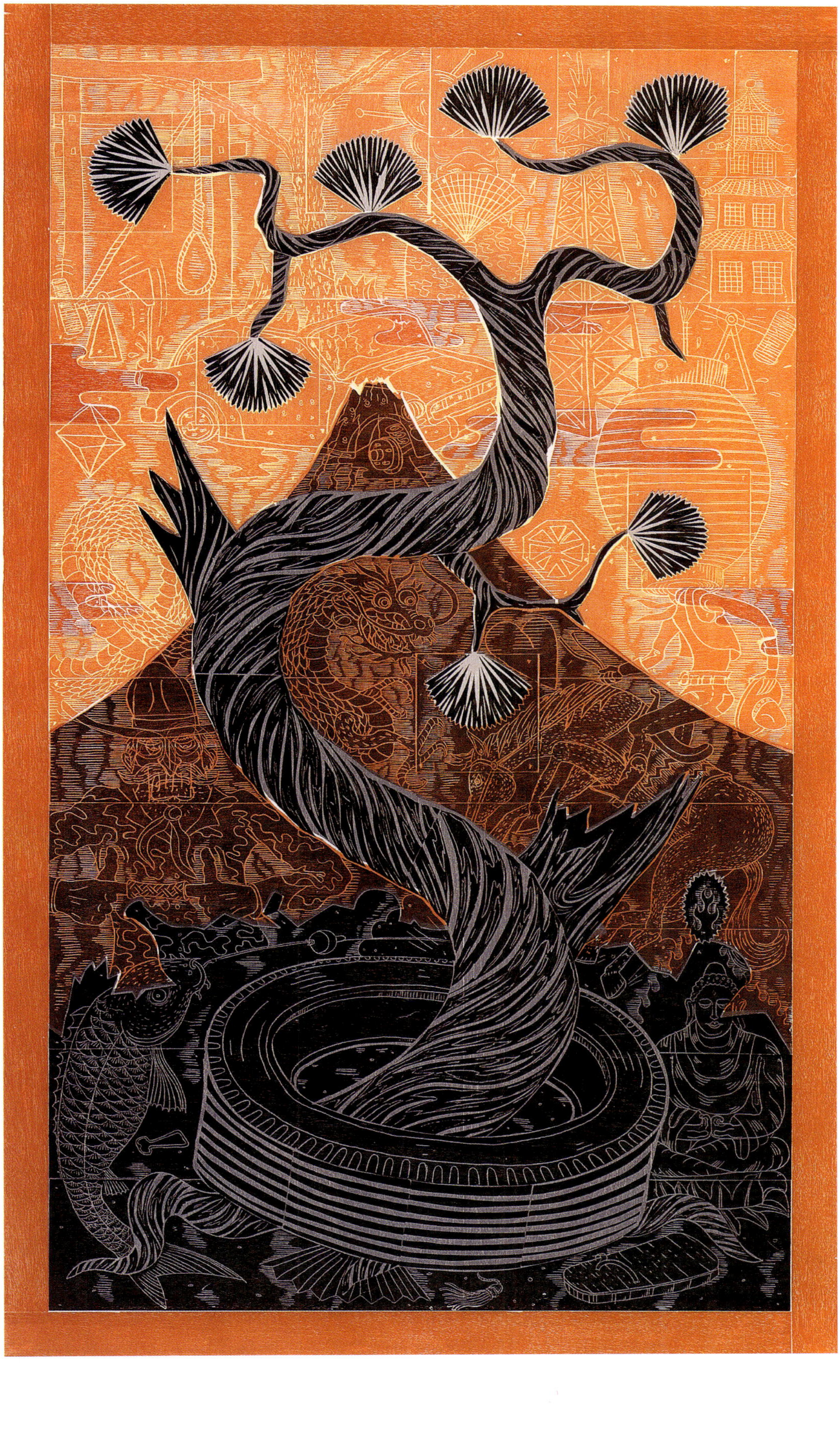

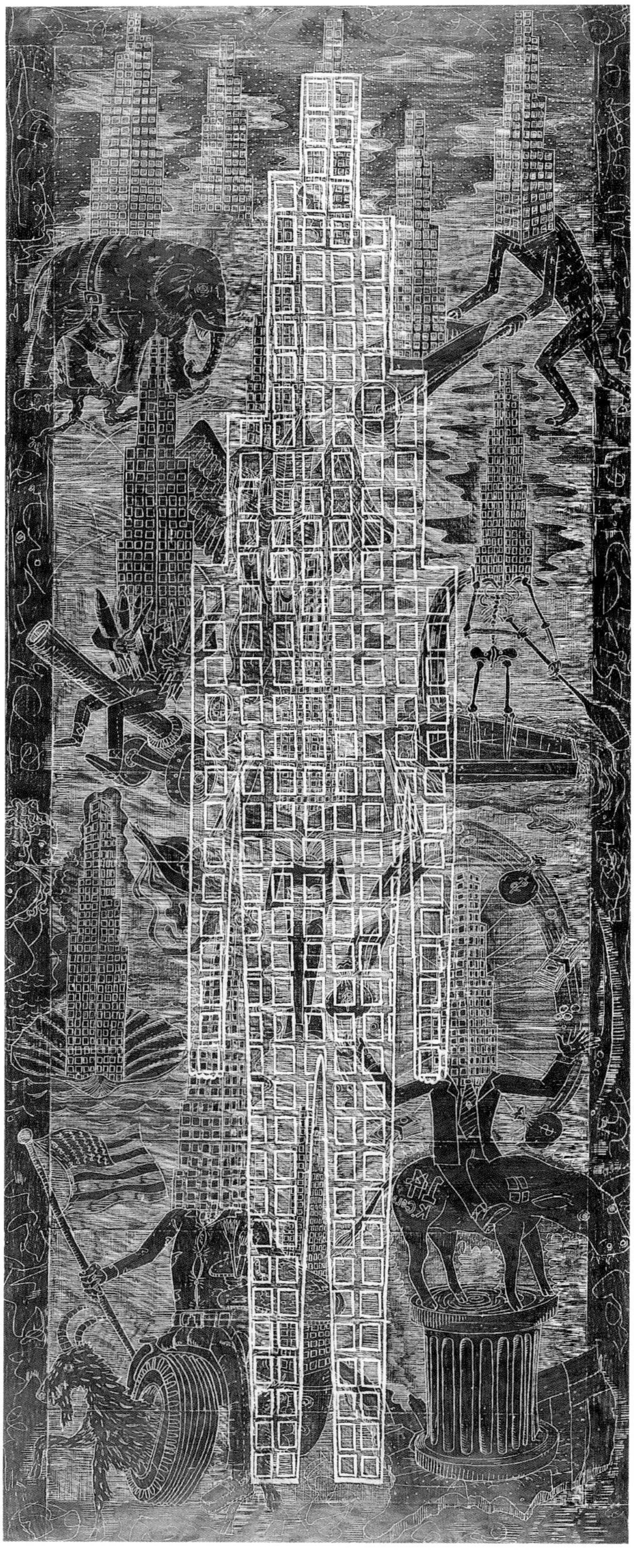

PLATE 34

SKYLINE, edition AP
2000
Woodblock rubbing
100 x 45 inches

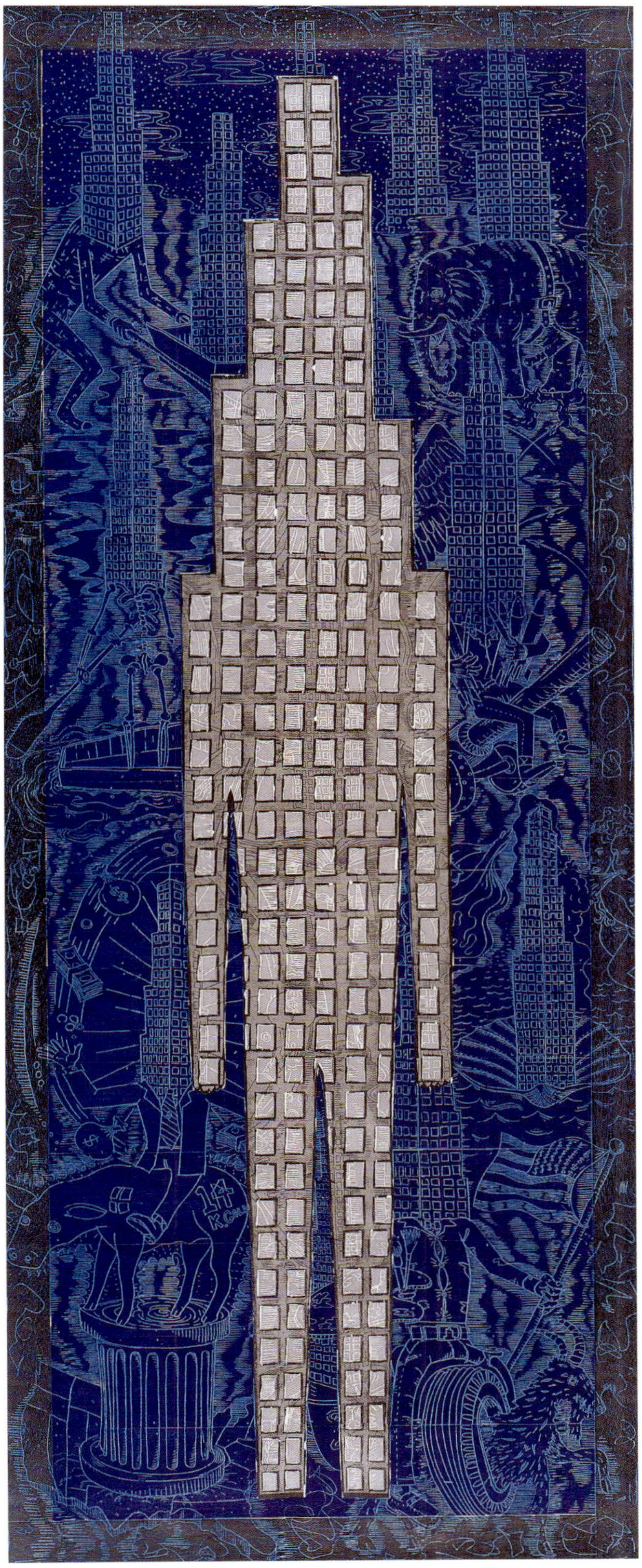

PLATE 35

SKYLINE, edition 4/15
2000–2002
Four color woodcut
92 x 37 inches

PLATE 36

BOTANICA, edition 10/15
2003
Nine-color woodcut
62 x 37 inches

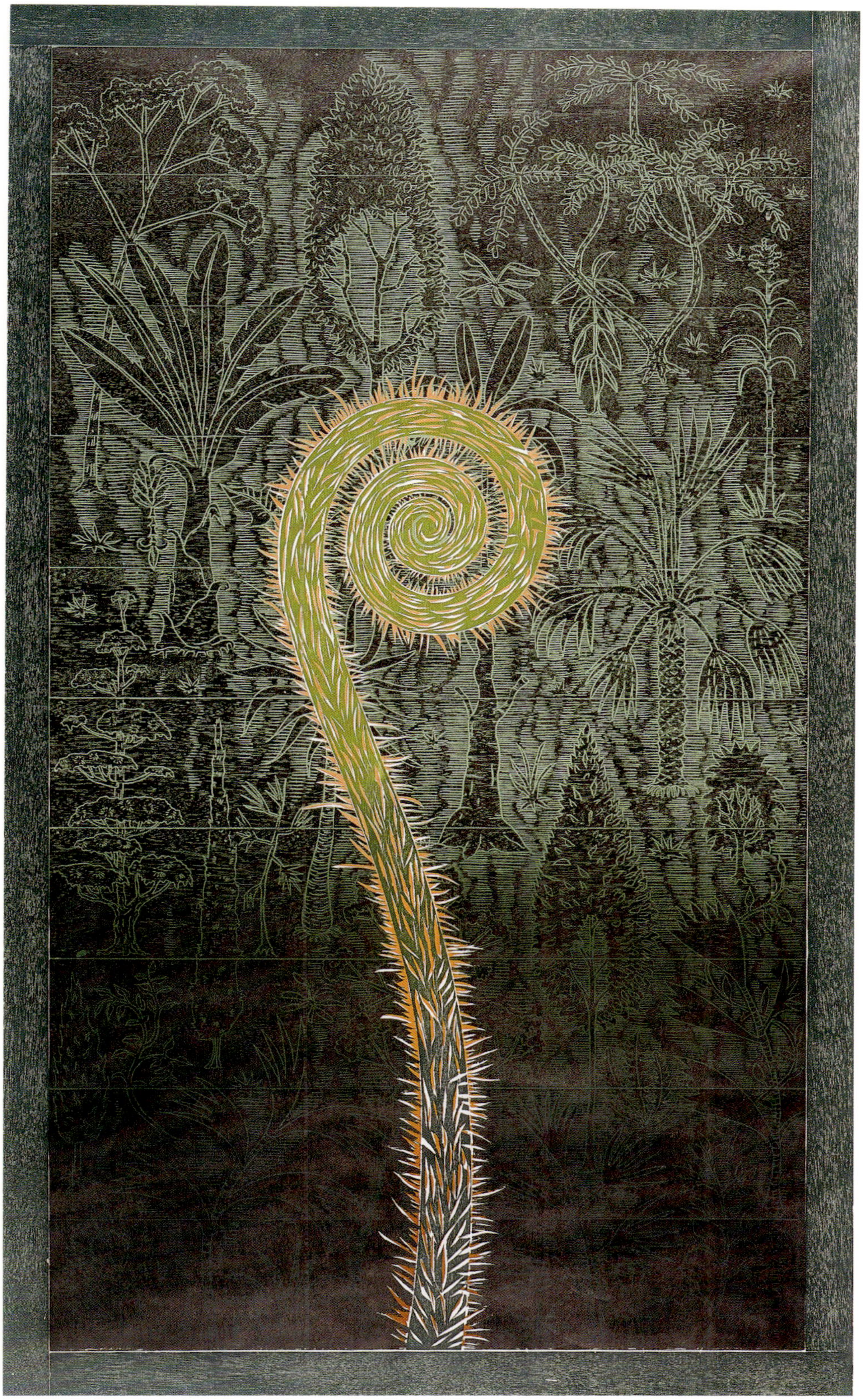

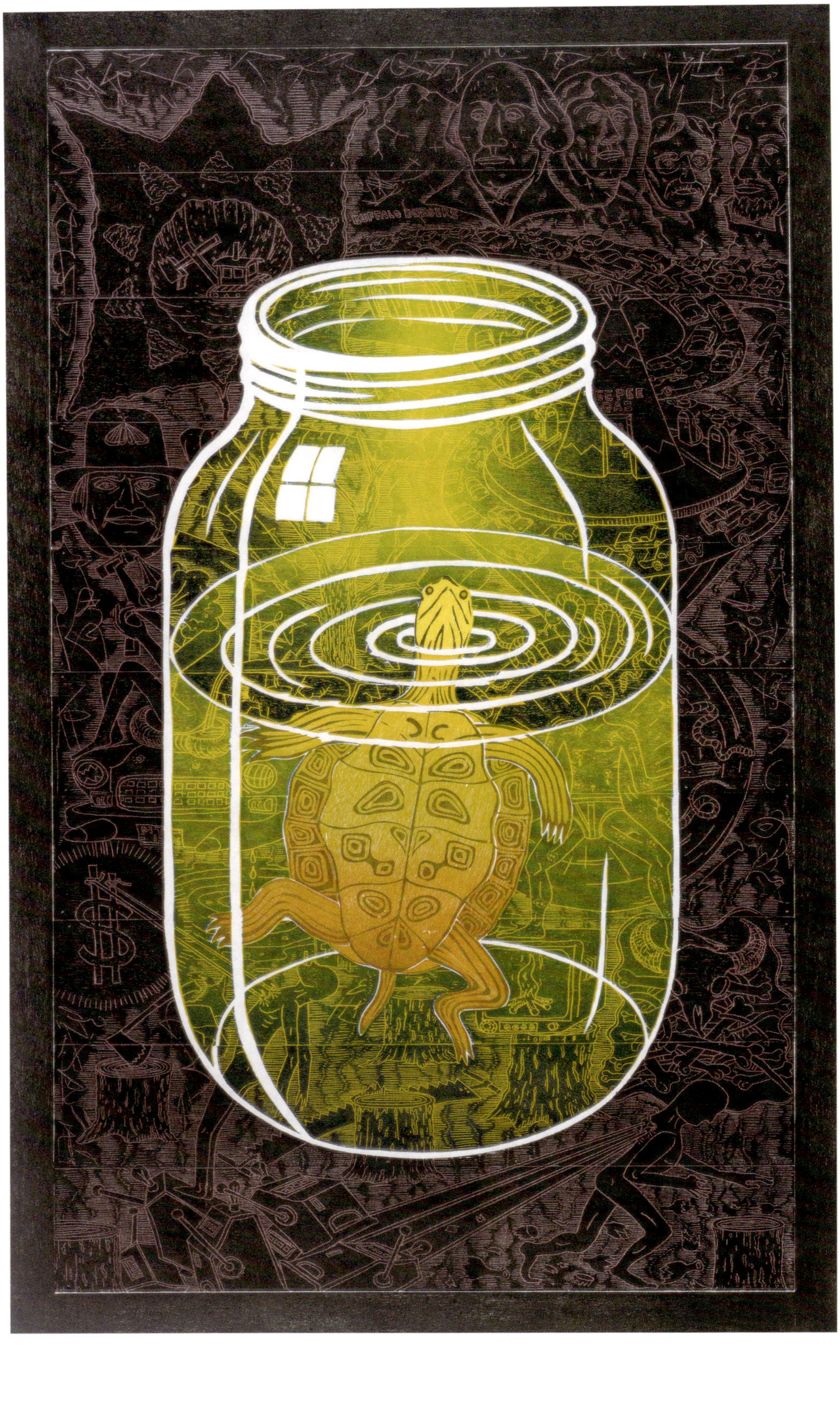

PLATE 37

Crystal Lake, edition 6/15
2001
Twelve-color woodcut
62 x 37 inches

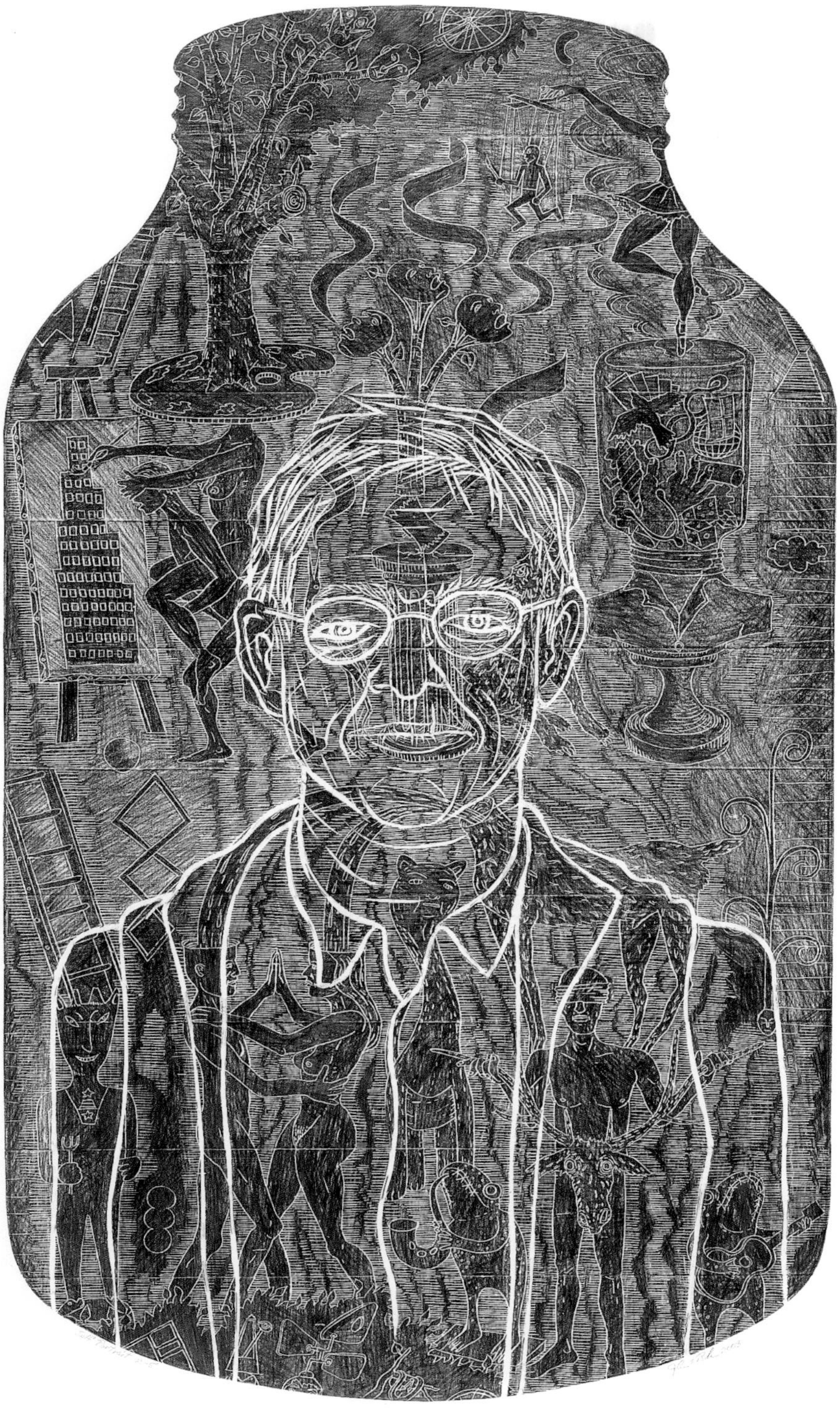

PLATE 38

SELF-PORTRAIT, edition 2/5
2003
Woodblock rubbing with crayon
56 x 32 inches

PLATE 39

TAJ MAHAL

2003

Jelutong wood with acrylic paint

48 x 48 x 2¾ inches overall

PLATE 40

NORTH OF SOUTH

2005

Wood panel with acrylic paint

72 x 72 x 3½ inches overall

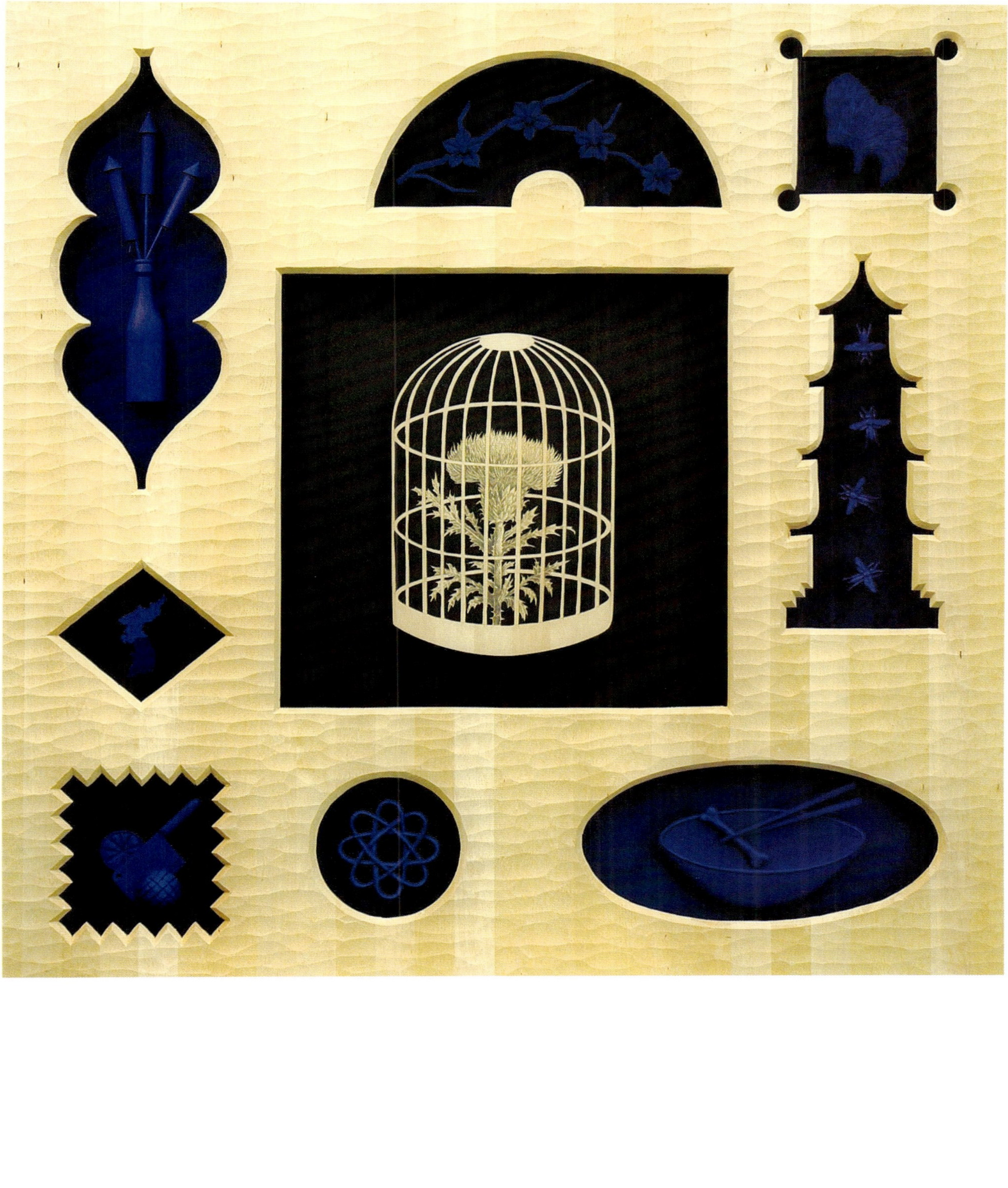

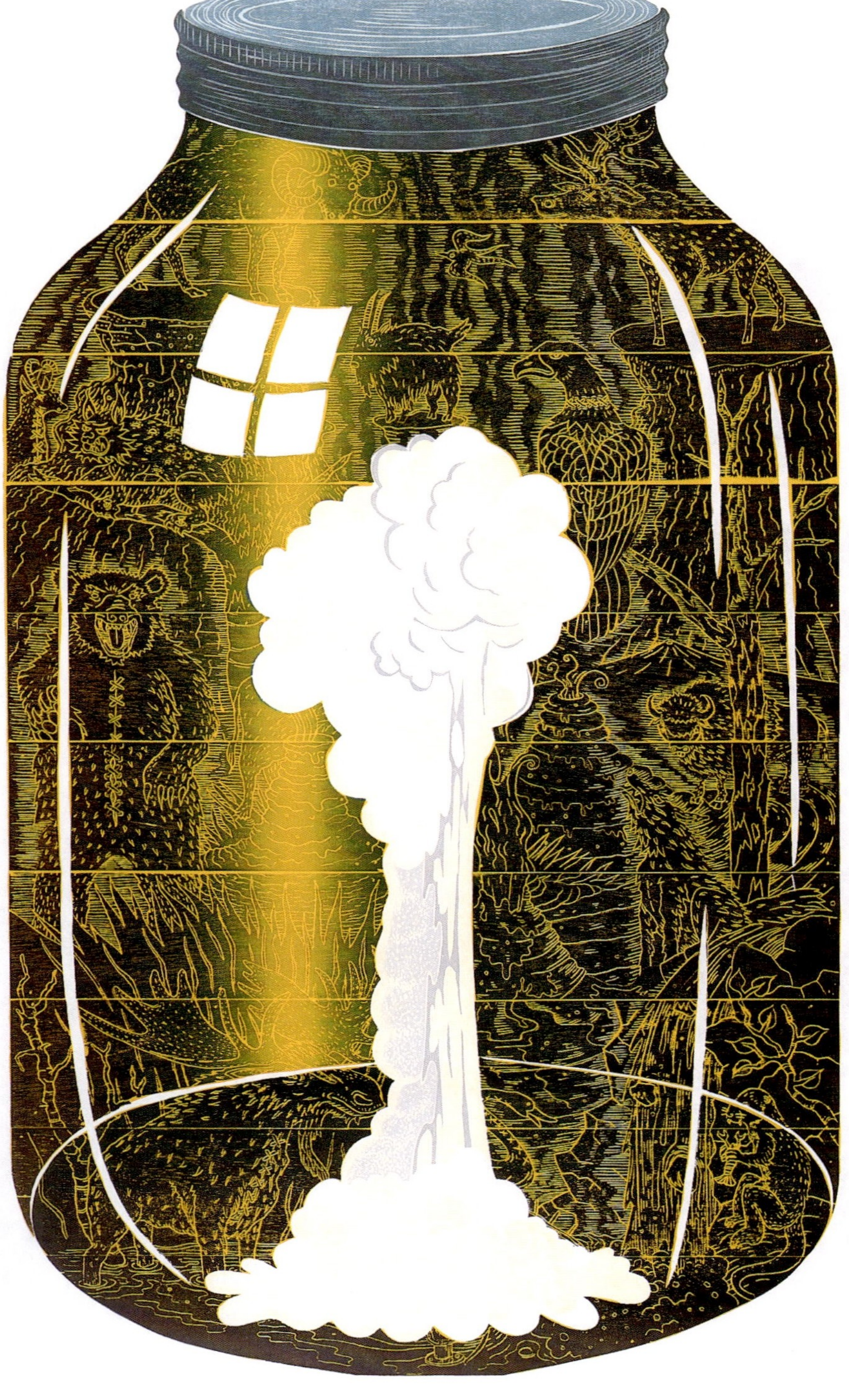

PLATE 41

The Preserve, edition 6/15
2005
Eleven-color woodcut
62 x 37 inches

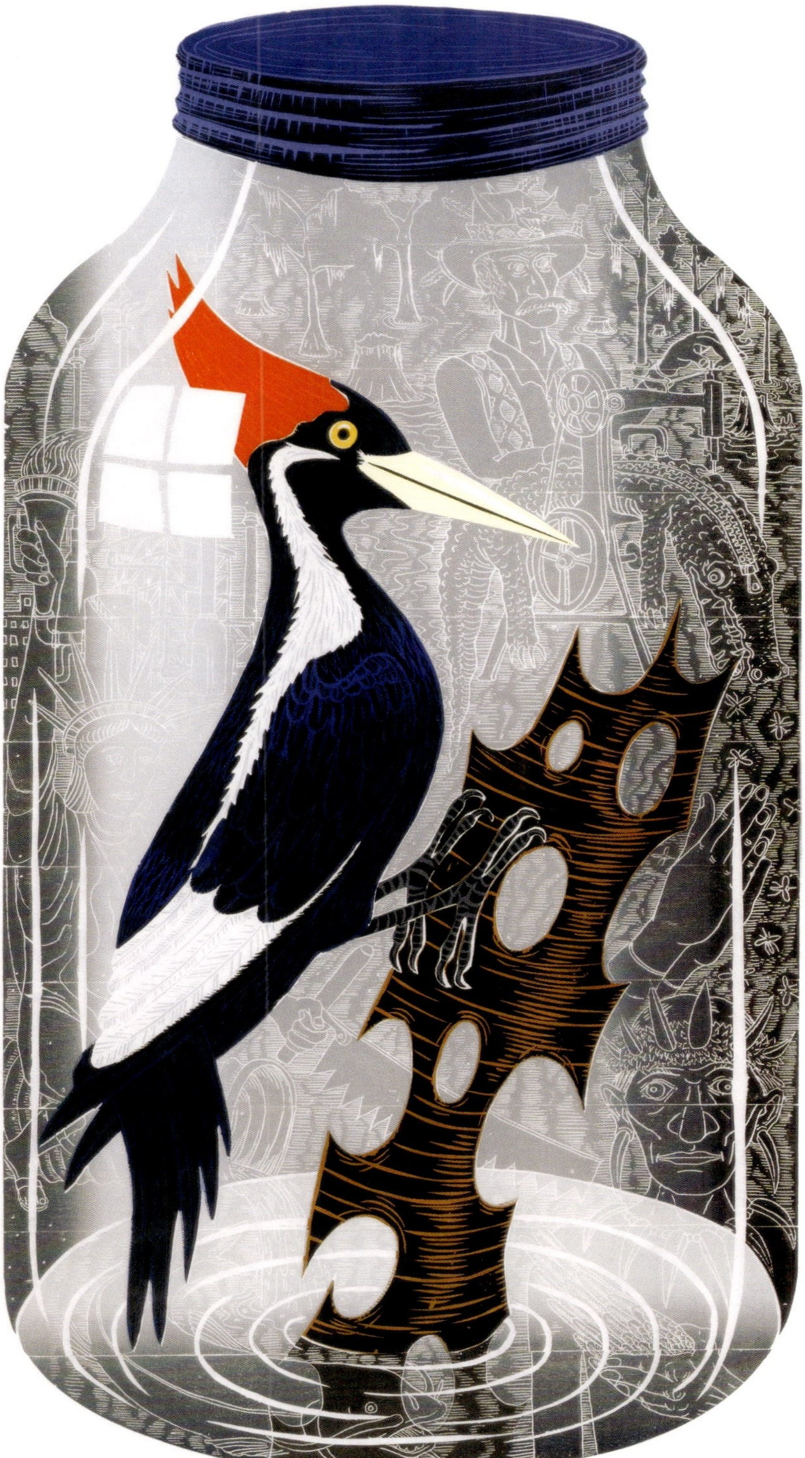

PLATE 42

The Singer Tract, edition 6/15
2005
Eleven-color woodcut with pochoir
67¾ x 37 inches

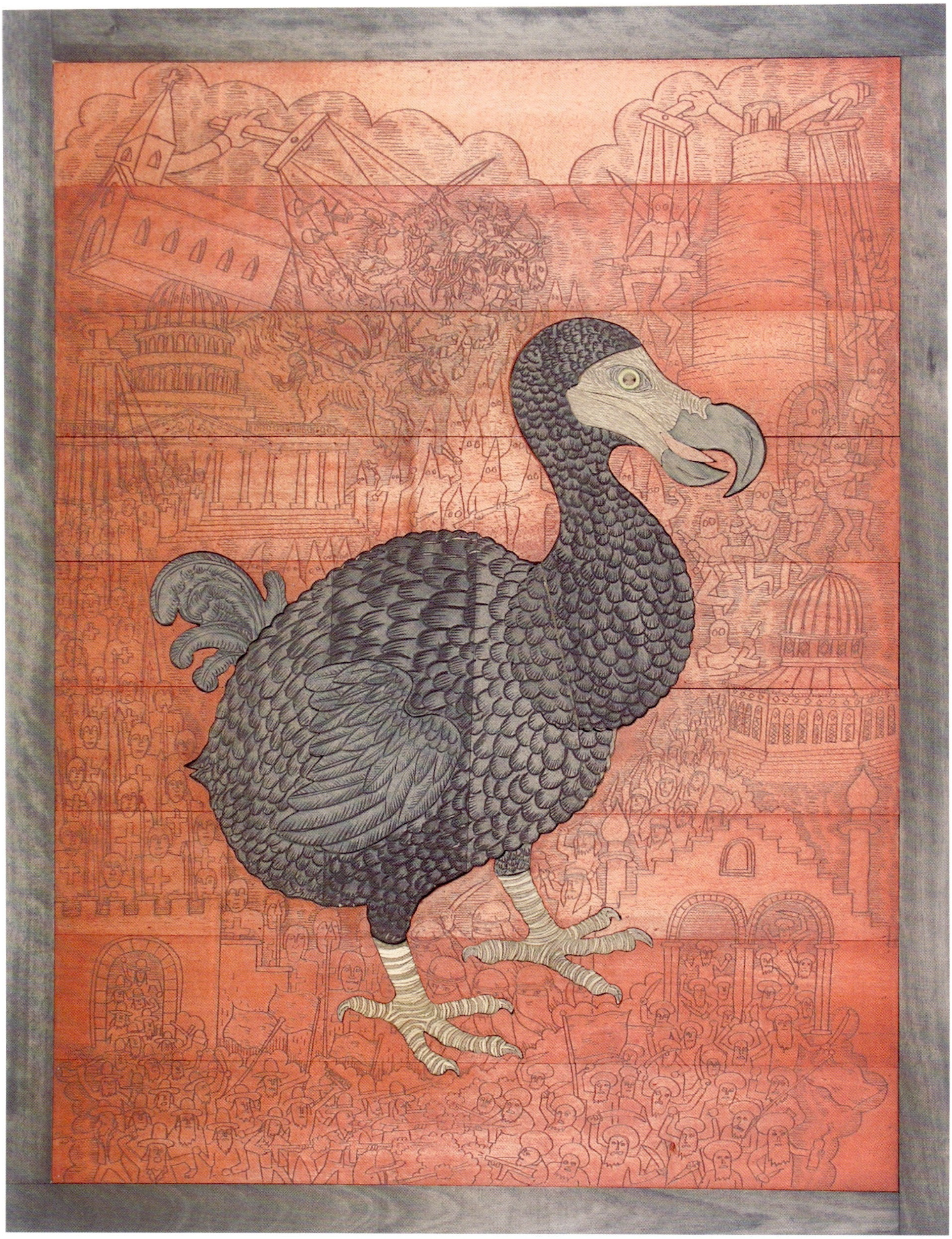

PLATE 43

Phoenix Rising

2006

Wood block

Image: 50 x 37 inches

Overall: 53 x 40 inches

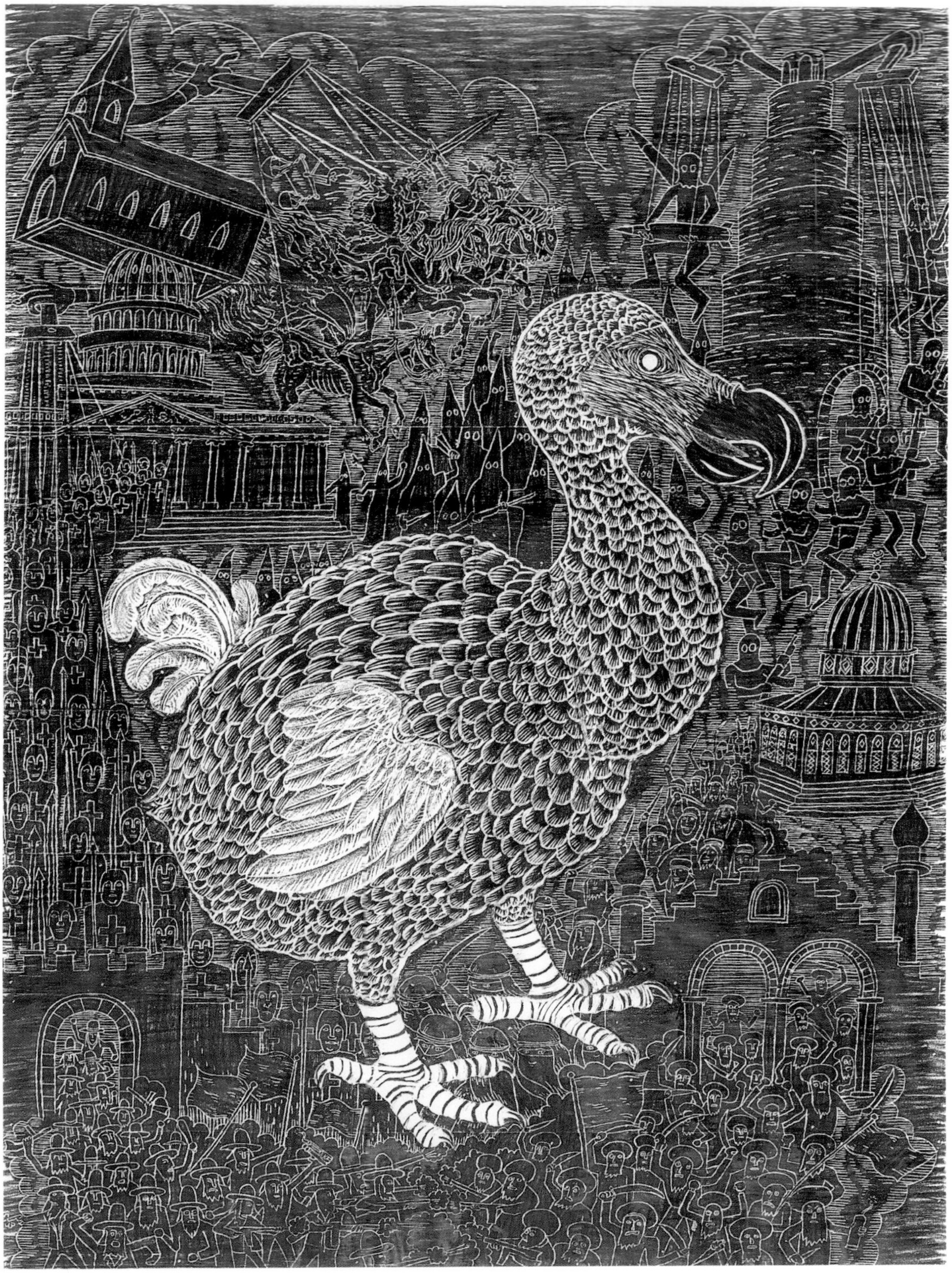

PLATE 44

Phoenix Rising, edition AP
2006
Woodblock rubbing
50 x 37 inches

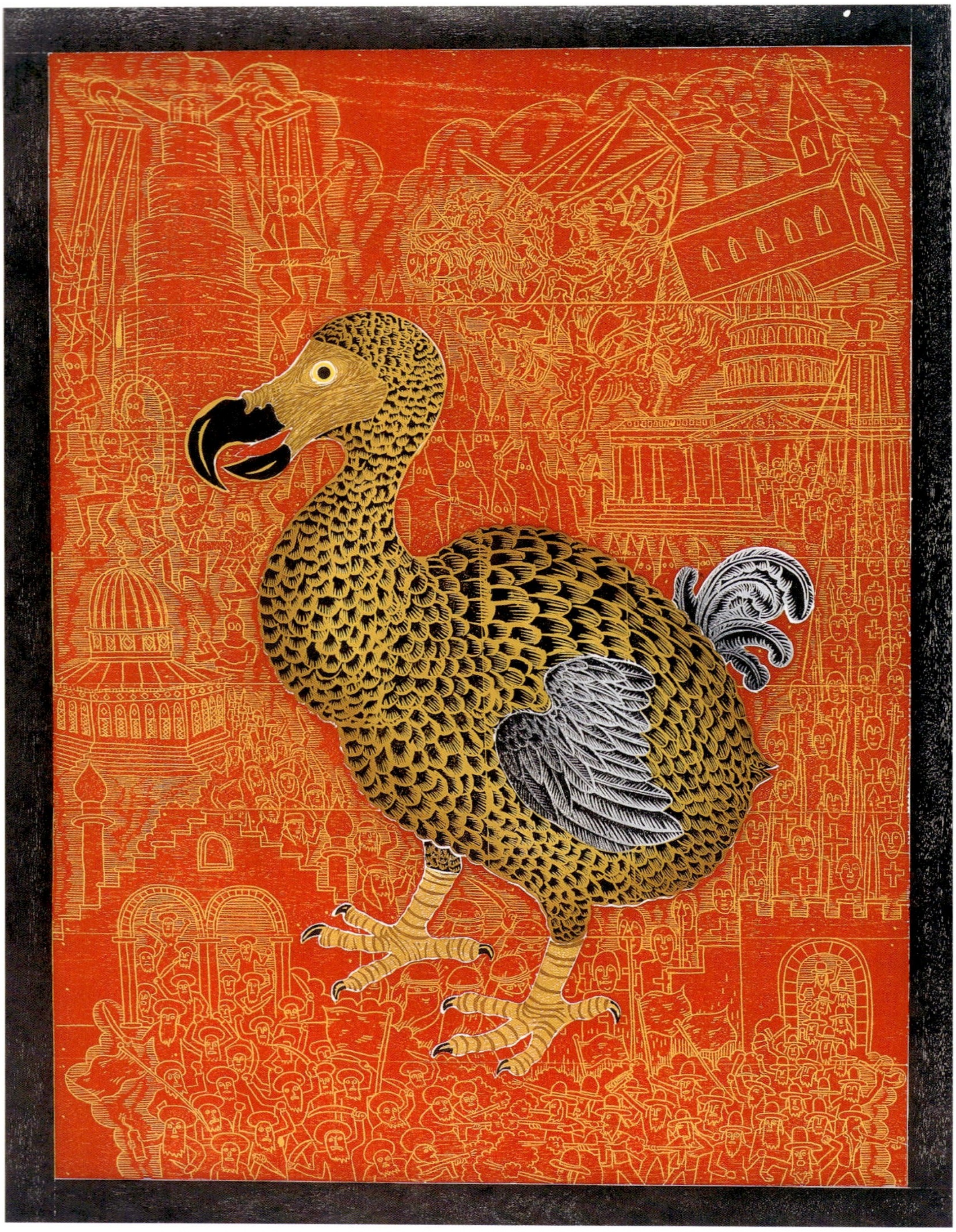

PLATE 45

PHOENIX RISING, edition TP
2006
Seven-color woodcut with pochoir
50 x 37 inches

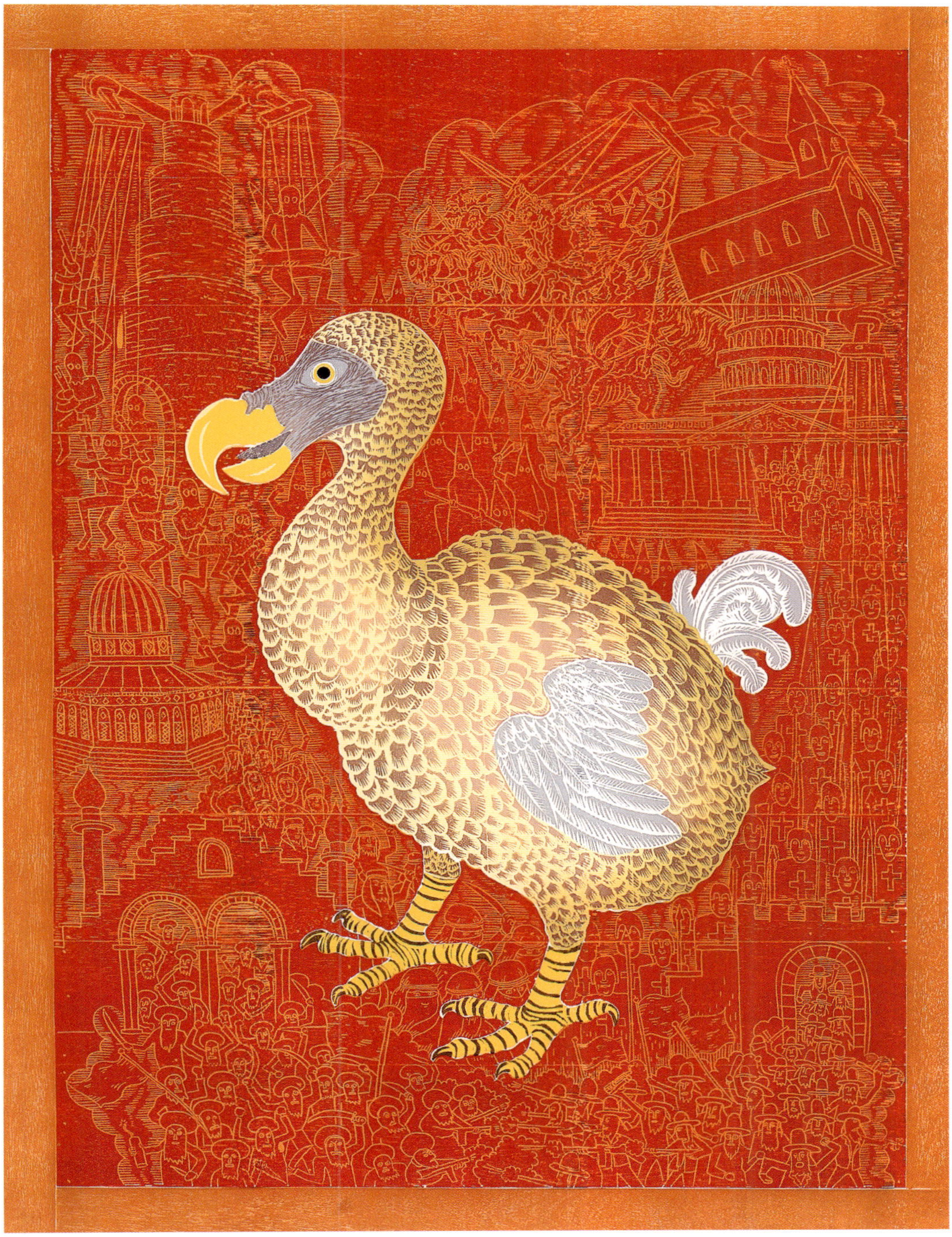

PLATE 46

PHOENIX RISING, edition TP
2006
Seven-color woodcut with pochoir
50 x 37 inches

PLATE 47

SUBMULOC II, edition AP
2006
Woodblock rubbing in nero crayon
60 x 36 inches

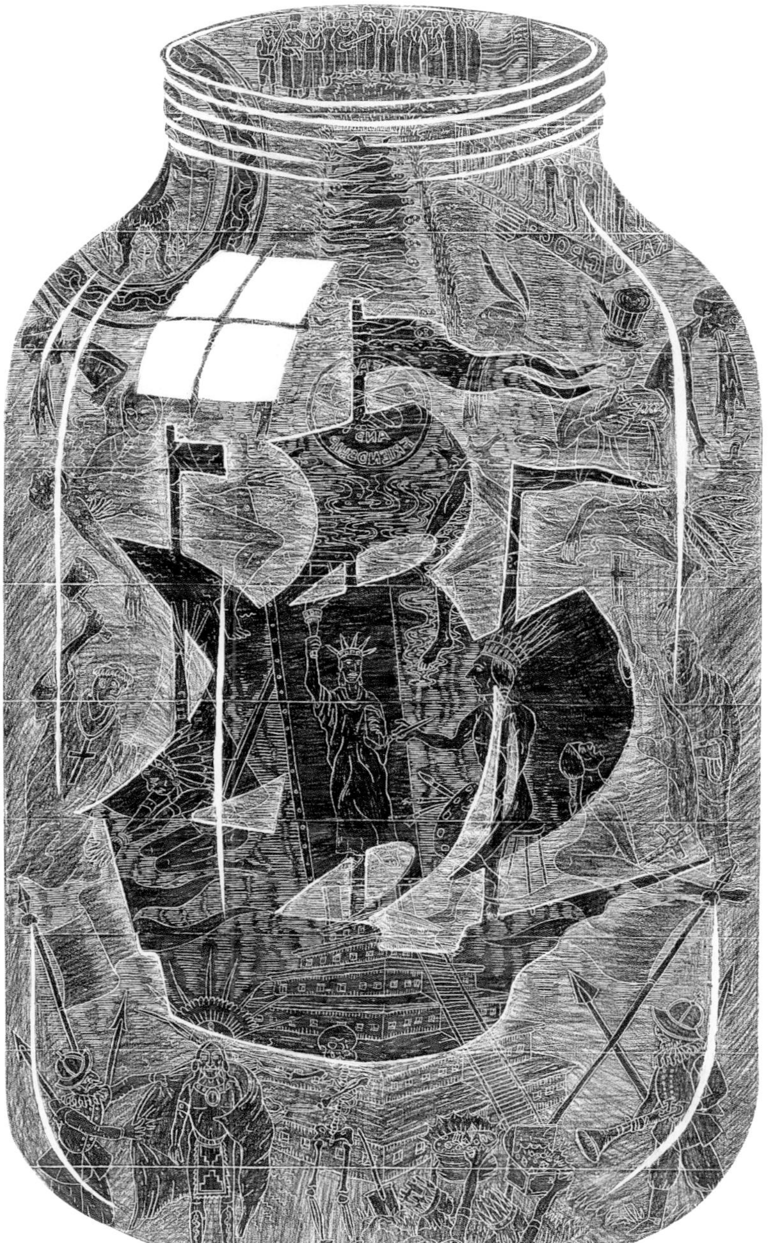

PLATE 48

Borderline
2007
Wood sculpture with acrylic paint
72 x 31 x 8 inches

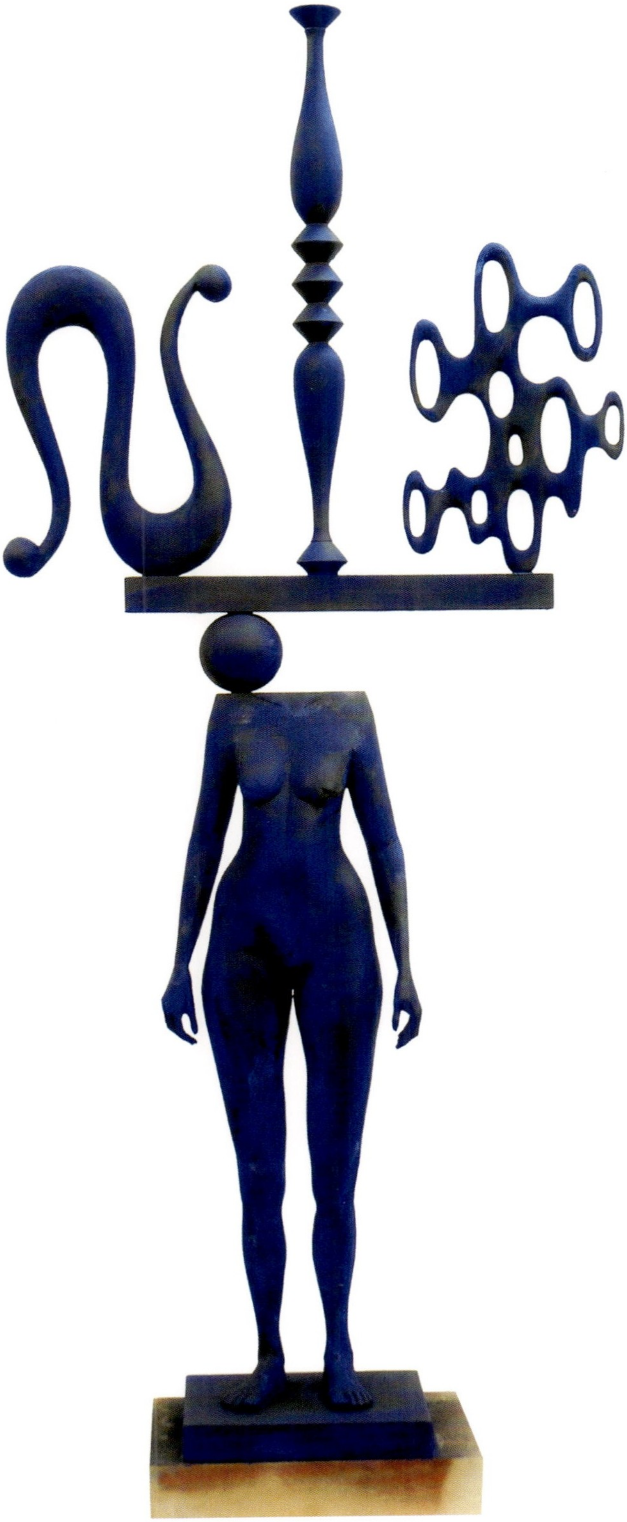

PLATE 49

THE NIGHT PRISM, edition 4/20
2007
Color woodcut
74½ x 37 inches

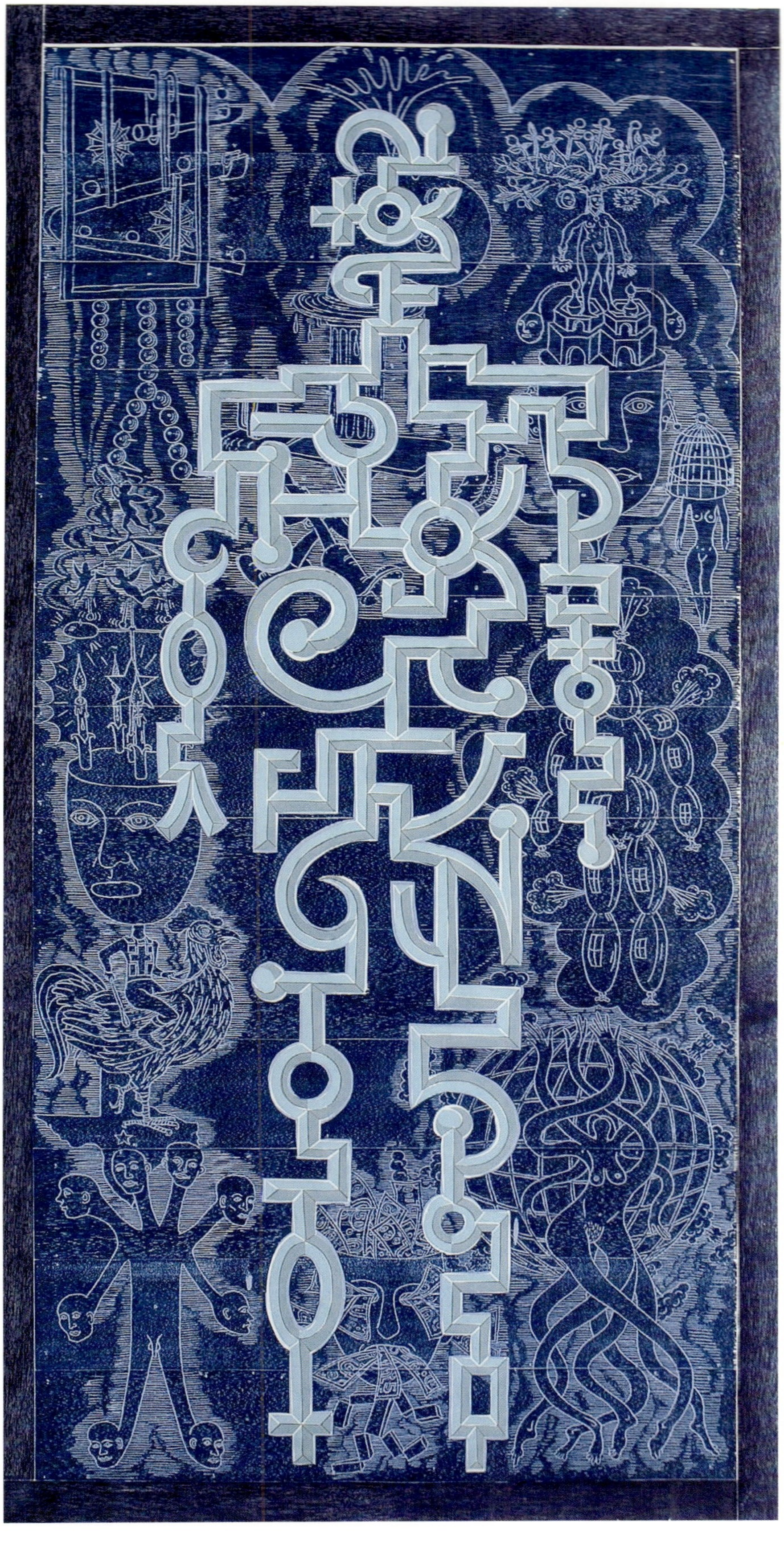

PLATE 50

REMEMBER THE MAINE

2007

Blown and lampworked glass with carved wood elements

23 x 14 x 14 inches overall

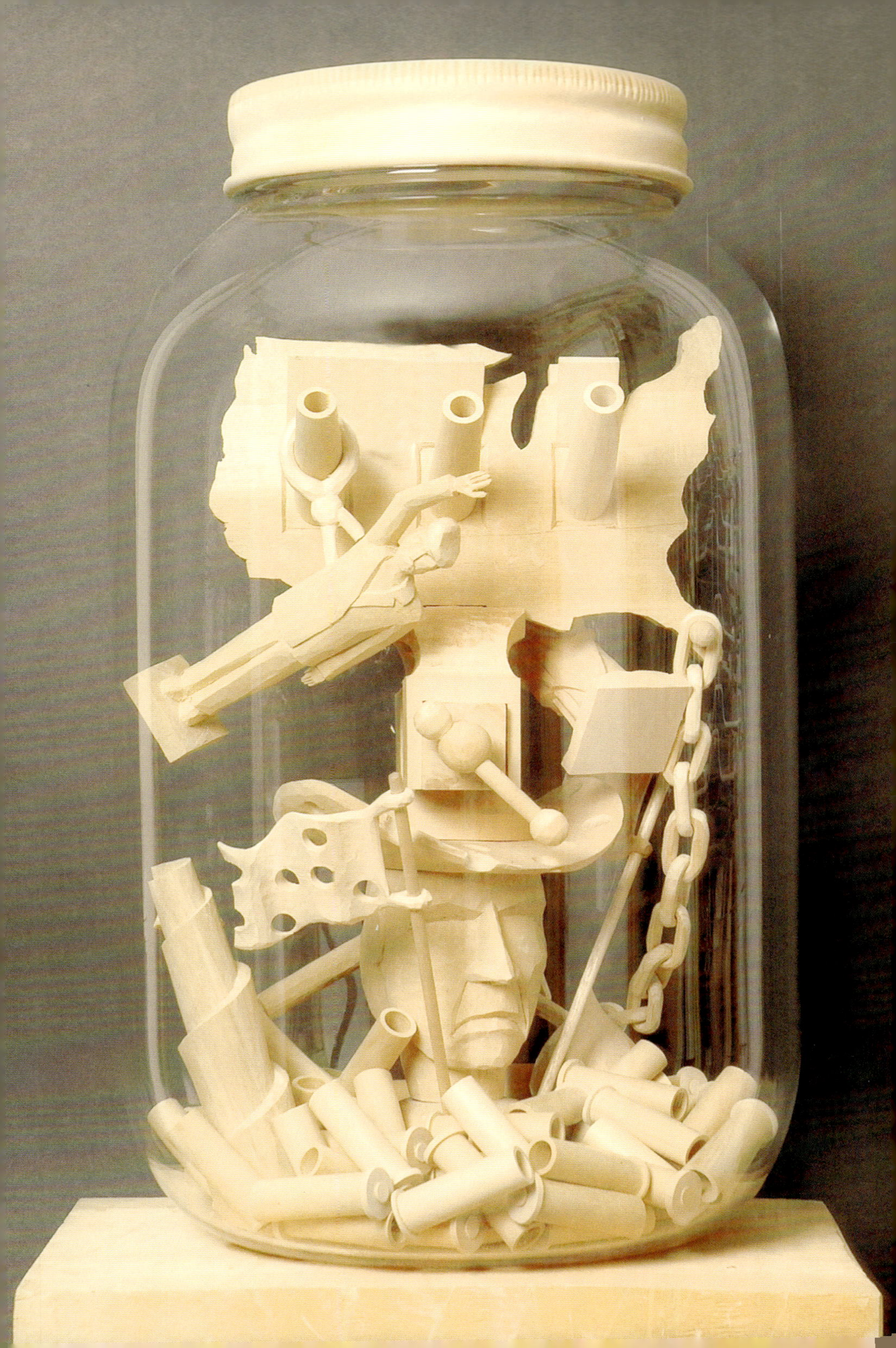

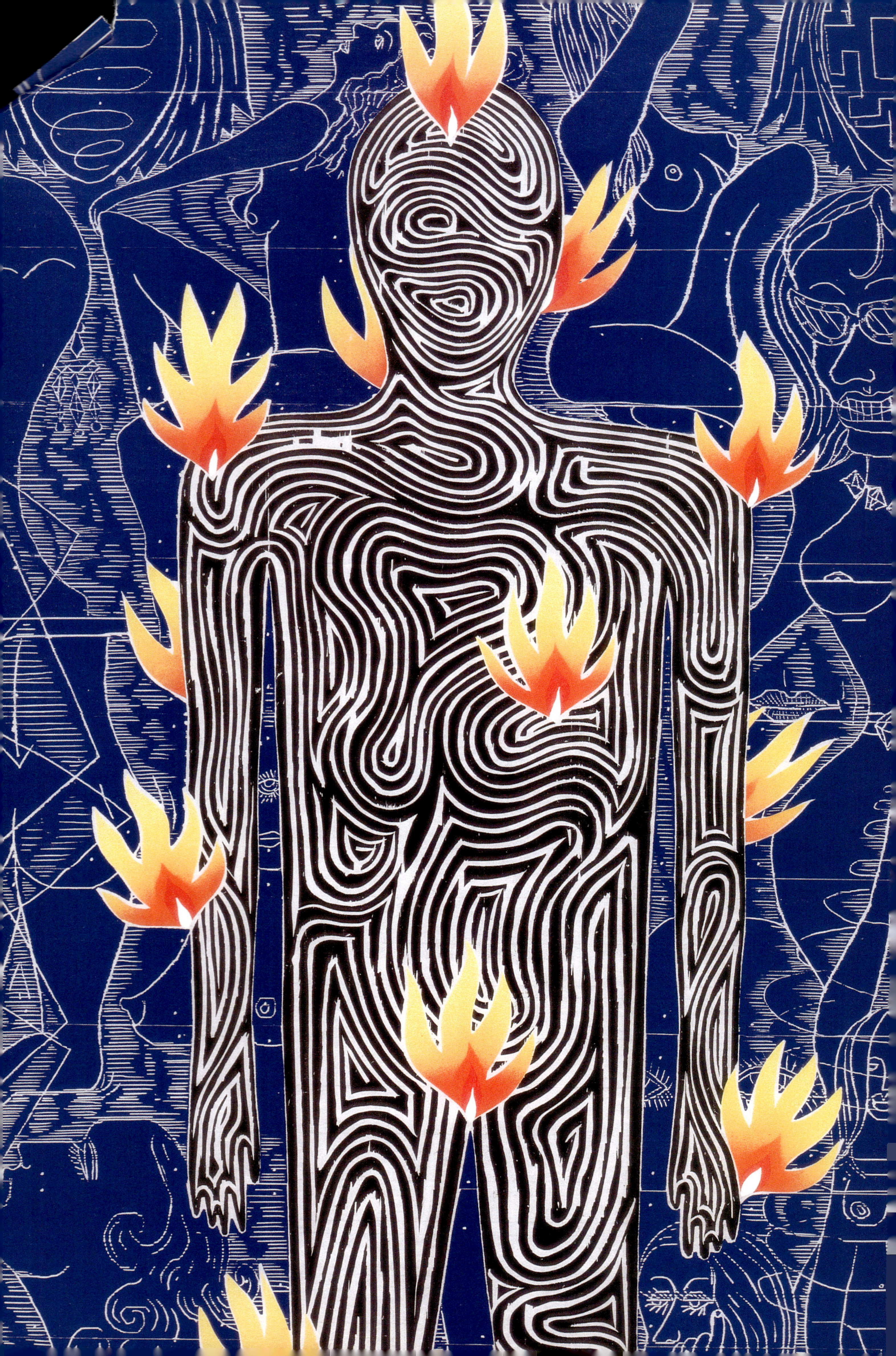

Checklist of the Exhibition

Prints & Rubbings

My First Print, edition 6/13
1980
Three color woodcut
26 x 34 inches
Collection of Jordan D. Schnitzer
2007.376
PLATE 10

Beirut, workshop proof edition 2/3
1983
Two color woodcut
62 ½ x 36 inches
Collection of Jordan D. Schnitzer
1999.3
PLATE 6

Jihad, edition 7/30
1984
Four color lithograph
44 ½ x 30 inches
Collection of Jordan D. Schnitzer
2002.12
PLATE 15

Avenue of the Americas, edition RTP
1985
Two color woodcut
50 x 34 inches
Collection of Jordan D. Schnitzer
2006.20
PLATE 16

Red Jesus, edition 28/30
1986
Three color woodcut
74 x 37 inches
Collection of Jordan D. Schnitzer
1999.5
PLATE 17

Prisoner, edition WP I
1987
Three color woodcut
74 x 37 inches
Collection of Jordan D. Schnitzer
2002.9
PLATE 20

The Have and the Have Nots, 3/14
1987
Two color woodcut
67 x 38 inches
Collection of Jordan D. Schnitzer
2006.61
PLATE 19

Crossroads, edition 2/15
1987
Two color woodcut
74 x 37 inches
Collection of Jordan D. Schnitzer
2002.14
PLATE 18

Cherry Blossom Time, workshop proof
edition 1/1
1988
Ten-color woodcut
63½ x 37 inches
Collection of Jordan D. Schnitzer
2002.13
PLATE 21

East/West, edition PP 3/4
1988
Six-color woodcut
74 x 73½ inches
Collection of the Jordan Schnitzer Family Foundation
1999.33
PLATE 5

Trails Plowed Under, edition 2/15
1989
Three color woodcut
63½ x 37 inches
Collection of Jordan D. Schnitzer
2002.15
PLATE 22

The Language of the Times, 4/36
1990
Woodcut and drypoint
80 x 52 inches
Collection of Jordan D. Schnitzer
2006.53
PLATE 13

The Shillelagh Tree, edition 7/15
1990
Five-color woodcut
52 x 36 inches
Collection of Jordan D. Schnitzer
2002.20
PLATE 23

Great Falls, edition 14/15
1991
Five-color woodcut
83¾ x 66 inches
Collection of Jordan D. Schnitzer
1999.4
PLATE 11

The Times, edition 13/15
1991
Eleven-color woodcut
53½ x 36¼ inches
Collection of Jordan D. Schnitzer
40
PLATE 24

Tattoo, edition 4/15
1992
Five-color woodcut, lithograph, chine-collé
74 x 37 inches
Collection of Jordan D. Schnitzer
2002.19
PLATE 26

A Common Tongue, edition 6/15
1992
Eight-color woodcut
62 x 36½ inches
Collection of Jordan D. Schnitzer
2002.21
PLATE 25

American Eagle / The Great Divide,
edition 10/15
1993
Eleven-color woodcut
60½ x 36½ inches
Collection of Jordan D. Schnitzer
1999.2
PLATE 2

The Lamp, edition 1/1 Archive impression
1994
Twelve-color woodcut with rubber stamp and hand coloring
62 x 37 inches
Collection of the Jordan Schnitzer Family Foundation
1999.36
PLATE 12

The Mechanic, edition 13/15
1994
Six-color woodcut
73 x 37 inches
Collection of Jordan D. Schnitzer
41
PLATE 27

The Coal Mine, edition 6/15
1996
Four color woodcut
62 x 37 inches
Collection of the Jordan Schnitzer Family Foundation
1999.34
PLATE 28

Fact and Fiction, edition 9/15
1997
Eight-color woodcut
74 x 58 inches
Collection of Jordan D. Schnitzer
1998.54
PLATE 30

The Glass Furnace, AP 4/4
1997
Fifteen-color woodcut
18 x 23¾ inches
Collection of Jordan D. Schnitzer
588
PLATE 1

Argosy, edition 10/15
1998 (signed 1999)
Eight-color woodcut
62½ x 37 inches
Collection of the Jordan Schnitzer Family Foundation
1999.32
PLATE 3

Heart Mountain, Wyoming, edition 6/15
2000
Seven-color woodcut
62 x 37 inches
Collection of the Jordan Schnitzer Family Foundation
2000.87
PLATE 33

Skyline, edition AP
2000
Woodblock rubbing
100 x 45 inches
Collection of Jordan D. Schnitzer
2000.171
PLATE 34

Skyline, edition 4/15
2000–2002
Four color woodcut
92 x 37 inches
Collection of Jordan D. Schnitzer
2002.63
PLATE 35

The Deep End, edition 9/15
2000
Thirteen-color woodcut and chine-collé
62 x 37 inches
Collection of the Jordan Schnitzer Family Foundation
2000.88
PLATE 9

Crystal Lake, edition 6/15
2001
Twelve-color woodcut
62 x 37 inches
Collection of Jordan D. Schnitzer
2002.25
PLATE 37

Botanica, edition 10/15
2003
Nine-color woodcut
62 x 37 inches
Collection of Jordan D. Schnitzer
2003.42
PLATE 36

Self-Portrait, edition 2/5
2003
Woodblock rubbing with crayon
56 x 32 inches
Collection of Jordan D. Schnitzer
2007.444
PLATE 38

The Preserve, edition 6/15
2005
Eleven-color woodcut
62 x 37 inches
Collection of Jordan D. Schnitzer
2005.103
PLATE 41

The Singer Tract, edition 6/15
2005
Eleven-color woodcut with pochoir
67 ¾ x 37 inches
Collection of Jordan D. Schnitzer
2005.167
PLATE 42

Phoenix Rising, edition TP
2006
Seven-color woodcut with pochoir
50 x 37 inches
Collection of Jordan D. Schnitzer
2007.474
PLATE 45

Phoenix Rising, edition AP
2006
Woodblock rubbing
50 x 37 inches
Collection of Jordan D. Schnitzer
2007.476
PLATE 44

Phoenix Rising, edition 1/10
2006
Seven-color woodcut with pochoir
50 x 37 inches
Collection of Jordan D. Schnitzer
2006.431
PLATE 4

Phoenix Rising, edition TP
2006
Seven-color woodcut with pochoir
50 x 37 inches
Collection of Jordan D. Schnitzer
2007.475
PLATE 46

Submuloc II, edition AP
2006
Woodblock rubbing in nero crayon
60 x 36 inches
Collection of Jordan D. Schnitzer
2007.378
PLATE 47

The Night Prism, edition 4/20
2007
Color woodcut
74 ½ x 37 inches
Shark's Ink., Lyons, Colorado
Collection of Jordan D. Schnitzer
2008.3
PLATE 49

SCULPTURE

Borderline
2007
Wood sculpture with acrylic paint
72 x 31 x 8 inches
Courtesy of the artist
PLATE 48

Ladder, Ring, Leaf
1999
Wood sculpture with acrylic paint
38 x 16 x 4 inches overall
Collection of Jordan D. Schnitzer
2001.48
PLATE 32

Nine Quarter Circle
1996
Wood sculpture with graphite
95 x 73 x 17 inches overall
Courtesy of the artist
PLATE 29

Zona Rosa II
2005
Wood sculpture with acrylic paint
65 x 53 x 9 inches overall
Courtesy of the artist
PLATE 7

WOOD PANELS

North of South
2005
Wood panel with acrylic paint
72 x 72 x 3½ inches overall
Collection of Jordan D. Schnitzer
2007.300
PLATE 40

Scrimshaw
2004
Wood panel with acrylic paint
71 x 71 x 3¼ inches overall
Collection of Jordan D. Schnitzer
2007.301
PLATE 8

Taj Mahal
2003
Jelutong wood with acrylic paint
48 x 48 x 2¾ inches overall
Collection of Jordan D. Schnitzer
2005.162
PLATE 39

The Singer Tract
2005
Wood panel with acrylic paint
36 x 72 x 3 inches overall
Collection of Jordan D. Schnitzer
2007.303
PLATE 14

WOOD BLOCK

Phoenix Rising
2006
Wood block
Image: 50 x 37 inches
Overall: 53 x 40 inches
Collection of Jordan D. Schnitzer
2007.477
PLATE 43

GLASS JARS

Remember the Maine
2007
Blown and lampworked glass with carved wood elements
23 x 14 x 14 inches overall
Collection of Jordan D. Schnitzer
2007.443
PLATE 50

The Inside
1998
Blown and lampworked glass with carved wood elements
23 x 14 x 14 inches overall
Collection of Jordan D. Schnitzer
2007.302
PLATE 31

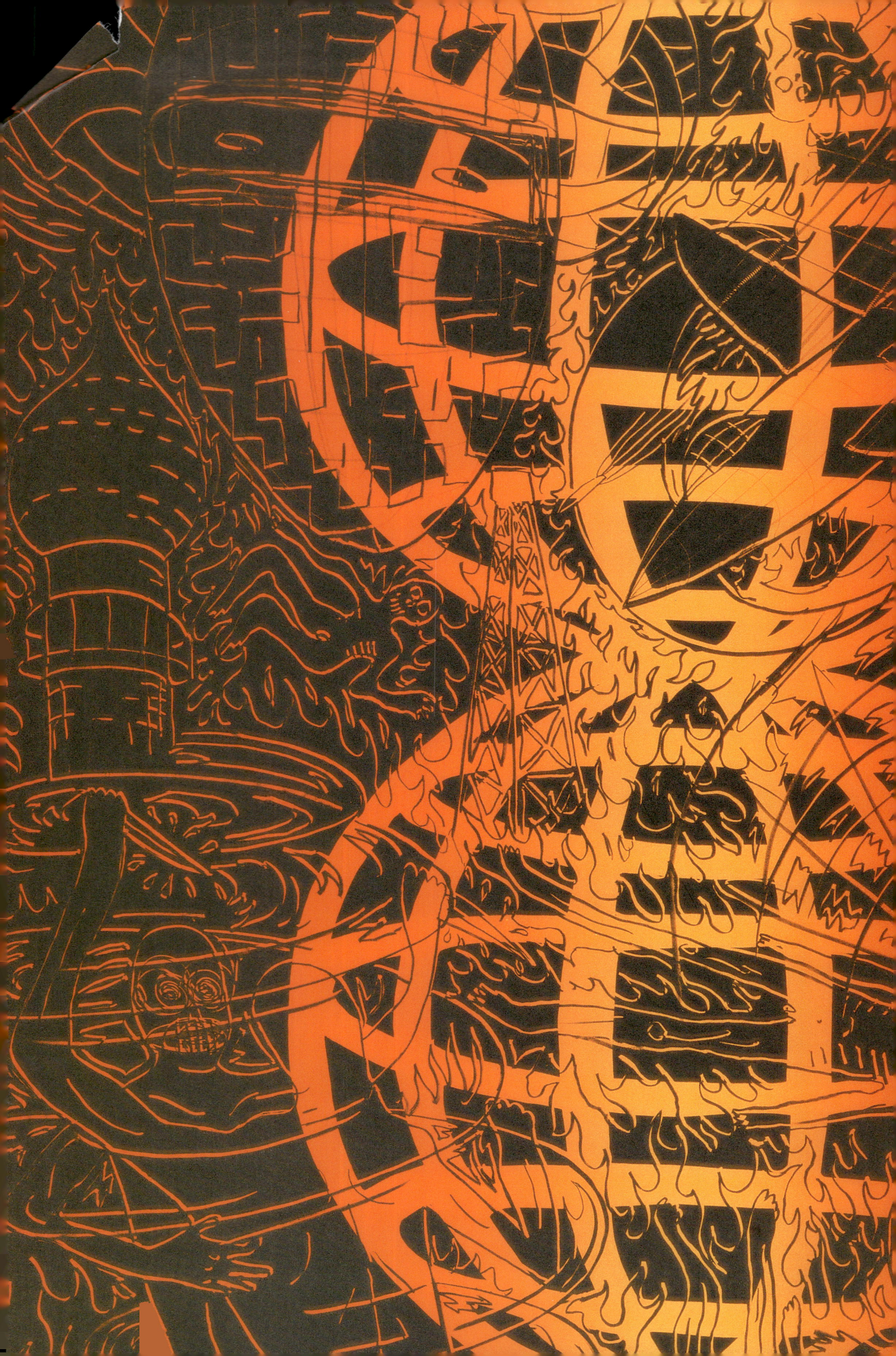

Artist's Chronology and Exhibition History

BORN

1946, Ames, Iowa

EDUCATION

1968 Kansas City Art Institute and School of Design, Kansas City, Missouri, BFA

1971 Skowhegan School of Sculpture and Painting, Skowhegan, Maine

1972 University of California, Davis, California, MFA

TEACHING

1971–72 University of California, Davis; Teaching Assistant

1972–73 Gloucestershire College of Art and Design, Cheltenham, England

1973–75 Humboldt State University, Arcata, California; Sculpture Instructor

1975 Mira Costa College, Carlsbad, California; Ceramics Instructor

1976 University of Cincinnati, Cincinnati, Ohio; Visiting Artist

1976–84 Montana State University, Bozeman, Montana; Assistant Professor, Sculpture

1984–87 Montana State University, Bozeman. Adjunct Assistant Professor; Graduate Student Consultant

1989 Tandem Press, University of Wisconsin, Madison, Wisconsin; Visiting Artist

Utah State University, Logan, Utah; Visiting Artist

1997, 2002, and 2004 Indiana University Art Museum, Bloomington. Visiting Artist

2007 Pilchuck Glass School, Stanwood, Washington. Artist in Residence

SCHOLARSHIPS

1970 Mary Lou Osbourne Fund, University of California, Davis

1970–71 Federal Fellowship Education Allowance Fund

1971 Skowhegan School of Sculpture and Painting

1972–73 Gloucestershire College of Art and Design, Cheltenham, England Teaching Fellowship

GRANTS AND AWARDS

1970 Second Annual Shasta College Invitational Art Exhibit, Redding, California: Purchase Award

1971 Fifth Annual Juried Art Exhibition, University of California, Davis: Purchase Award

1980 National Endowment for the Arts: Individual Artist Grant

1984 Awards in the Visual Arts: National Artists Award

COMMISSIONS

1988

Washington State Arts Commission, University Hospital, Olympia, Washington

1989

Principal Financial Group, Des Moines, Iowa: *Three Generations*

1991

Ahmanson Commercial Development, Chicago, Illinois: *The Loop*, 1990

1999

Lewis & Clark College, Portland, Oregon: *Music in the Sky*; *The Hawk & the Dove*, both 1999

Swedish Hospital, Seattle, Washington: *The Accompaniment*; *The Waltz*, both 1999

2002

Meridian Plaza, Sacramento, California. *Sacramento*; *Pomo Hupa Yurok*; *Mission*; *Gold Rush*; *The Big Four*, all 2002

2006–07

Harsch Investment Properties, South Shore Center, Alameda, California: *Untitled* # 3076.1, 2007; *Untitled* # 3077.1, 2007

SOLO EXHIBITIONS

1972

University of California, Davis, *John E. Buck: MFA*

1974

Mira Costa College, Carlsbad, California

Humboldt State University, Arcata, California

1975

University of Kentucky Art Museum, Lexington, Kentucky

1979

Hansen Fuller Goldeen Gallery, San Francisco: *John Buck: Polychrome Wood Sculpture*

Allan Frumkin Gallery, Chicago, Illinois

1980

Zolla/Lieberman Gallery, Chicago

1981

Morgan Gallery, Kansas City, Missouri

Hansen Fuller Goldeen Gallery, San Francisco, *John Buck*

1982

Concord Gallery, New York City

Mandeville Art Gallery, University of California, San Diego: *John Buck: A Month of Sundays*. Traveled to Main Art Gallery, California State University, Fullerton. Brochure.

1983

Fuller Goldeen Gallery, San Francisco

Yellowstone Art Center, Billings, Montana: *John Buck*. Traveled to Zolla/Lieberman Gallery; Gallery of Contemporary Art, University of Colorado, Colorado Springs; Aspen Center for the Visual Arts; Seattle Art Museum. Catalogue.

1984

Asher Faure Gallery, Los Angeles

Brunswick Gallery, Missoula, Montana, *John Buck*

1985

Paris Gibson Square, Center for Contemporary Arts, Great Falls, Montana: *John Buck: Woodblock Prints*

Fuller Goldeen Gallery, San Francisco

Santa Cruz County Museum of Art, Santa Cruz, California: *John Buck*

Carlo Lamagna Gallery, New York City: *John Buck*

Foster/White Gallery, Seattle: *John Buck*

1986

Carlo Lamagna Gallery, New York City: *John Buck*

Zolla/Lieberman, Chicago: *John Buck*

1987

Contemporary Arts Center, Honolulu, Hawaii: *John Buck: New Works from Kona*

San Antonio Art Institute, San Antonio, Texas. Brochure.

Robischon Gallery, Denver

Asher/Faure Gallery, Los Angeles

1988

Kemper Gallery, Kansas City Art Institute, Kansas City, Missouri

Moss-Chumley Gallery, Dallas, Texas

Volcano Art Center, Volcano, Hawaii

Studio 7, Holualoa, Hawaii

John Berggruen Gallery, San Francisco: *John Buck: Recent Sculpture*

Carlo Lamagna Gallery, New York City

Galerie Ninety-Nine, Bay Harbour Islands, Florida: *John Buck: Paintings, Sculpture, Works on Paper*

Anne Reed Gallery, Ketchum, Idaho

1990

J. Noblett Gallery, Boyes Hot Springs, California

Zolla/Lieberman Gallery, Chicago: *John Buck: New Sculpture*

1991

Morgan Gallery, Kansas City, Missouri: *John Buck*

Esprit Sculpture Garden, John Berggruen Gallery, San Francisco: *John Buck: Large Scale Bronzes: An Outdoor Exhibition*

John Berggruen Gallery, San Francisco: *Recent Sculpture: An Indoor Exhibition*

Allene Lapides Gallery, Santa Fe, New Mexico: *John Buck: Woodblock Prints*

Ann Jaffe Gallery, Bay Harbor Islands, Florida: *John Buck: New Sculpture*

1992

Allene Lapides Gallery, Santa Fe: *John Buck*

1993

Zolla/Lieberman Gallery, Chicago

Achenbach Foundation for the Graphic Arts, M. H. de Young Memorial Museum, San Francisco: *John Buck: Woodblock Prints*. Traveled; Catalogue.

Robischon Gallery, Denver

John Berggruen Gallery, San Francisco: *John Buck: Sculpture and Works on Paper*

1994

Allene Lapides Gallery, Santa Fe: *John Buck*

Yellowstone Art Center, Billings: *In Context: John Buck*

Palm Springs Desert Museum, Palm Springs: *John Buck: Sculpture*. Brochure.

1995

Greg Kucera Gallery, Seattle, Washington

Beall Park Art Center, Bozeman, Montana: *John Buck: Print Exhibition*

Robischon Gallery, Denver: *John Buck: Sculpture and Prints*

Cohen Berkowitz Gallery, Kansas City, Missouri: *John Buck: Sculpture and Prints*

1996

Zolla/Lieberman Gallery, Chicago: *John Buck, New Work*

1998

Greg Kucera Gallery, Seattle: *John Buck: Carved Wood and Blown Glass Sculpture*

1999

DC Moore Gallery, New York City: *John Buck*. Catalogue.

Gallery of Contemporary Art, Lewis & Clark College, Portland: *John Buck: Recent Sculpture and Woodblock Prints*. Traveled.

Madison Art Center, Madison, Wisconsin: *Selections from the Collection: John Buck*

2000

Gallery Camino Real, Boca Raton, Florida: *John Buck*

Museum of Northwest Art, La Conner, Washington: *John Buck: Self Contained*

2001

David Floria Gallery, Aspen, Colorado: *John Buck: New Sculpture, Reliefs & Wood Block Prints*

Imago Galleries, Palm Desert, California: *John Buck*

Zolla/Lieberman Gallery, Chicago: *John Buck: New Work*

2003

DC Moore Gallery, New York City: *John Buck: Sculpture and Prints*

Sangre De Cristo Arts & Conference Center, Pueblo, Colorado: *John Buck: A Selection of Prints, 1980–2003 and Recent Sculpture*

2004

Robischon Gallery, Denver: *John Buck*

Greg Kucera Gallery, Seattle: *John Buck*

2005

The Robert and Gennie DeWeese Gallery, Bozeman, Montana: *John Buck: Sculpture and Prints*

Imago Galleries, Palm Desert, California: *John Buck*

Boulder Museum of Contemporary Art, Boulder, Colorado: *John Buck Prints*

Jackson Hole Center for the Arts, Jackson, Wyoming: *John Buck*

Zolla/Lieberman Gallery, Chicago: *John Buck*

2006

Gallery Camino Real, Boca Raton, Florida: *John Buck*

Schneider Museum of Art, Southern Oregon University, Ashland: *John Buck*

2008

Northwest Museum of Arts & Culture, Spokane, Washington: *John Buck: Iconography*

SELECTED GROUP EXHIBITIONS

1970

Shasta College, Redding, California: *Second Annual Shasta Art Exhibition*

University of California, Davis: *Twenty-Four Hour Show*

1971

Art Center of the World Gallery, Davis, California: *Doing Stuff with Feathers*

Memorial Union Art Gallery, University of California, Davis: *Fifth Annual Juried Exhibition*

University of California, Davis: *Obscure Artists of Davis*

University of Nevada, Reno, Nevada: *A Group Show*

Wenger Gallery, San Francisco: *Eight from Davis*

1972

Artists Contemporary Gallery, Sacramento, California: *Sculpture*

The Museum of Modern Art, New York City

Honig-Cooper and Harrington Arts, San Francisco *Awards Invitational*

San Francisco Art Institute

San Francisco State College, San Francisco: *Group Ceramic Show*

University Art Museum, University of California, Berkeley: *Bay Area Underground*

University of California, San Diego: *Ceramics*

Wenger Gallery, San Francisco: *Plastic When Moist*

1973

Artists Contemporary Gallery, Sacramento, California: *Vacaville Crossing*

The Candy Store, Folsom, California: *Here We Go Gathering Nuts in May*

University of Colorado, Boulder

1974

Humboldt State University, Arcata, California: *Two Man Faculty Exhibit*

Stephens College, Columbia, Missouri: *Clay Magic*

University of Nevada, Las Vegas: *Sculpture and Drawing Show*

1975

Morningside College, Sioux City, Iowa: *Invitational Group Show*

1977

Fine Arts Gallery, Central Washington State College, Ellensburg: *Work in 3 Dimensions: 1977 Invitational for Nine Northwest Artists*. Catalogue.

Fort Mason Center, San Francisco: *San Francisco Art Institute Annual*

Hansen Fuller Gallery, San Francisco: *Introductions*

Montana State University, Bozeman: *Faculty Show*

San Francisco Art Institute; *San Francisco Art Institute Ceramics Annual*

University of Montana, Missoula: *Drawing Invitational*

1978

Richard L. Nelson Gallery, University of California, Davis: *Artists Working in Wood*. Catalogue.

1979

Denver Art Museum, Denver, Colorado: *The First Western States Biennial Exhibition*. Traveled to San Francisco Museum of Modern Art; National Gallery of Art, Washington, DC; University of Hawaii, Honolulu. Catalogue.

Art Gallery, California State University, Chico

Palo Alto Cultural Center, Palo Alto, California

de Saisset Art Gallery and Museum, University of Santa Clara, Santa Clara, California

Allan Frumkin Gallery, Chicago: *New Wood Sculpture from the West*

1980

Triton Museum of Art, Santa Clara

Indianapolis Museum of Art, Indianapolis, Indiana: *Painting & Sculpture Today 1980*. Catalogue.

Yellowstone Art Center, Billings: *Montana: Current Ideas*

The Art Gallery, California State University, Fullerton: *Visions & Figurations*. Catalogue.

Hansen Fuller Goldeen Gallery, San Francisco: *The Peaceable Kingdom*

Zolla/Lieberman Gallery, Chicago: *John Buck: Sculpture & David Story: Paintings*

Alaska Center for the Visual Arts, Anchorage

Fendrick Gallery, Washington, DC

1981

SebastianMoore Gallery, Denver, Colorado: *Bay Area Artists*

University of North Dakota Galleries, Grand Forks: *The Figure: A Celebration*. Traveled.

P.S. 1, Long Island City, New York: *Figurative Sculpture*

Monique Knowlton Gallery, New York City

1982

Palm Springs Desert Museum, Palm Springs: *The West as Art: Changing Perceptions of Western Art in California Collections*. Catalogue.

Fresno Art Center, Fresno, California: *Forgotten Dimensions ... A Look at Sculpture in California Now*. Traveled through Spring 1984 by the Art Museum Association of America. Catalogue.

Municipal Art Gallery, Los Angeles: *Painted Sculpture*

Richard L. Nelson Gallery, University of California, Davis: *Sculptors at UC Davis: Past and Present*. Catalogue.

Turman Gallery, Indiana State University, Terre Haute: *Wood Into the 80s*. Catalogue.

Transamerica Corporation, San Francisco: *It Figures*

Gallery of Art, The University of Missouri, Kansas City: *Cuts: An Exhibition of Woodcut and Relief Prints*. Catalogue.

Boise Gallery of Art, Boise, Idaho: *Black & White & Read All Over*

Madison Art Center, Madison, Wisconsin

1983

Art Gallery, New Mexico State University, Las Cruces: *John Buck / Deborah Butterfield: An Exhibition of Paintings and Sculpture*. Brochure.

Corcoran Gallery of Art, Washington, DC: *Second Western States Exhibition: The 38th Corcoran Biennial Exhibition of American Painting*. Traveled through 1984. Catalogue.

The Museum of Modern Art, New York City: *Prints from Blocks: Gauguin to Now*

Chicago International Art Exposition, Navy Pier: *Chicago Sculpture International: Mile 2*. Catalogue.

Zolla/Lieberman Gallery, Chicago: *John Buck and Linda Herritt*

Art Gallery, California State University, Fullerton: *The House That Art Built*. Catalogue.

1984

The Brooklyn Museum, Brooklyn, New York: *The American Artist as Printmaker: 23rd National Print Exhibition*. Catalogue.

Institute of Contemporary Art, Virginia Museum of Fine Arts, Richmond: *Impressions 1: Experimental Prints*. Traveled to The Noyes Museum, Oceanville, New Jersey. Catalogue.

Custer County Art Center, Miles City, Montana: *Contemporary Sculpture in Montana*

Memorial Union Art Gallery, University of California, Davis: *Works on Paper: Graduate Students from UC Davis, 1965–1982*

Fuller Goldeen Gallery, San Francisco: *50 Artists / 50 States*

Morgan Gallery, Kansas City, Missouri

1985

Fuller Goldeen Gallery, San Francisco: *Stars*

San Francisco Museum of Modern Art: *The 20th Century: The San Francisco Museum of Modern Art Collection*

Nelson-Atkins Museum of Art, Kansas City, Missouri: *Highlights from Kansas City Art Institute Alumni*

Birmingham Museum of Art, Birmingham, Michigan: *John Buck and Deborah Butterfield*

California Palace of the Legion of Honor, San Francisco: *Recent Acquisitions of the Achenbach Foundation for the Graphic Arts, Part Two 1940–1984*

Bruce Velick Gallery, San Francisco: *Light and Heavy Light: Contemporary Use of Shadow in the Visual Arts*

Creative Growth Gallery, Oakland, California: *Art Auction*

Albright-Knox Art Gallery, Buffalo, New York: *Awards in the Visual Arts 4*. Traveled; Catalogue.

Transamerica Pyramid, San Francisco: *Artists Look at Architecture*

Monterey Peninsula Museum of Art, Monterey, California: *Works in Wood*

Pamela Auchincloss Gallery, Santa Barbara, California: *Revolving Show: John Buck, Yvonne Jacquett*

University Art Gallery, California State University, Chico: *Couples: Party of Two*

Bernice Steinbaum Gallery, New York City: *Adornments*. Catalogue.

Herbert Palmer Gallery, Los Angeles: *Sculptors and their Prints*

1986

The Brooklyn Museum: *Public and Private: American Prints Today*. Traveled; Catalogue.

Galerie Ninety-Nine, Bay Harbor Islands, Florida: *John Buck, Darryl Hughto*

Corcoran Gallery of Art, Washington, DC: *Spectrum: The Generic Figure*. Catalogue.

Visual Arts Center of Alaska, Anchorage: *Symbols & Narratives: National Print Invitational*

Euphrat Gallery, De Anza College, Cupertino, California: *Fine Wood*

Foster/White Gallery, Seattle: *Prints by New York Artists*

Bank of America, San Francisco, *Couples in Art*

Gerald Peters Gallery, Santa Fe, New Mexico: *Amnesty International USA 25th Anniversary Art Auction*. Catalogue.

Robischon Gallery, Denver: *Woodcut*

Pittsburgh Center for the Arts, Pittsburgh, Pennsylvania: *Deborah Butterfield / John Buck: A Collaborative Work*. Traveled; Catalogue.

Maryland Institute College of Art, Baltimore: *Artist / Printmaker*

Gallery of Art, University of Northern Iowa, Cedar Falls: *Born in Iowa: The Homecoming Exhibition*. Traveled; Catalogue.

Mitchell Museum, Mount Vernon, Illinois: *Recent Graphics from American Print Shops*. Traveled; Catalogue.

Palo Alto Cultural Center: *Between Painting and Sculpture*

The Art Store Gallery, Oakland, California: *Shoebox Show*

Carlo Lamagna Gallery, New York City: *Traps: Elements of Psychic Seduction*

Helander Gallery, Palm Beach, Florida: *New Work, New York*

1987

Galerie Ninety-Nine, Bay Harbor Islands: *New Year / New Works*

Virginia Museum of Fine Arts, Richmond: *Recent Graphics from American Print Shops*

Zolla/Lieberman Gallery, Chicago: *Outstanding Work by Gallery Artists*; also *New Glory in Sculpture*

Gallery Paule Anglim, San Francisco: *One Exhibition / Two Galleries*

Monterey Peninsula Museum of Art, Monterey, California: *The Artist and the Myth*

Federal Reserve Board Fine Arts Gallery, Washington, DC: *Artists Who Teach*. Catalogue.

Helander Gallery, Palm Beach *Works of Wood*

1988

Mary Porter Sesnon Art Gallery, University of California, Santa Cruz: *Wood Sculpture*

John Berggruen Gallery, San Francisco: *Selected Sculpture*; also *Group Sculpture Exhibition*; and *Selected Acquisitions*

Greenville County Museum of Art, Greenville, South Carolina: *Imprimatur*. Traveled to North Carolina Museum of Art, Raleigh. Brochure.

Helander Gallery, Palm Beach: *Figure It Out: Visual Body Language*

The Brunswick Contemporary Arts Center, Missoula, Montana: *Art as Political Vision*. Traveled in Montana.

Mia Gallery, Seattle, Washington: *On the Edge*

Zolla/Lieberman Gallery, Chicago: *Important Work by Gallery Artists*

Stephen Wirtz Gallery, San Francisco: *Selections from the Experimental Workshop, San Francisco*

Brody's Gallery, Washington, DC: *Impressions*

Moody Gallery of Art, University of Alabama, Tuscaloosa: *Visions of Printmakers: New Works*. Brochure.

Cheney Cowles Museum, Spokane, Washington: *Editions: East and West*

Boulder Center for the Visual Arts, Boulder, Colorado: *Selected Prints: Shark's Incorporated*. Catalogue.

Sheehan Gallery, Whitman College, Walla Walla, Washington: *Cast in Walla Walla*

Helander Gallery, Palm Beach: *East Side – West Side*; also *Don't Knock Wood*

Robischon Gallery, Denver: *Small Sculpture*

Carlo Lamagna Gallery, New York City: *Saga(s)*

1989

Anne Jaffe Gallery, Bay Harbor Islands, Florida: *25th Anniversary Gala Exhibition*

Associated American Artists, New York City: *Three Contemporary Presses*. Catalogue.

Landfall Press, Chicago and New York: *Prints by Sculptors*

Walker Art Center, Minneapolis: *First Impressions: Early Prints by Forty-Six Contemporary Artists*. Traveled; Catalogue.

Waddell Studio, Ryegate, Montana: *Art and Book Exhibition*

Anne Reed Gallery, Ketchum, Idaho: *Sculpture: Visions Transformed*

John Berggruen Gallery, San Francisco: *Sculpture*

Cheney Cowles Museum, Spokane: *Masters of the Inland Northwest*

Madison Art Center, Madison, Wisconsin: *Coming of Age: Twenty-One Years of Collecting by the Madison Art Center*

The Old Police Station, Hilo, Hawaii: *Visions of the Volcano*, organized by The Volcano Art Center. Traveled to The Contemporary Museum, Honolulu; Stones Gallery, Lihue, Kauai; Hui Noeau Visual Arts Center, Makawao, Maui.

1990

The Honolulu Advertiser Gallery, Honolulu, Hawaii: *Visions of the Volcano*

Palm Springs Desert Museum, Palm Springs: *Northwest X Southwest: Painted Fictions*. Traveled; Catalogue.

Nora Eccles Harrison Museum of Art, Utah State University, Logan: *Group Exhibition: John Buck, Deborah Butterfield, Jay Schmidt*. Traveled to Center for Contemporary Art, Santa Fe.

Museum of Contemporary Art, Chicago: *Toward the Future: Contemporary Art in Content*

Hockaday Center for the Arts, Kalispell, Montana: *Montana 3-D*. Catalogue.

Mark Masuoka, Las Vegas, Nevada, *John Buck & Hiroki Morinoui*

Security Pacific Corporation, Los Angeles: *Of Nature and Nation: Yellowstone – Summer of Fire*

Anne Reed Gallery, Ketchum: *Sculpture: Visions Transformed II*

Center for Contemporary Art, Santa Fe: *Deborah Butterfield, John Buck*; also *Second Invitational Exhibition and Auction*

Natsoulas/Novelozo Gallery, Davis, California: *All Creatures, Great & Small*

Stephen F. Austin University, Nacogdoches, Texas: *John Buck and Igor Mitoraj*

Thomas Barry Fine Arts, Minneapolis: *Prints from Tandem Press*

Anne Jaffe Gallery, Bay Harbor Islands: *The Second Anniversary Annual*

1991

University of Hawaii, Hilo: *Fourth International Shoebox Sculpture Exhibition*. Traveled; Catalogue.

Atlanta College of Art, Atlanta, Georgia: *Contemporary Bronze: Process and Object*

Robischon Gallery, Denver: *Gallery Artists*

Anne Reed Gallery, Ketchum: *Sculpture: Visions Transformed III*

Muckenthaler Cultural Center, Fullerton, California: *Sculptural Perspectives for the Nineties*

Greg Kucera Gallery, Seattle: *Bad Politics*

Robischon Gallery, Denver: *Gallery Artists Summer Show*; also *Small Scale Sculpture*

John Berggruen Gallery, San Francisco: *Selected Sculpture*

1992

Salt Lake City Art Center, Salt Lake City, Utah: Dreams *and Shield: Contemporary Spiritual Art*. Traveled.

Haynes Fine Art Gallery, Montana State University, Bozeman: *Narration Through Form*

I. Wolk Gallery, St. Helena, California: *"23" Artists from John Berggruen Gallery*

John Berggruen Gallery, San Francisco: *Sculpture*

Anne Reed Gallery, Ketchum: *Visions Transformed IV*

Zolla/Lieberman Gallery, Chicago

Oliver Art Center, California College of Arts and Crafts, Oakland: *From Plastic Form to Printer's Plate: Contemporary Sculptors / Printmakers*

Seattle Art Museum: *Permanent Collection Exhibition*

John Berggruen Gallery, San Francisco: *Objects of Affection*

1993

Greg Kucera Gallery, Seattle: *Sculpture from Walla Walla Foundry*

Newport Harbor Art Museum, Newport Beach, California: *Beyond the Bay: The Figure*

Anne Reed Gallery, Ketchum: *Visions Transformed V*

Laguna Gloria Art Museum, Austin: *Human Nature / Human Form: Figurative Dimensions in Clay, Metal, Stone, and Wood*

1994

Robischon Gallery, Denver

The Oakland Museum, Oakland, California: *Here and Now: Bay Area Masterworks from the Di Rosa Collection*. Catalogue.

Zolla/Lieberman Gallery, Chicago Art Fair

1995

Robert Kidd Gallery, Birmingham, Michigan: *Figurative Concepts: John Buck, Manuel Neri, Gary Kulak*

Schmidt-Bingham Gallery, New York City: *Embody*

1996

Paris Gibson Square Museum of Art, Great Falls, Montana: *Two in Montana, Deborah Butterfield and John Buck, Sculpture and Woodblock Prints*. Traveled.

National Museum of American Art, Smithsonian Institution, Washington, DC: *Contemporary Printmaking in America: Collaborative Prints and Presses*

1997

Yale University Art Gallery, New Haven, Connecticut: *Hawaiian Eye: Collecting Contemporary Art with Thurston Twigg-Smith*

Zolla/Lieberman Gallery, Chicago: *Zolla/Lieberman Artists*

Holter Museum of Art, Helena: *Ports of Entry*. Traveled to Copper Village Museum and Arts Center, Anaconda, Montana.

Bemis Center for Contemporary Arts, Omaha, Nebraska: *John Buck and Deborah Butterfield / Sculpture*

Leigh Yawkey Woodson Art Museum, Wausau, Wisconsin: *Contemporary Sculpture: The Figurative Tradition*

Sheehan Gallery, Whitman College, Walla Walla: *Cast Contemporary Sculpture from the Walla Walla Foundry*

Botanica Gallery, Bozeman: *John Buck: Prints and Sculpture*

Printworks Gallery, Chicago: *A Game of Chance*. Traveled.

1998

The LEF Foundation, St. Helena, California: *Sculptural Perspectives for the New Millennium*

Schmidt Bingham Gallery, New York City: *Camouflage*

John Berggruen Gallery, San Francisco: *Wild Things: Artists' Views of the Animal Kingdom*

Gerald Peters Gallery, Santa Fe: *New Works by Contemporary Artists*

Triart Gallery, J. B. Speed Museum, Louisville, Kentucky: *Prints by Shark's*

1999

Cleveland Museum of Art, Cleveland, Ohio: *Cleveland Collects Contemporary Art*

Oakland Museum of California: *What Is Art For?*

San Jose Museum of Art: *Into the 21st Century: Selections from the Permanent Collection*

Austin Museum of Art, Laguna Gloria, Austin, Texas: *Holding Light: Contemporary Glass Sculpture*. Brochure.

2000

Miami University Art Museum, Oxford, Ohio: *Off the Wall: Sculptural Markers in the 20th Century*

Oskar Friedl Gallery, Chicago: *The Buddha Show*

William Havu Gallery, Denver: *Select Prints Shark's Ink*

2001

The Art Gym, Marylhurst University, Marylhurst, Oregon: *Pressure Points*. Traveled.

Elizabeth Leach Gallery, Portland: *In Public*

Jane Haslem Gallery, Washington, DC: *A Century of American Woodcuts*

Lewis & Clark College, Portland: *Strike: Printmakers as Social Critics*

DC Moore Gallery, New York City: *Self-Made Men*

San Jose Museum of Art: *Collecting Our Thoughts: The Community Responds to Art in the Permanent Collection*

Seattle Arts Commission, Seattle, Washington: *Printworks 2001*

Scottsdale Museum of Contemporary Art, Scottsdale, Arizona: *The Cultural Desert*

Sky Harbor Airport, Phoenix, Arizona: *Limited Editions*

Stewart Gallery, Boise, Idaho: *Red, Yellow, Black*

2002

Artemisia Gallery, Chicago: *To Kiss the Spirits*

The Contemporary Museum, Honolulu, Hawaii: *Contemporarities 2002*

Flanders Graphics, Minneapolis: *Prints from Shark's Ink*. Catalogue.

Gallery of Contemporary Art, University of Colorado Springs: *Shark's Ink, 1976–2001, A 25 Year Retrospective*

Greg Kucera Gallery, Seattle: *States of the Union: Before and After*

Holter Museum of Art, Helena: *9th Annual Minitreasures Exhibition & Auction*

J. Johnson Gallery, Jacksonville Beach, Florida: *Contemporary Printmakers*

Paris Gibson Square Museum of Art, Great Falls: *Escape to Jamaica*

Robischon Gallery, Denver: *Solace*

San Jose Museum of Art: *Collection Highlights*

Southeastern Center for Contemporary Art, Winston-Salem, North Carolina: *Preview Exhibit: Spring Art Auction 2002*

2003

Anderson Ranch Arts Center, Snowmass Village, Colorado: *22nd Annual Art Auction*. Catalogue.

di Rosa Preserve, Napa, California: *Off the Preserve*. Catalogue.

Huntington Museum of Art, Huntington, West Virginia: *Through American Eyes: Two Centuries of American Art from the Huntington Museum of Art*. Traveled; Catalogue.

Jean Albano Gallery, Chicago: *Exquisite Snake*

Montana State University, Bozeman: *Mountain West Contemporary Art Auction*

Tacoma Art Museum: *Building Tradition: Gifts in Honor of the Northwest Art Collection*. Catalogue.

Yellowstone Art Museum, Billings: *Expanded Horizons*. Catalogue.

2004

Arkansas Arts Center, Little Rock: *National Drawing Invitational*

Art Students League of Denver: *Sculpture Invitational, Visiting Artist Series*

Davis Museum and Cultural Center, Wellesley College, Wellesley, Massachusetts: *American Identities: Twentieth-Century Prints from the Nancy Gray Sherrill, Class of 1954, Collection*. Catalogue.

di Rosa Preserve, Napa: *The True Artist*

Evanston Art Center, Evanston, Illinois: *Roberta Lieberman: A Sharp Eye; An Art Dealer's 40 Year Journey*

John Natsoulas Gallery, Davis, California: *Four Sculptors*

Museum of Art, Washington State University, Pullman: *Sculpture from the Walla Walla Foundry*

Yellowstone Art Museum, Billings: *Expanded Horizons*. Catalogue.

2005

Arvada Center for the Arts and Humanities: *Five Presses*

di Rosa Preserve, Napa: *Fourth Annual Benefit Exhibition and Auction*

Exhibitrek, Boulder, Colorado: *Shark & His Ink*

Savannah College of Art & Design, Savannah, Georgia: *Print, Process, Collaboration*

Stewart Gallery, Boise: *The Fine Art of Prints*

San Jose Museum of Art: *Visual Politics: Art of Engagement*

Yellowstone Art Museum, Billings: *Making Connections*. Catalogue.

2006

Arvada Center for the Arts and Humanities: *The Dog and Pony Show*

di Rosa Preserve, Napa: *Fifth Annual Benefit Exhibition and Auction: California Dreamin'*. Catalogue.

Katzen Art Center, American University, Washington, DC: *Visual Politics: Art of Engagement*

Yellowstone Art Museum, Billings, MT, *38th Annual Art Auction*. Catalogue; also *Montana Collection*

2007

Art Association of Jackson Hole, Jackson, Wyoming: *Contemporary Prints from Shark's Ink*

The Contemporary Museum, Honolulu: *Contempo 2007: Animal Instincts*

di Rosa Preserve, Napa: *Moon Proof Madness*

Hawaii State Art Museum, Honolulu: *uncommon objects*

Holter Museum of Art, Helena: *Holter Art Auction 2007*

Northwest Museum of Arts & Culture, Spokane: *Works from the Heart Contemporary Art Exhibition and Auction*

Nu'uanu Gallery at Marks Garage, Honolulu, Hawaii: *Hiroki Morinue & John Buck*

Robischon Gallery, Denver: *Decades*

Ucross Foundation Art Gallery, Clearmont, Wyoming: *Range of Expression II: A Montana Invitational*. Catalogue.

Yellowstone Art Museum, Billings: *The Human Touch*

Zolla/Lieberman Gallery, Chicago: *Killer B's*

2008

Holter Museum of Art, Helena: *Speaking Volumes: Transforming Hate*

SELECTED LECTURES / WORKSHOPS

1972

Gloucester College of Art and Design, Cheltenham, England

1973

University of London, Goldsmiths

University of California Davis

1974

University of Wisconsin, Madison

Mira Costa College, Carlsbad, California

1975

University of Kentucky, Lexington

1976

University of Iowa, Iowa City, Iowa

1977

University of Texas, Austin

University of Texas, San Antonio

1979

University of New Mexico, Albuquerque

1980

Chicago Art Institute, Chicago

1981

University of Oklahoma, Norman

1982

University of California, San Diego

1994

Yellowstone Art Center, Billings, Montana

2001

Anderson Ranch Arts Center, Snowmass Village, Colorado

di Rosa Preserve, Napa, California

2003

Madison Print Club, Madison, Wisconsin

2006

University of Minnesota, Minneapolis. Juror, Minnesota National Print Biennial

SELECTED PUBLIC COLLECTIONS

Achenbach Foundation for the Graphic Arts
Albright-Knox Gallery, Buffalo, New York
Arkansas Arts Center, Little Rock, Arkansas
Art Institute of Chicago, Chicago, Illinois
Atlantic Richfield Company, Dallas, Texas
Boise Art Museum, Boise, Idaho
Bank of America Corporation, San Francisco, California
Brooklyn Museum, Brooklyn, New York
Children's Hospital, Denver, Colorado
Contemporary Art Center, Honolulu, Hawaii
Dain Bosworth Inc., Minneapolis, Minnesota
Denver Art Museum, Denver, Colorado
Fine Arts Museums of San Francisco, California
First Union Bank Corporation, San Francisco
Fort Wayne Museum of Art, Fort Wayne, Indiana
Grand Valley State University, Allendale, Michigan
Haggerty Museum of Art, Marquette University, Milwaukee, Wisconsin
Honolulu Advertiser Collection, Honolulu, Hawaii
Huntington Museum of Art, Huntington, West Virginia
Joslyn Art Museum, Omaha, Nebraska
Lewis & Clark College, Portland, Oregon
Library of Congress, Washington, DC
Madison Art Center, Madison, Wisconsin
Mayo Clinic, Rochester, Minnesota
Memphis Brooks Museum of Art, Memphis, Tennessee
Meridian Plaza, Sacramento, California
Milwaukee Art Museum, Milwaukee, Wisconsin
Museum of Contemporary Art, Chicago
Museum of Modern Art, New York City
Palm Springs Desert Museum, Palm Springs, California
Prudential Life Insurance Company, Newark, New Jersey
San Francisco Museum of Modern Art, San Francisco
San Jose Museum of Art, San Jose, California
Seattle Art Museum, Seattle, Washington
Swedish Hospital, Seattle, Washington
Tacoma Art Museum, Tacoma, Washington
Texas Tech University, Lubbock
The St. Paul Companies, Minneapolis, Minnesota
Tri-City Corporate Center, San Bernardino, California
University Art Museum, Berkeley, California
University of Washington Hospital, Seattle
Frederick R. Weisman Collection, Los Angeles
Wright State University, Dayton, Ohio
Yellowstone Art Museum, Billings, Montana

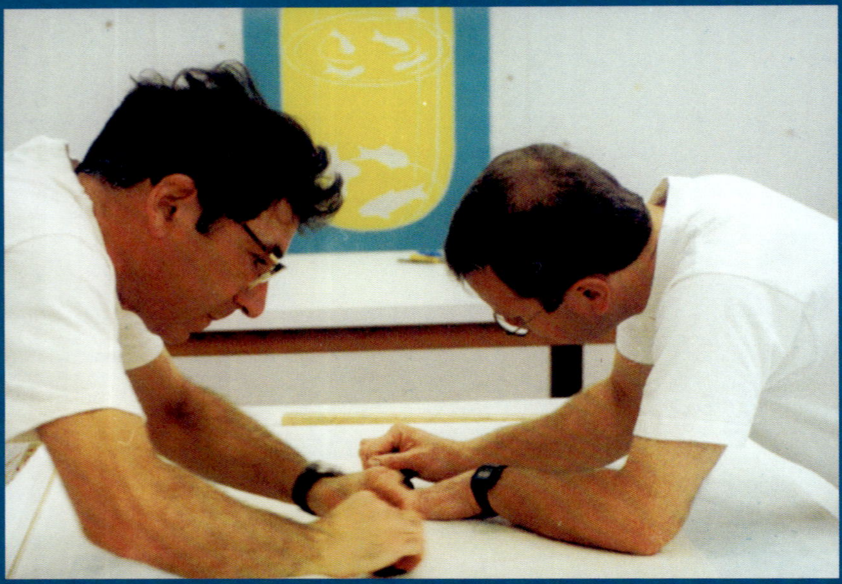

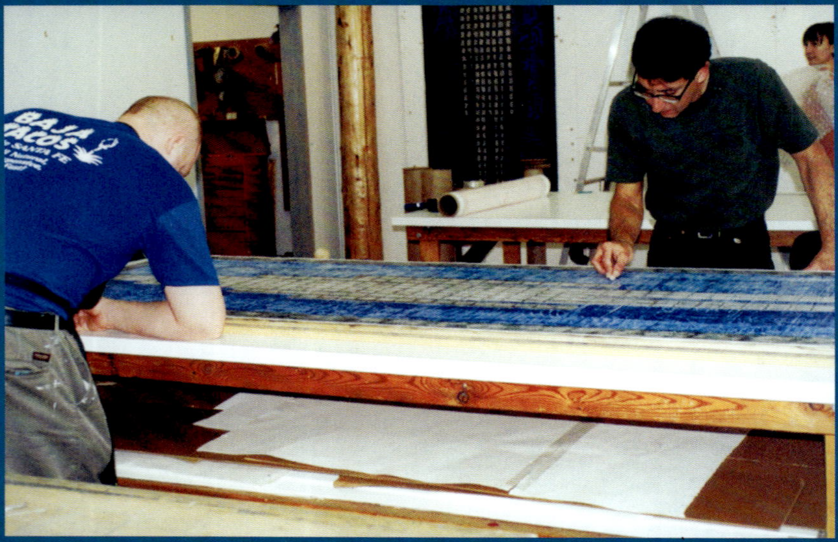

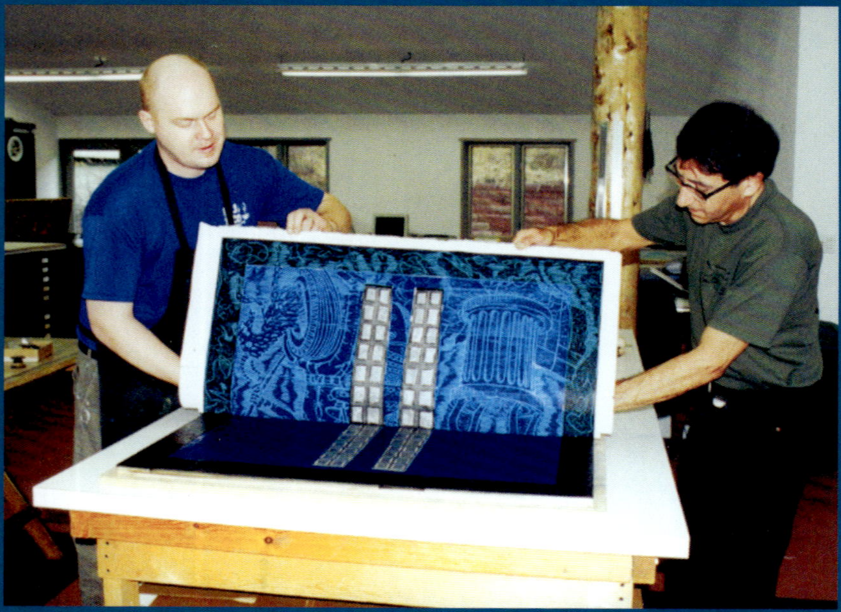

John Buck prints in production at Shark's Ink., Lyons, Colorado.

Top: Bud Shark and Matthew Christie printing *The Deep End* by hand-burnishing the back of the paper.

Middle: Evan Colbert and Bud Shark add final touches to the hand-burnishing of a *Skyline* print.

Bottom: Evan Colbert and Bud Shark pull a completed *Skyline* print from the block.

Photos courtesy Barbara Shark

Working with John Buck

by Bud Shark

I first met John Buck at the University of Colorado in 1983. He was a visiting artist and had made a woodblock that the printmaking department was having trouble printing. They asked me to come and see the block and perhaps help them print it. I met John and saw the block and was knocked out by it . . . I wanted to print it. I had seen some reproductions of a couple of recent prints of John's, maybe one was the review of his *La Grande Eclipse* in the *Print Collectors Newsletter.*[1] I boldly said that I could print it for them . . . "no problem." I had never printed a woodcut of that scale before but I was a cocky young printer and figured that if I could print a small woodcut or a large lithograph I could certainly print this. Of course, it turned out to be much more difficult than I imagined and took many, many proofs, trying various inks, papers, and printing techniques to find the way to do it, but I did. The print was *Beirut,* and it began a fruitful collaborative relationship between John and me that now spans twenty-four years and more than forty woodcut editions.

The imagery and content of John's prints initially sparked my interest in his work—but the bold graphic quality and a very specific kind of integration of the materials, the images, and the process keep me interested and challenged. John made his first woodblocks with the goal of making rubbings, not prints. So his approach and the techniques he has improvised for making the woodblocks are very different from those of someone trained in printmaking. This unique approach, when combined with his imagery and content, produces powerful graphic statements and distinctive woodcuts.

The Woodblocks

John's woodblocks are constructed like large jigsaw puzzles. The parts can be lifted out and inked in various colors, reassembled, and then all the pieces and colors are printed at one time.

The lines in the background are incised into the wood using a sharp object like a nail, hard pencil, or ballpoint pen. The lines are much more fluid than could be carved with a chisel or knife and clearly show the artist's hand. This method creates a very shallow line, so when ink is rolled on the surface of the block it prints as a fine white line. Because the line is so shallow we print the key blocks by hand-burnishing rather than in a press, which would slowly crush the wood and fill in the lines. We have used a variety of tools to do the burnishing . . . starting with metal spoons, and moving on to drawer-pulls and knobs of various sizes and shapes, and objects like folding bones. The hand-burnishing requires very firm and constant pressure to be applied to the back of the whole of the sheet of paper. On Buck-size prints this is hard physical work *and* takes time, mocking one of our studio mottos: "It's not hard, it just takes time."

Beginning with *The Sound of the Sea* in 1994, John wanted to have the incised lines in the backgrounds of the prints to have color. We began using "doorskins" or thin wood-veneer plywood to print color under parts of the background or central image. These background printings are usually done on the press. With the two doorskins for *Skyline* (2000–2002), the tallest of John's prints at 92 inches, we can only print about two-thirds of the blocks and then need to turn them 180 degrees to print the remaining third, a tricky operation. The more complex color prints require virtually every roller, brayer, and ink knife, plus all the countertop workspace in the studio to roll out the inks and ink up all the various wood-block parts.

WORKING WITH JOHN

My collaborative relationship with John is unlike those with the other artists I print and publish. Most come to the studio for a specific time to work on a print or prints. John ships me a completed block and only rarely is he here in the studio while we are proofing. Some blocks have arrived without notice, some have been preceded by a phone call telling me that one or more blocks are on their way.

John and I typically have several phone calls to discuss thoughts about how he would like to approach the new print. Talking about colors, overprintings, background colors, borders, and blend rolls is very difficult using language alone. Once John asked for a color that was "like Japanese money." I had recently been to Japan and had some Yen to look at that I thought would have us on the right track. But John had been looking at some "old Yen" and the colors I used were way off. In some discussions John has referred me to specific pages in nature guides or other books to find the colors that he wants to use, as for the turtle in *Crystal Lake*, or the moths in *The Night Sky (Luna)* and *The Night Sky (Polyphemus)*.

We get the block, we talk, we give it a try . . . Then I proof up something along the lines of what I think John's been suggesting and send it off to him to look at for awhile. A couple of times we've managed to get a proof that works just right on the first try. Most times it takes several more phone calls and more trial proofs FedEx'd back and forth before the print is finalized. I know when it's going to be a tough one to resolve when John says *I don't know . . . what do you think?* (I think it will take several more proofs!) Though there have been a few instances where we never get an acceptable print and the block was abandoned.

Since *Beirut*, with its simple red and

black colors and bold graphic imagery, the prints have evolved in their sophistication and use of color. Through the improvisational nature of collaboration we've progressed by small jumps, adding basic colors like blue, yellow, and orange. And then to bigger jumps, using dozens of colors and multiple blocks on sheets of paper that have been joined together. As the Master Printer, I have had to find ways to make it possible for John to get the visual effect he desires. For *The Lamp* (1994) I built a cone-shaped roller to roll the inks, creating the glow around the outside of the jar. The fireflies' light was achieved by airbrushing yellow watercolor on each tail after printing. In *Cherry Blossom Time* (1988) the ink on the cherry blossoms was dabbed onto the blocks using our fingers. I've made daubers from foam rubber and cheesecloth to apply inks and blend colors. We've made rubber stamps to print small, intricate areas like the moths in *The Times*. We have also drawn from our repertoire of printmaking tricks like pochoir to add isolated bits of color with stencils, and have used lithography and collage as in the flames in *Tattoo* and chine-collé on *The Deep End*.

John Buck's woodcuts are "low-tech" prints, and in this era of highly evolved imaging systems I find working on the prints, actually making them with my hands, to be extremely satisfying and rewarding. Because they start with hand-carved and incised planks of wood, it makes perfect sense that the prints should remain true to their source and be hand-made objects. There is an integrity to the physical presence of the dense layers of colored ink saturating the paper that imparts a power to the images John creates. It is these powerful images that first drew me to John's work and made me want to make these woodcuts with him. I am very proud to have been able to help bring them to life and to publish them for others to see and appreciate.

Finally, I want to say that the prints could not have been accomplished without the help of many others who have helped with the printing of John's editions. Many thanks to Barbara Shark, Roseanne Colachis, Evan Colbert, Matt Christie, Jean Pless, Lisa Merrin, Jim Robb, Aleta Braun, and Ron Trujillo for their assistance.

1. For current issues of the *Print Collectors Newsletter* see the magazine *Art on Paper*.

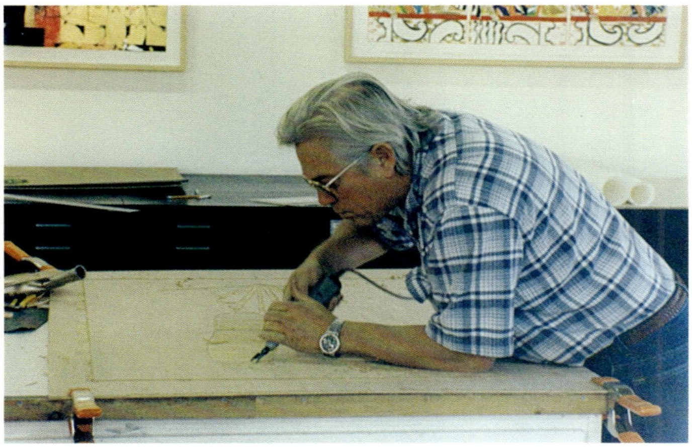

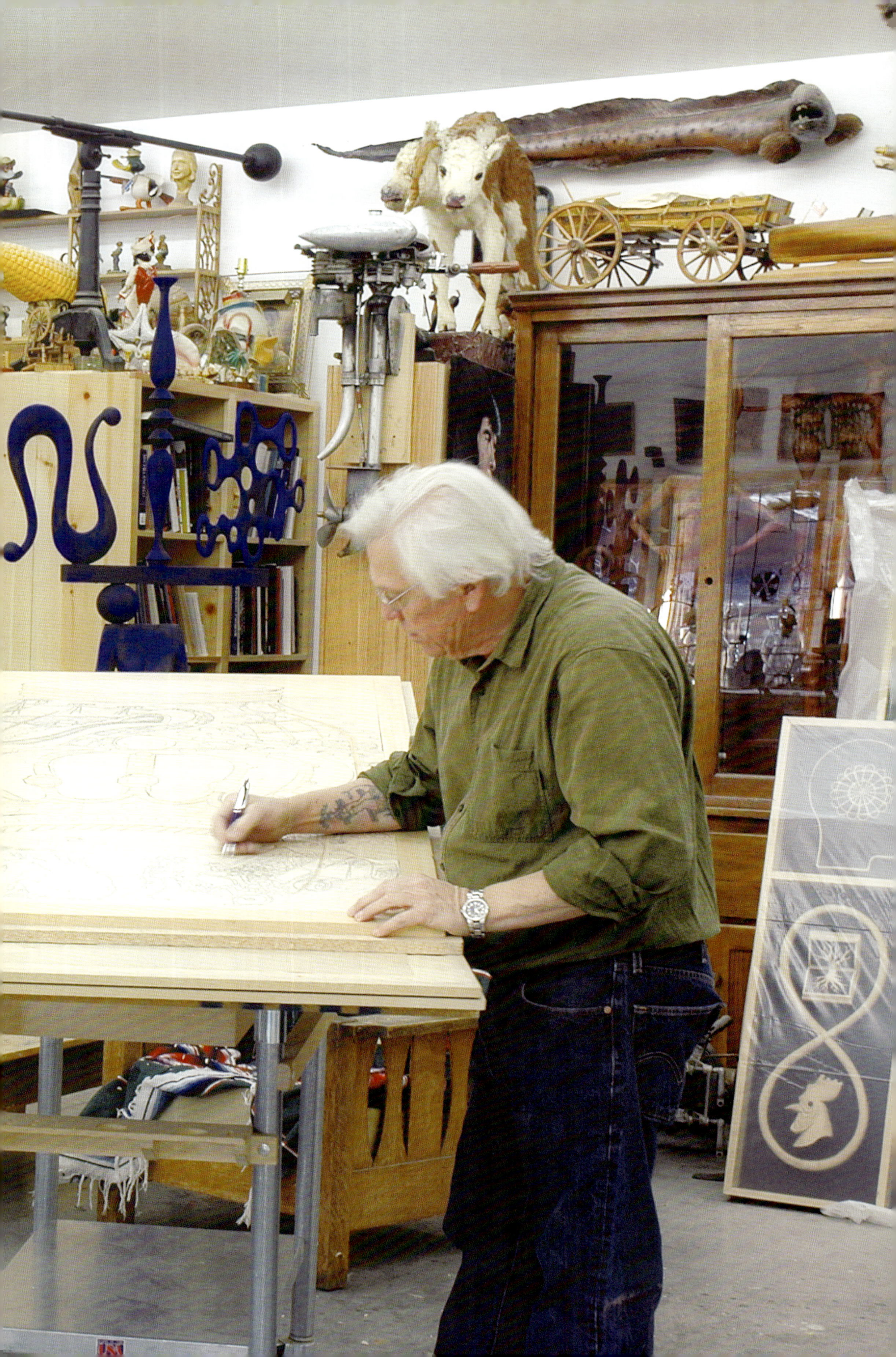

Catalogue Raisonné

JOHN BUCK: PRINTS

1980–2007

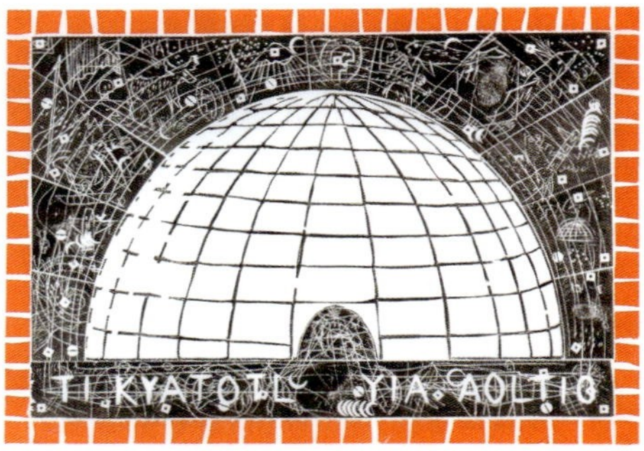

1.
MY FIRST PRINT, edition 6/13
1980
Three color woodcut
26 x 34 inches
Printed on Sekishu paper, edition of 13
Ted Gardeline and Jane Gray
Visual Arts Center of Alaska, Anchorage, Alaska
Collection of Jordan D. Schnitzer
2007.376

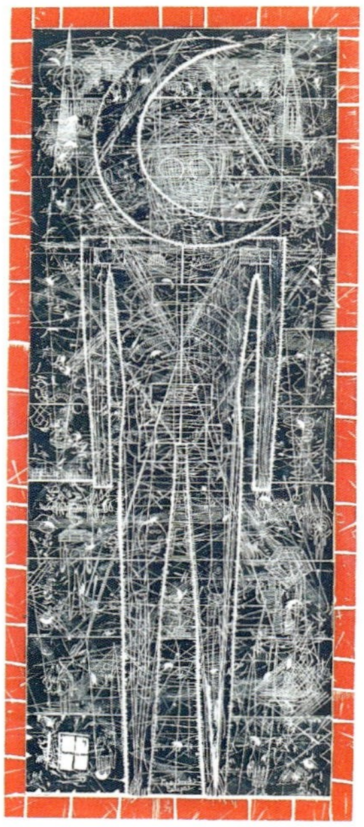

2.
UNTITLED (LA GRANDE ECLIPSE)
1982
Three color woodcut
75 x 38 inches
Printed on Suzuki handmade paper, edition of 20, plus 1 right to print proof, 1 PP, 6 AP, 5 TP, 3 Landfall Press impressions
Jack Lemon, David Holzman, and Barbara Spies
Landfall Press, Inc., Chicago, Illinois

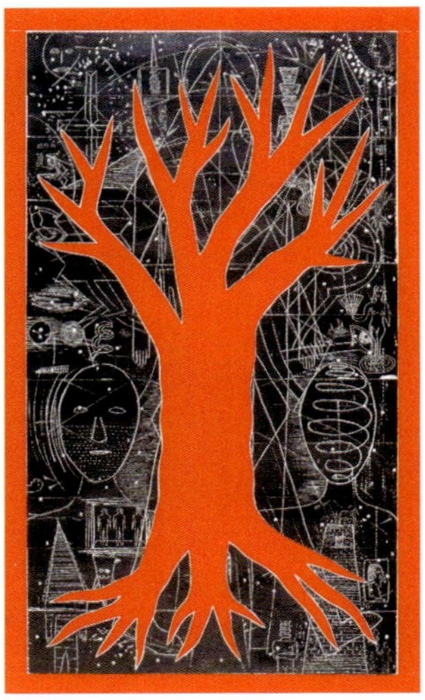

3.
BEIRUT, workshop proof edition 2/3
1983
Two color woodcut
62½ x 36 inches
Printed on Suzuki handmade paper, edition of 30, plus 5 AP, 2 PP, 3 workshop proofs, 1 University of Colorado impression
Bud Shark, Barbara Shark, and Jean Pless
Shark's Ink., Lyons, Colorado
Collection of Jordan D. Schnitzer
1999.3

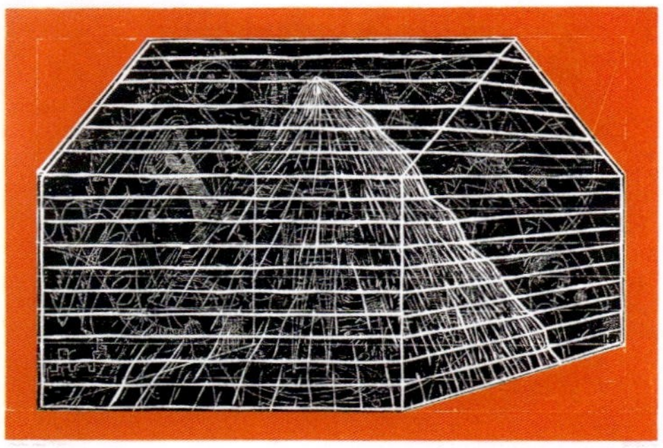

4.
MOUNTAIN HOME, edition PP 3/4
1983–84
Three color woodcut
43 x 60 inches
Ink on Masa paper, edition of 10, plus 1 RTP, 4 AP, 4 Landfall Press impressions, 1 cancellation proof
Jack Lemon
Landfall Press, Inc., Chicago, Illinois
Collection of Jordan D. Schnitzer
2006.18

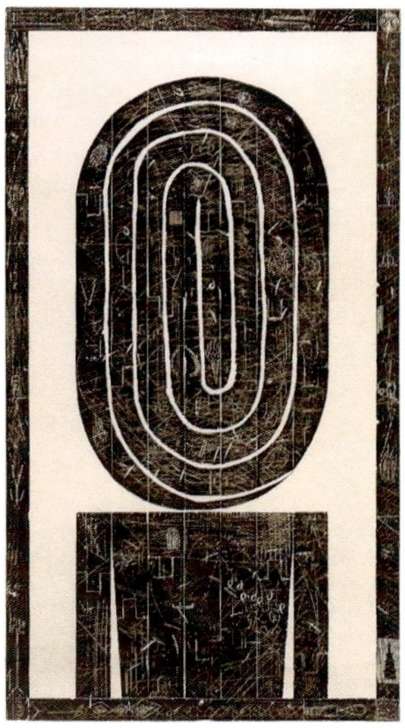

5.
TROPIC OF CAPRICORN, edition HC
1983–84
One color woodcut
60 x 34 inches
Printed on Okawara paper, edition of 10, plus 2 TP, 1 BAT, 1 HC, 2 PP, 5 AP, 2 Landfall Press impressions
Jack Lemon, Mark Genrich, and Barbara Spies
Landfall Press, Inc., Chicago, Illinois
Collection of Jordan D. Schnitzer
2006.19

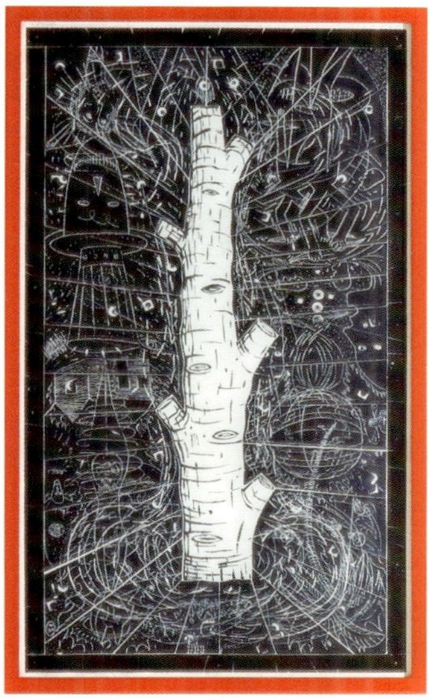

7.
BIG STICK
1984
Two color woodcut
61 x 35 inches
Printed on Suzuki handmade paper, 2 AP only
Unknown printer
Experimental Workshop, San Francisco, California

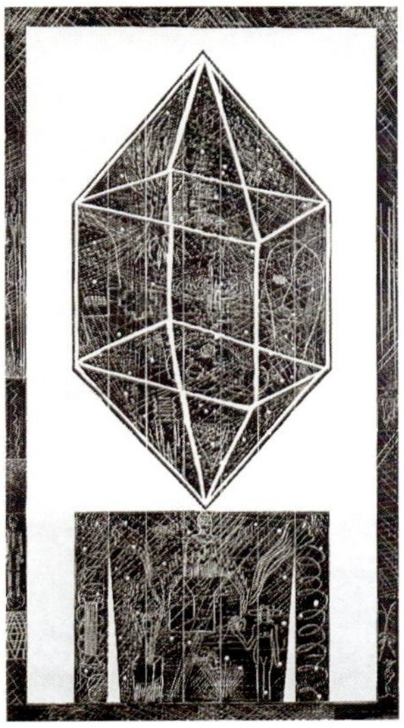

6.
TROPIC OF CANCER
1984
One color woodcut
61 x 36½ inches
Printed on Okuwara paper, edition of 10, plus 1 BAT, 2 TP, 5 AP, 2 PP, 2 Landfall Press impressions
Jack Lemon, Mark Genrich, and Barbara Spies
Landfall Press, Inc., Chicago, Illinois

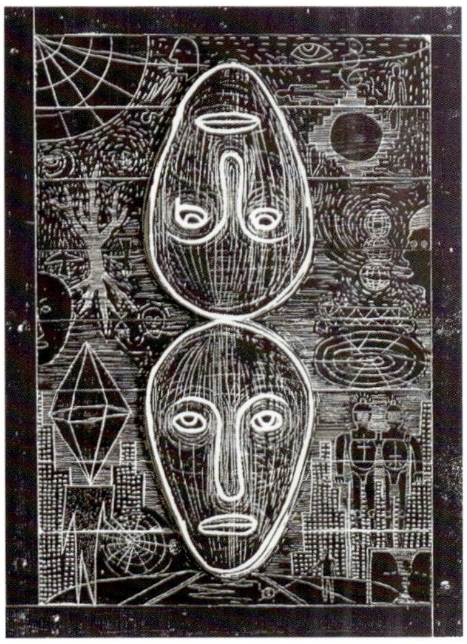

8.
EQUATOR
1984
Two color woodcut
37 x 27 inches
Printed on Rives BFK, edition of 20, plus 2 AP, 1 BAT, 2 PP
Wil Foo and John Stemmer
Experimental Workshop, San Francisco, California

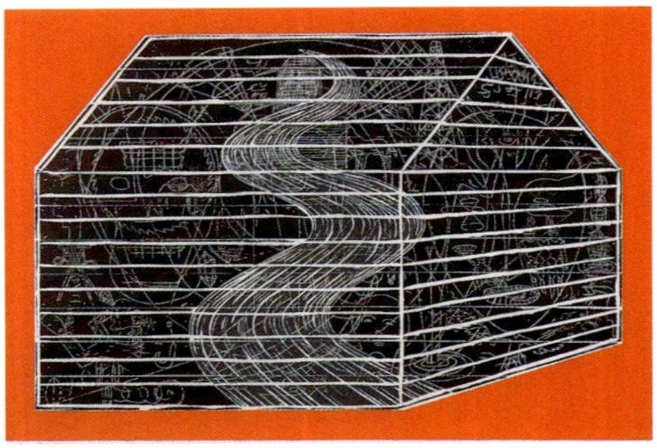

9.
GREEN RIVER, edition PP 3/4
1984
Three color woodcut
43 x 60 inches
Printed on Kozo paper, edition of 10, plus 1 BAT, 4 AP, 4 Landfall Press impressions, 1 cancellation proof
Jack Lemon and Steve Campbell
Landfall Press, Inc., Chicago, Illinois
Collection of Jordan D. Schnitzer
2006.17

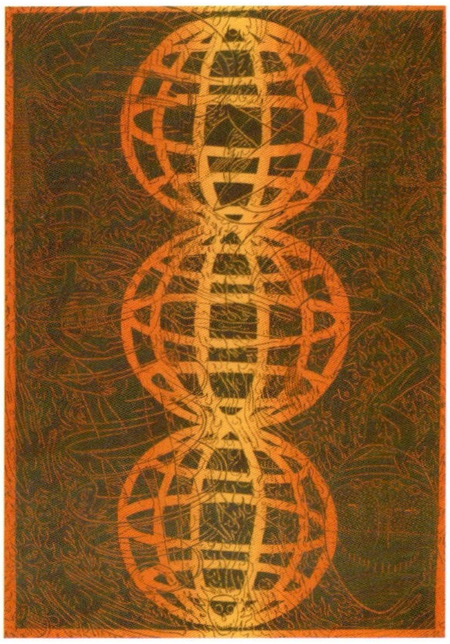

10.
JIHAD, edition 7/30
1984
Four color lithograph
44½ x 30 inches
Printed on Rives BFK white paper, edition of 30, plus 2 TP, 5 AP, 2 PP, 3 workshop proofs
Bud Shark assisted by Matthew Christie
Shark's Ink., Lyons, Colorado
Collection of Jordan D. Schnitzer
2002.12

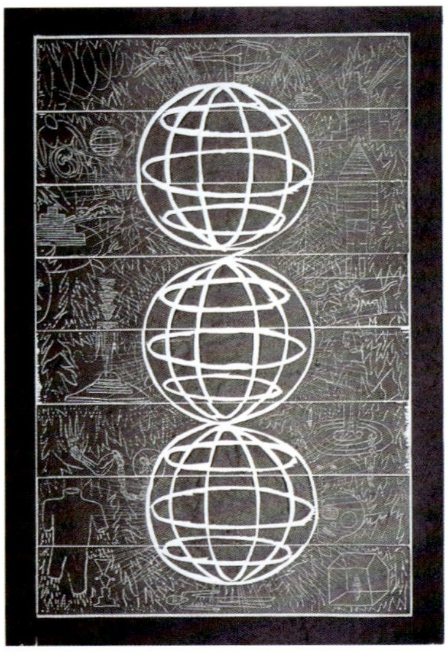

11.
TRIPOLI
1984
Two color woodcut
38 x 26 inches
Edition of 30, plus 2 PP, 1 BAT
Thomas Majeski assisted by Kenneth Jimmerson
University of Nebraska Print Workshop, Omaha, Nebraska

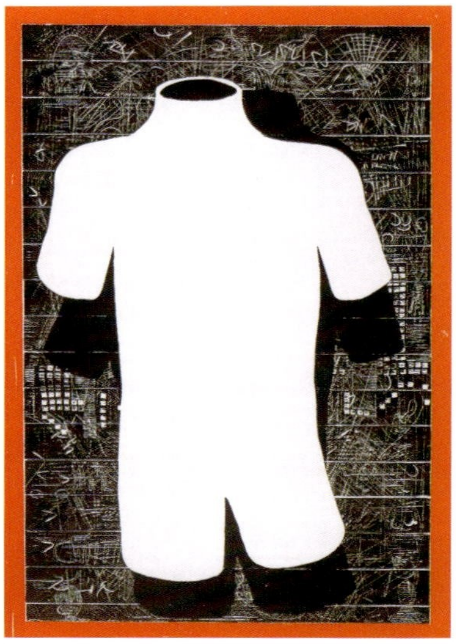

12.
AVENUE OF THE AMERICAS, edition RTP
1985
Two color woodcut
50 x 34 inches
Printed on Suzuki handmade paper, edition of 20, plus 2 TP, 1 RTP, 2 AP
Jack Lemon and Barbara Spies
Landfall Press, Inc., Chicago, Illinois
Collection of Jordan D. Schnitzer
2006.20

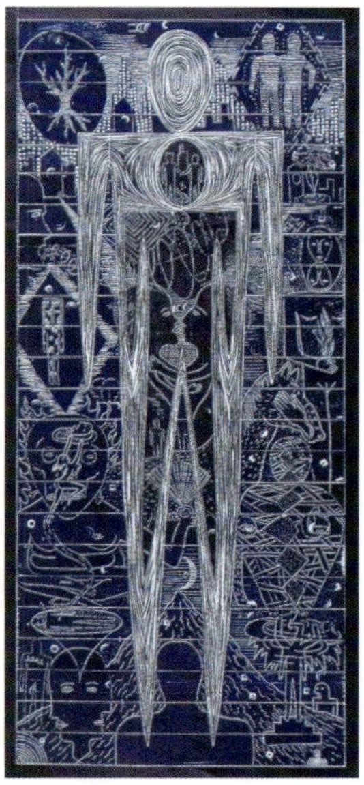

13.
FATHER & SON
1985
Two color woodcut
82 ½ x 36 ½ inches
Printed on Suzuki handmade paper, edition of 30, plus 4 AP, 1 WP, 2 PP, 1 TP
Bud Shark, Roseanne Colachis, Jean Pless, and Barbara Shark
Shark's Ink., Lyons, Colorado

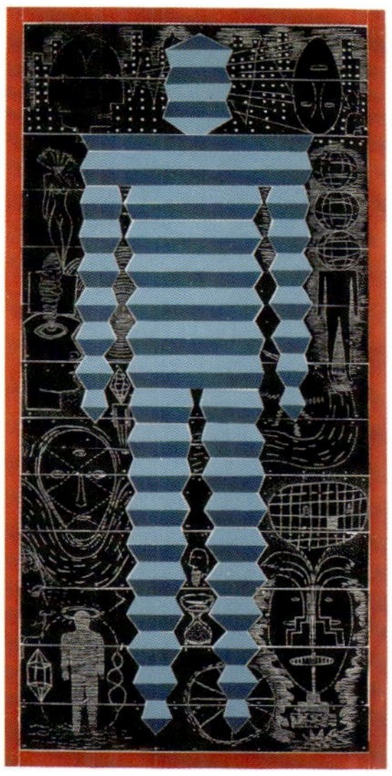

15.
PACIFICA
1985
Four color woodcut
72 x 37 inches
Printed on Suzuki handmade paper, edition of 20, plus 2 AP, 3 PP, 1 TP
Matthew Christie, Sascha Immerman, and Mollie Favour
Anderson Ranch Arts Center, Snowmass Village, Colorado

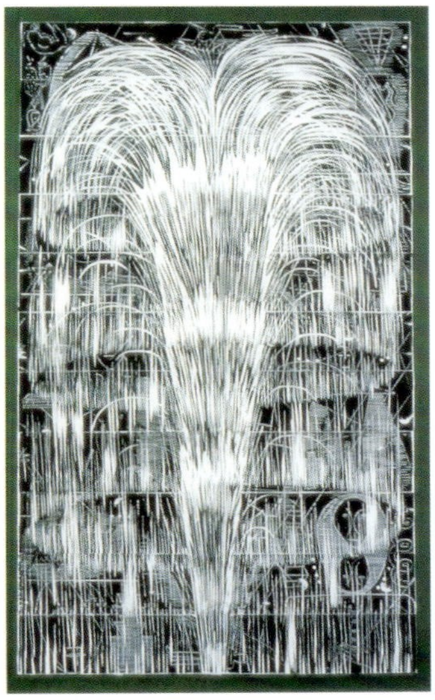

14.
FOUNTAIN
1985
Two color woodcut
62 x 37 inches
Printed on Suzuki handmade paper, edition of 20, plus 2 AP, 3 PP, 1 TP
Matthew Christie, Sascha Immerman, and Mollie Favour
Anderson Ranch Arts Center, Snowmass Village, Colorado

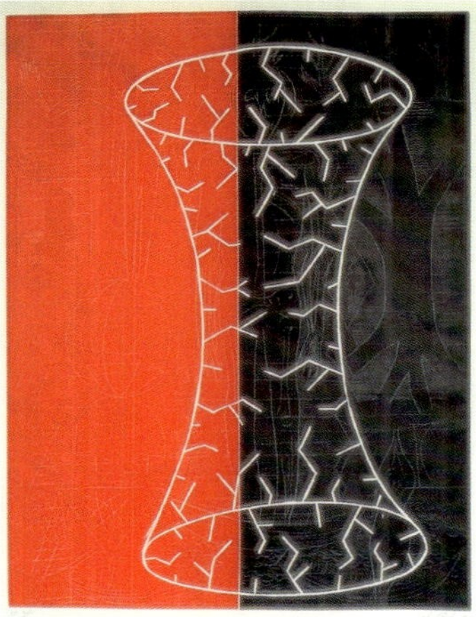

16.
BASKET STUDY
1986
Two color Plexiglas engraving
37 x 30 inches
Ink on paper, edition of 16
John Buck and David Wharton
Sun Valley Arts Center, Ketchum, Idaho

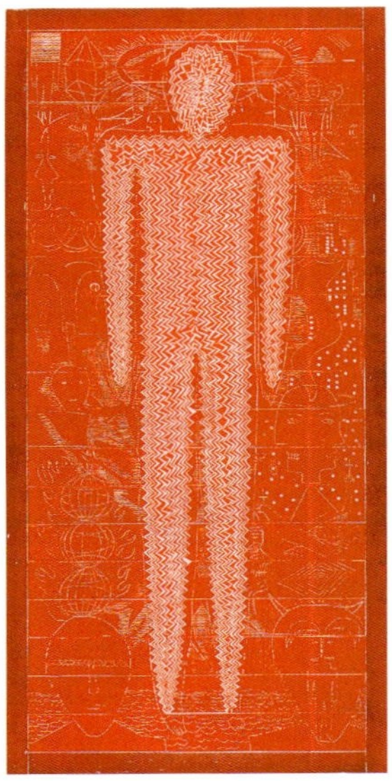

17.
RED JESUS, edition 28/30
1986
Three color woodcut
74 x 37 inches
Printed on Suzuki handmade paper, edition of 30, plus 1 TP, 5 AP, 4 PP, 3 workshop proofs
Bud Shark, Roseanne Colachis, Jean Pless, and Barbara Shark
Shark's Ink., Lyons, Colorado
Collection of Jordan D. Schnitzer
1999.5

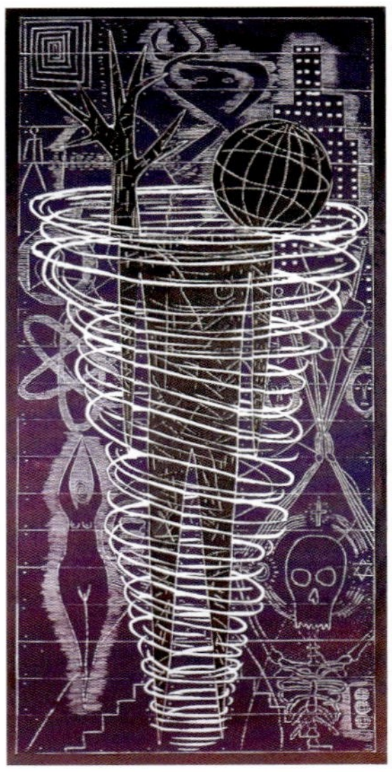

19.
BETWEEN THE WARS
1987
Two color woodcut
72 x 37 inches
Printed on Suzuki handmade paper, edition of 14
John Catterall
Center for the Graphic Arts, New Mexico University, Las Cruces, New Mexico

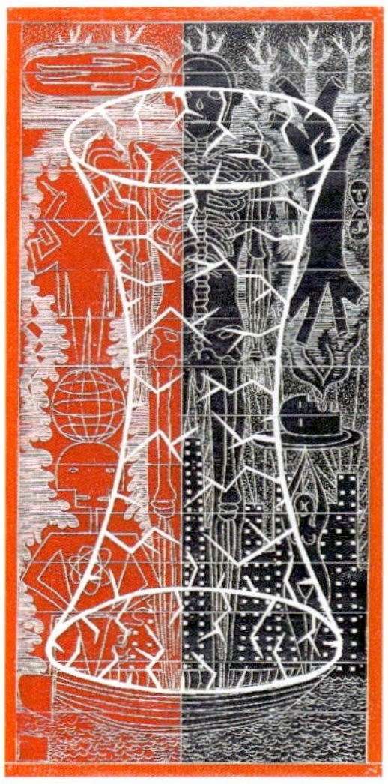

18.
BASKET, edition of 9/15
1987
Three color woodcut
72½ x 36½ inches
Printed on Suzuki handmade paper, edition of 15, plus 2 TP, 4 AP, 4 PP, 1 workshop proof
Roseanne Colachis, Jean Pless, Jim Robb, and Barbara Shark
Shark's Ink., Lyons, Colorado
Collection of Jordan D. Schnitzer
2002.10

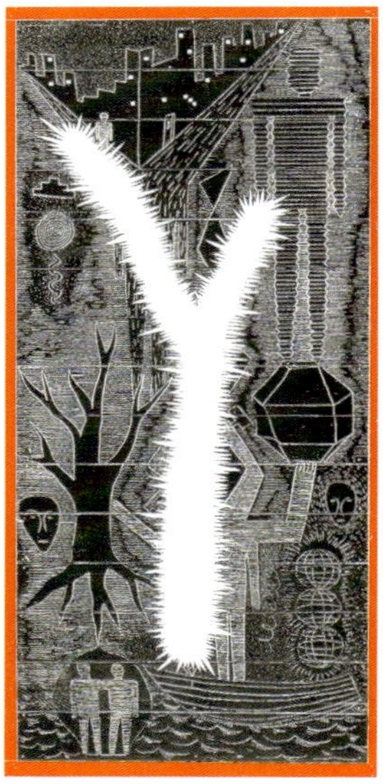

20.
CAPETOWN, edition 1/15
1987
Two color woodcut
74 x 37 inches
Printed on Suzuki handmade paper, edition of 15, plus 2 TP, 4 AP, 3 PP, 1 workshop proof
Roseanne Colachis, Jean Pless, and Barbara Shark
Shark's Ink., Lyons, Colorado
Collection of Jordan D. Schnitzer
2002.11

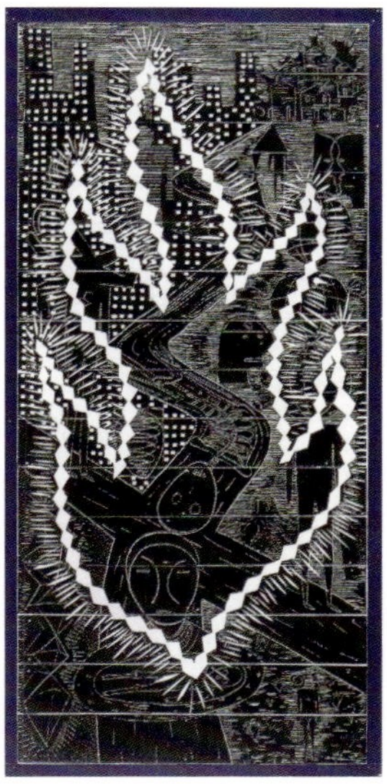

21.
CROSSROADS, edition 2/15
1987
Two color woodcut
74 x 37 inches
Printed on Suzuki handmade paper, edition of 15, plus 2 TP, 4 AP, 3 PP, 1 workshop proof
Roseanne Colachis, Jean Pless, and Barbara Shark
Shark's Ink., Lyons, Colorado
Collection of Jordan D. Schnitzer
2002.14

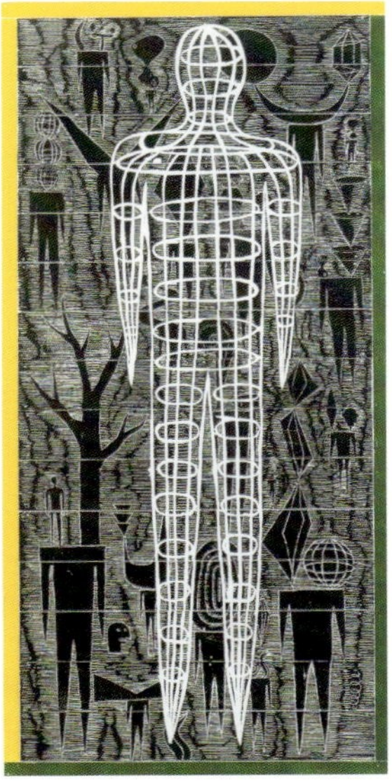

22.
PRISONER, edition WP 1/1
1987
Three color woodcut
74 x 37 inches
Printed on Suzuki handmade paper, edition of 15, plus 2 TP, 4 AP, 4 PP, 1 workshop proof
Roseanne Colachis, Jean Pless, Jim Robb, and Barbara Shark
Shark's Ink., Lyons, Colorado
Collection of Jordan D. Schnitzer
2002.9

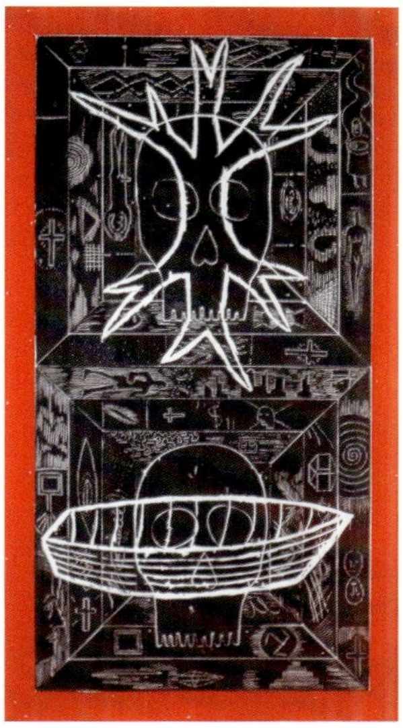

23.
THE HAVES AND THE HAVE NOTS, edition 3/14
1987
Two color woodcut
67 x 38 inches
Printed on Suzuki handmade paper, edition of 14
John Catterall
Center for the Graphic Arts, New Mexico University, Las Cruces, New Mexico
Collection of Jordan D. Schnitzer
2006.61

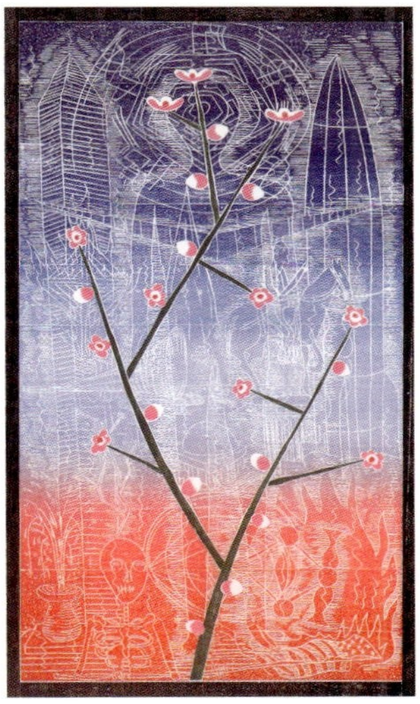

24.
CHERRY BLOSSOM TIME, edition WP 1/1
1988
Ten-color woodcut
63 ½ x 37 inches
Printed on Suzuki handmade paper, edition of 15, plus 2 TP, 4 AP, 4 PP, 1 workshop proof
Bud Shark, Barbara Shark, Roseanne Colachis, and Ron Trujillo
Shark's Ink., Lyons, Colorado
Collection of Jordan D. Schnitzer
2002.13

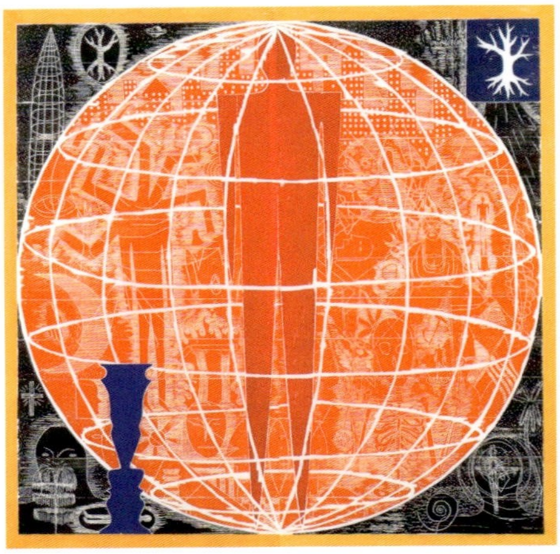

25.
EAST/WEST, edition PP 3/4
1988
Six-color woodcut
74 x 73½ inches
Printed on 2 sheets of Suzuki handmade paper, edition of 15 plus 2 TP, 4 AP, 4 PP, 1 workshop proof
Bud Shark, Barbara Shark, Roseanne Colachis, Ron Trujillo, and Jim Robb
Shark's Ink., Lyons, Colorado
Collection of the Jordan Schnitzer Family Foundation
1999.33

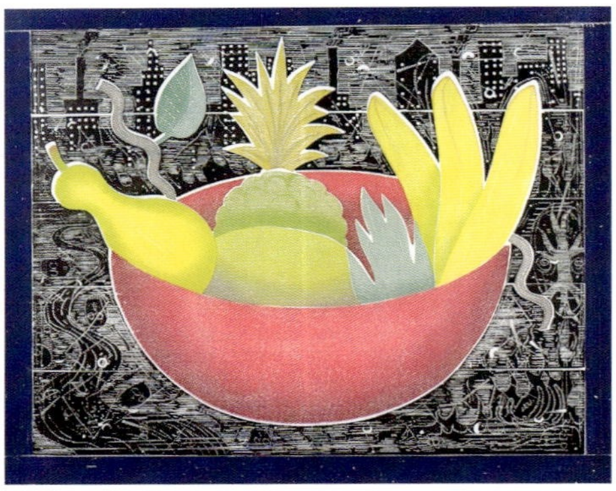

26.
GREEN FRUIT, edition PP 1/4
1989
Twenty-three color woodcut
31½ x 37 inches
Watercolor and ink on Suzuki handmade paper, edition of 20, plus 3 TP, 5 AP, 4 PP, 1 workshop proof
Bud Shark, Hiroki Morinoue, Barbara Shark, Roseanne Colachis, Matthew Christies, and Ron Trujillo
Shark's Ink., Lyons, Colorado
Collection of Jordan D. Schnitzer
2002.17

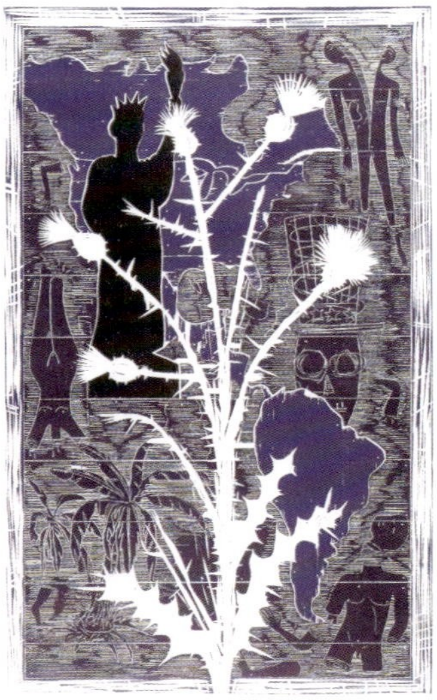

27.
TRAILS PLOWED UNDER, edition 2/15
1989
Three-color woodcut
63½ x 37 inches
Printed on Suzuki handmade paper, edition of 15, plus 3 TP, 4 AP, 4 PP
Bud Shark, Barbara Shark, Roseanne Colachis, and Matthew Christie
Shark's Ink., Lyons, Colorado
Collection of Jordan D. Schnitzer
2002.15

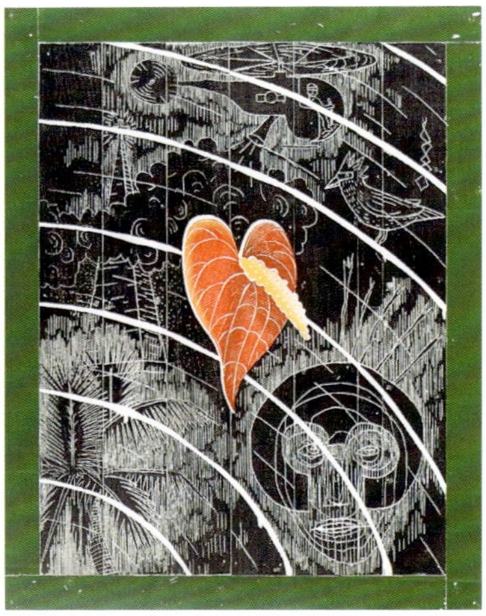

28.
ROUNDUP: ANTHURIUM, edition TP
1990
Eight-color woodcut
37¼ x 28 inches
Triptych, ink and watercolor on Suzuki handmade paper, edition of 15, plus 2 TP, 5 AP, 4 PP, 2 workshop proofs
Bud Shark, Hiroki Morinoue, Barbara Shark, Roseanne Colachis, Lisa Merrin, Aleta Braun, and Ron Trujillo
Shark's Ink., Lyons, Colorado
Collection of Jordan D. Schnitzer
1999.14c

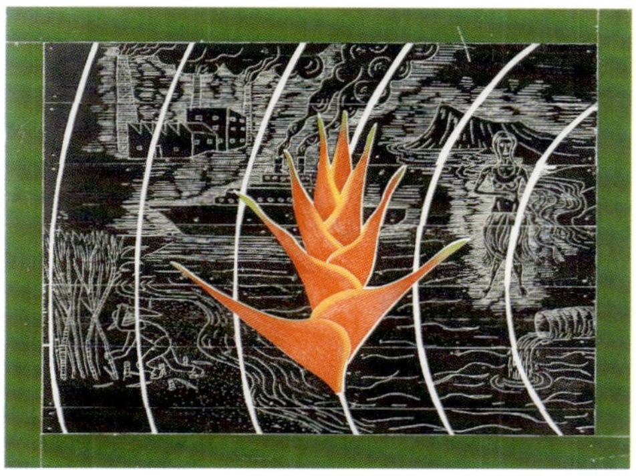

29.
ROUNDUP: HELICONIA, edition TP
1990
Six-color woodcut
28 x 37 ¼ inches
Triptych, ink and watercolor on Suzuki handmade paper, edition of 15, plus 2 TP, 5 AP, 4 PP, 2 workshop proofs
Bud Shark, Hiroki Morinoue, Barbara Shark, Roseanne Colachis, Lisa Merrin, Aleta Braun, and Ron Trujillo
Shark's Ink., Lyons, Colorado
Collection of Jordan D. Schnitzer
1999.14a

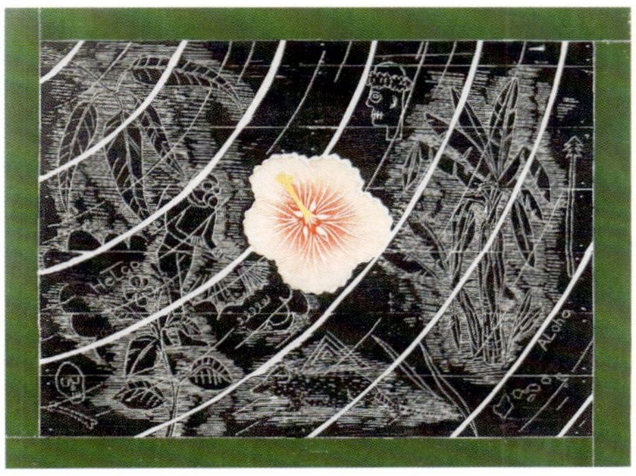

30.
ROUNDUP: HIBISCUS, edition TP
1990
Five-color woodcut
28 x 37 ¼ inches
Triptych, ink and watercolor on Suzuki handmade paper, edition of 15, plus 2 TP, 5 AP, 4 PP, 2 workshop proofs
Bud Shark, Hiroki Morinoue, Barbara Shark, Roseanne Colachis, Lisa Merrin, Aleta Braun, and Ron Trujillo
Shark's Inc., Lyons, Colorado
Collection of Jordan D. Schnitzer
1999.14b

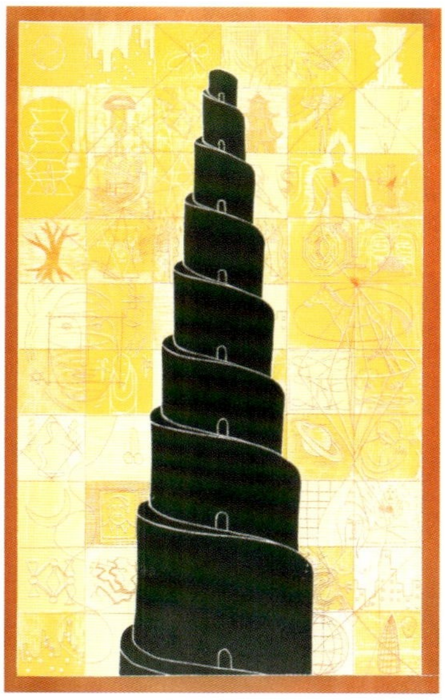

31.
THE LANGUAGE OF THE TIMES, edition 4/36
1990
Woodcut and drypoint
80 x 52 inches
Ink on Arches Cover White, edition of 36
Andrew M. Rubin
Tandem Press, Madison, Wisconsin
Collection of Jordan D. Schnitzer
2006.53

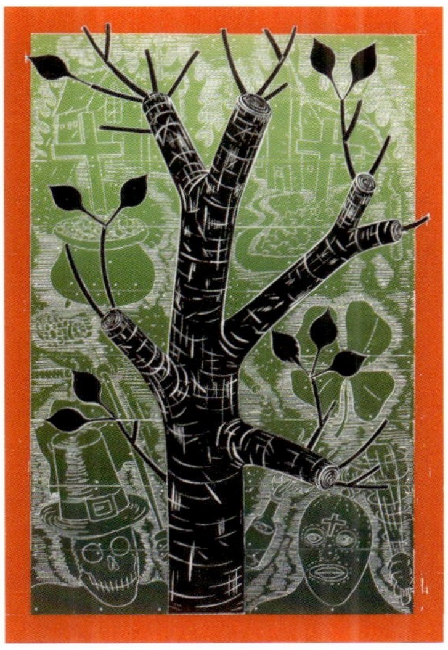

32.
THE SHILLELAGH TREE, edition 7/15
1990
Five-color woodcut
52 x 36 inches
Printed on Suzuki handmade paper, edition of 15, plus 2 TP, 5 AP, 4 PP, 3 workshop proofs
Bud Shark, Barbara Shark, Roseanne Colachis, Lisa Merrin, and Aleta Braun
Shark's Ink., Lyons, Colorado
Collection of Jordan D. Schnitzer
2002.20

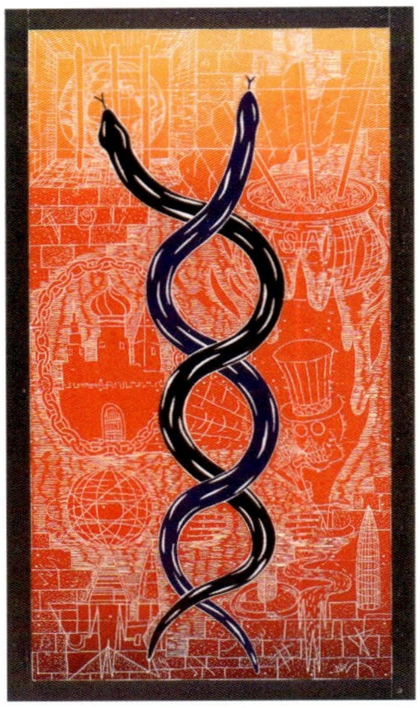

33.
A COMMON TONGUE, edition 6/15
1991 (signed 1992)
Eight-color woodcut
62 x 36½ inches
Printed on Suzuki handmade paper, edition of 15, plus 2 TP, 5 AP, 4 PP, 2 WP, 1 Rutgers Archives for Printmaking Studios impression
Bud Shark, Barbara Shark, Roseanne Colachis, Matthew Christie, and Lisa Merrin
Shark's Ink., Lyons, Colorado
Collection of Jordan D. Schnitzer
2002.21

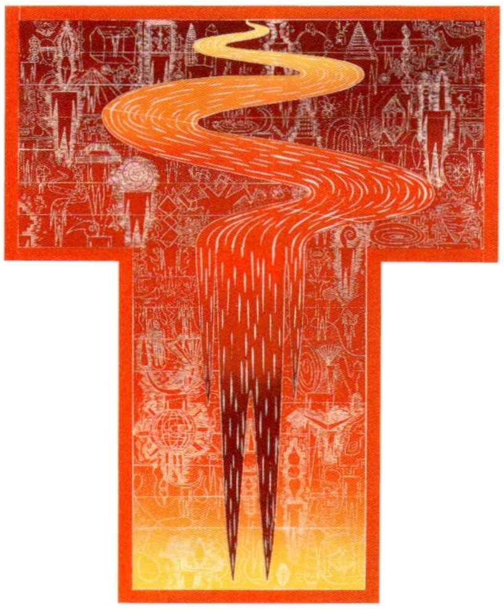

34.
GREAT FALLS, edition 14/15
1991
Five-color woodcut
83¾ x 66 inches
Printed on two sheets of Suzuki handmade paper, edition of 15, plus 1 TP, 5 AP, 4 PP, 1 Rutgers Archives for Printmaking Studios impression
Bud Shark, Barbara Shark, Roseanne Colachis, Matthew Christie, and Lisa Merrin
Shark's Ink., Lyons, Colorado
Collection of Jordan D. Schnitzer
1999.4

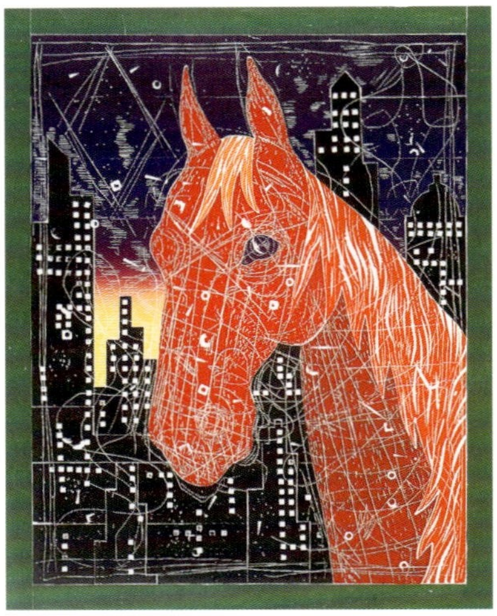

35.
THE BIG CITY, edition WP 2/2
1991
Ten-color woodcut
45 x 36 inches
Printed on Suzuki handmade paper, edition of 15, plus 2 TP, 5 AP, 4 PP, 2 workshop proofs, 1 Rutgers Archives for Printmaking Studios impression
Bud Shark, Barbara Shark, Roseanne Colachis, Matthew Christie, and Lisa Merrin
Shark's Ink., Lyons, Colorado
Collection of Jordan D. Schnitzer
2002.18

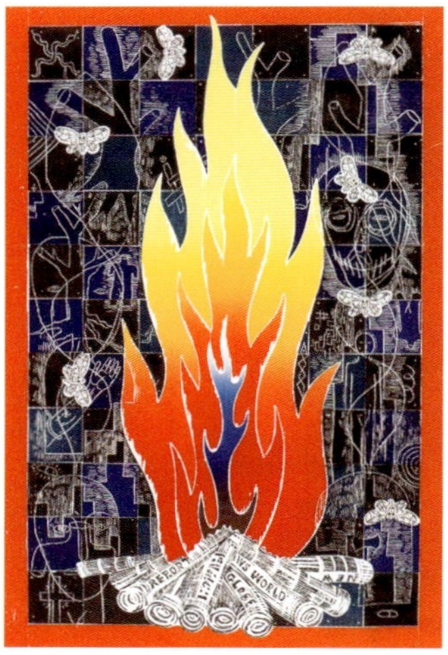

36.
THE TIMES, edition 13/15
1991
Eleven-color woodcut
53½ x 36¼ inches
Ink and rubber stamp on Suzuki handmade paper, edition of 15, plus 3 TP, 5 AP, 4 PP, 2 WP, 1 Rutgers Archives for Printmaking Studio impression
Bud Shark, Barbara Shark, Roseanne Colachis, Matthew Christie, and Lisa Merrin
Shark's Ink., Lyons, Colorado
Collection of Jordan D. Schnitzer
40

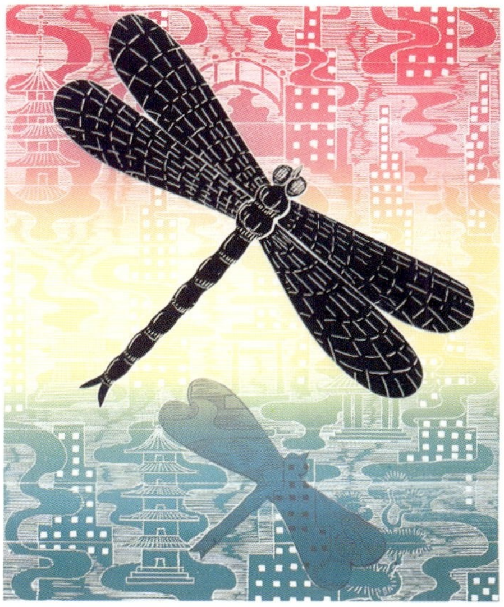

37.
A LITTLE AMERICA
1992
Multicolor woodcut and lithograph
36 x 30 inches
Printed on Rives BFK, edition of 18, plus 2 TP, 3 AP, 2 PP, 1 workshop proof, 1 Rutgers Archive for Printmaking Studios impression
Bud Shark and Matthew Christie
Business Committee for the Arts, Inc., New York

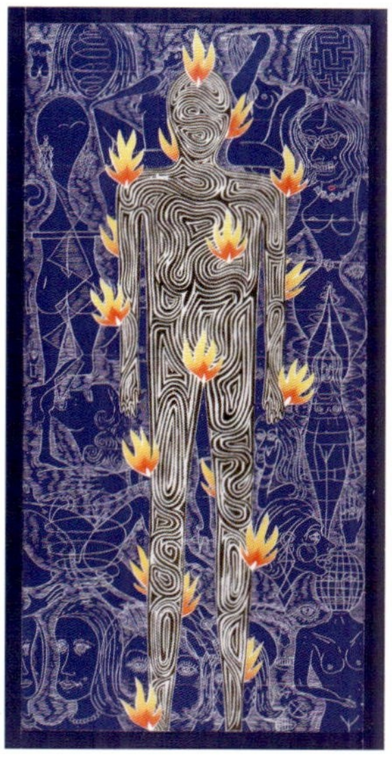

39.
TATTOO, edition 4/15
1992
Five-color woodcut, lithograph, chine-collé
74 x 37 inches
Printed on Sekishu handmade paper, edition of 15
Bud Shark assisted by Matthew Christie, chine-collé applied by Roseanne Colachis
Shark's Ink., Lyons, Colorado
Collection of Jordan D. Schnitzer
2002.19

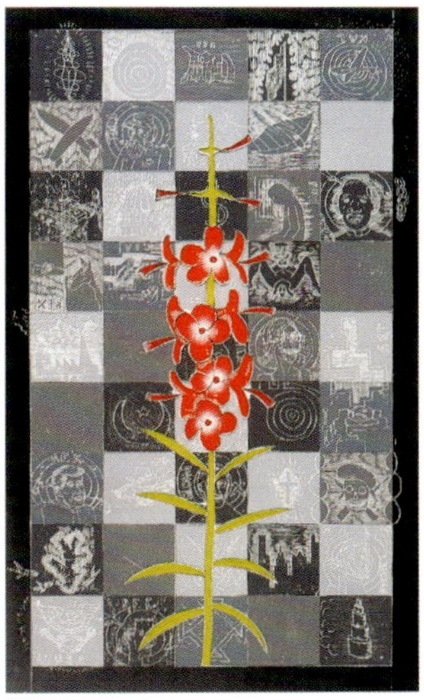

38.
FIREWEED, edition 2/25
1992
Seven-color woodcut and etching
66¾ x 39¾ inches
Printed on Arches paper, edition of 25, plus 2 TP, 1 RTP, 10 AP, 2 PP, 3 Publisher's proofs, 2 copyright proofs, 1 cancellation proof
Steve Campbell, Barbara Spies-Labus, and Betsy Hande
Landfall Press, Inc., Chicago, Illinois
Collection of Jordan D. Schnitzer
2006.21

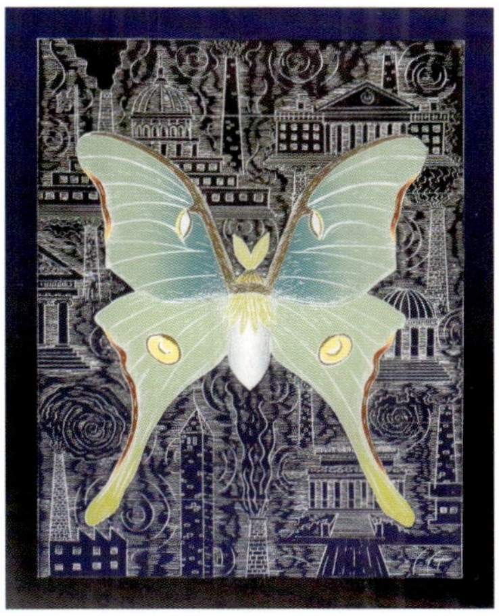

40.
THE NIGHT SKY (LUNA), edition WP 3/3
1992
Six-color woodcut
37¾ x 30 inches
Printed on Sekishu handmade paper, edition of 15, plus 2 TP, 5 AP, 2 PP, 3 workshop proofs, 1 Rutgers Archives for Printmaking Studios impression
Bud Shark assisted by Matthew Christie
Shark's Ink., Lyons, Colorado
Collection of Jordan D. Schnitzer
2002.23

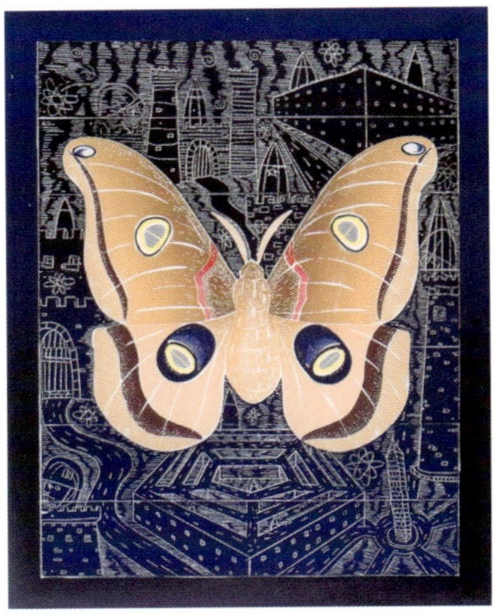

41.
The Night Sky (Polyphemus), edition 7/15
1992
Ten-color woodcut, linocut
37 x 30 inches
Printed on Sekishu handmade paper, edition of 15, plus 2 TP, 5 AP, 2 PP, 3 workshop proofs, 1 Rutgers Archives for Printmaking Studio impression
Bud Shark assisted by Matthew Christie
Shark's Ink., Lyons, Colorado
Collection of Jordan D. Schnitzer
2002.22

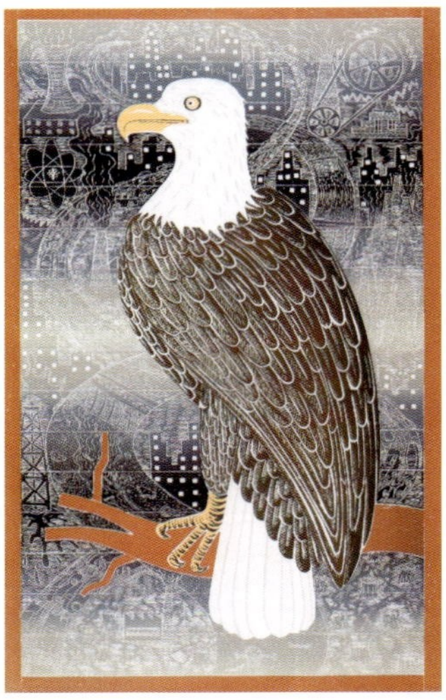

42.
American Eagle/The Great Divide, edition 10/15
1993
Eleven-color woodcut
60½ x 36½ inches
Printed on Sekishu handmade paper, edition of 15, plus 1 TP, 5 AP, 2 PP, 3 workshop proofs
Bud Shark assisted by Matthew Christie
Shark's Ink., Lyons, Colorado
Collection of Jordan D. Schnitzer
1999.2

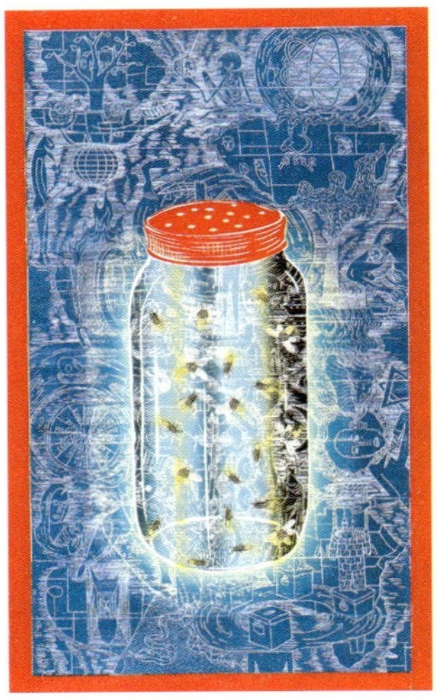

43.
The Lamp, edition Archive impression 1/1
1994
Twelve-color woodcut with rubber stamp and hand coloring
62 x 37 inches
Printed on Sekishu handmade paper, edition of 15, plus 5 AP, 3 WP, 2 PP, 2 TP, 1 Archive impression
Bud Shark assisted by Matthew Christie
Shark's Ink., Lyons, Colorado
Collection of the Jordan Schnitzer Family Foundation
1999.36

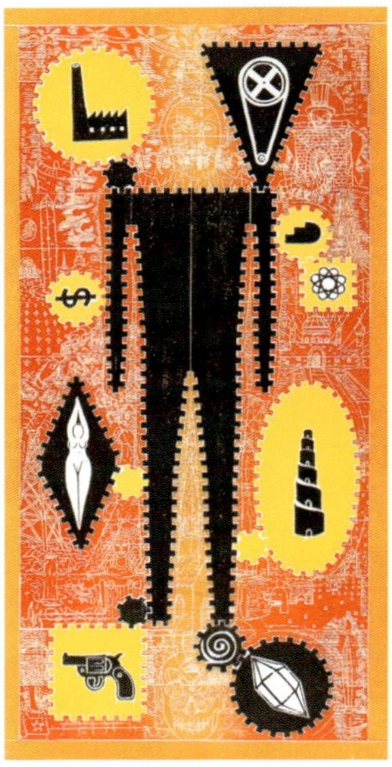

44.
The Mechanic, edition 13/15
1994
Six-color woodcut
73 x 37 inches
Printed on Sekishu handmade paper, edition of 15, plus 5 AP, 3 WP, 2 PP
Bud Shark assisted by Matthew Christie
Shark's Ink., Lyons, Colorado
Collection of Jordan D. Schnitzer
41

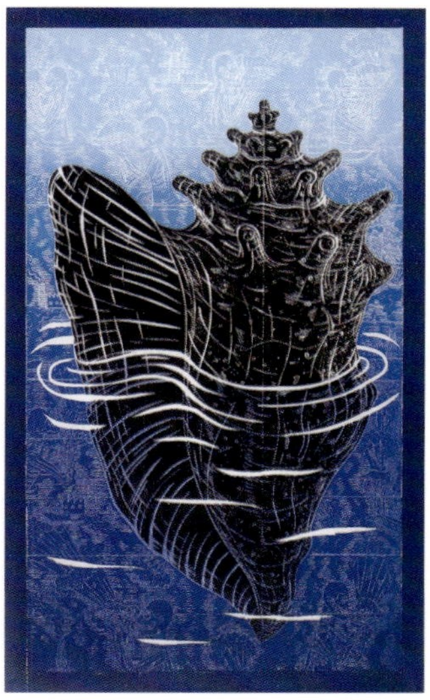

45.
THE SOUND OF THE SEA, edition 6/15
1994
Twelve-color woodcut
62 x 37 inches
Printed on Sekishu handmade paper, edition of 15, plus 5 AP, 3 WP, 2 PP, 2 TP
Bud Shark assisted by Matthew Christie
Shark's Ink., Lyons, Colorado
Collection of the Jordan Schnitzer Family Foundation
1999.37

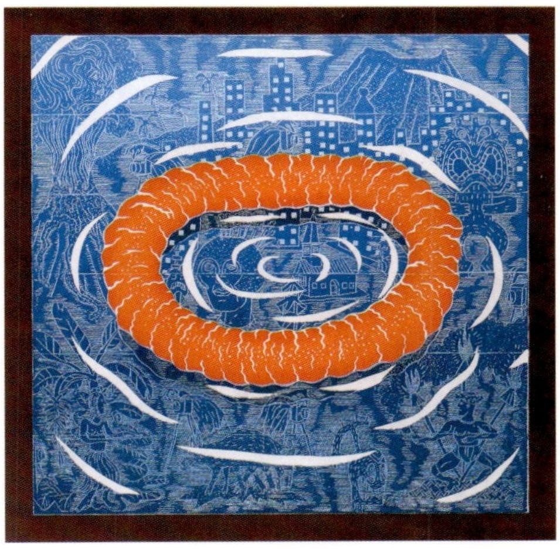

46.
LEI ILIMA, edition 8/15
1995
Twelve-color woodcut
37½ x 37 inches
Printed on White Thai Mulberry, edition of 15, plus 5 AP, 3 WP, 2 PP, 2 TP
Bud Shark assisted by Matthew Christie
Shark's Ink., Lyons, Colorado
Collection of Jordan D. Schnitzer
2002.16

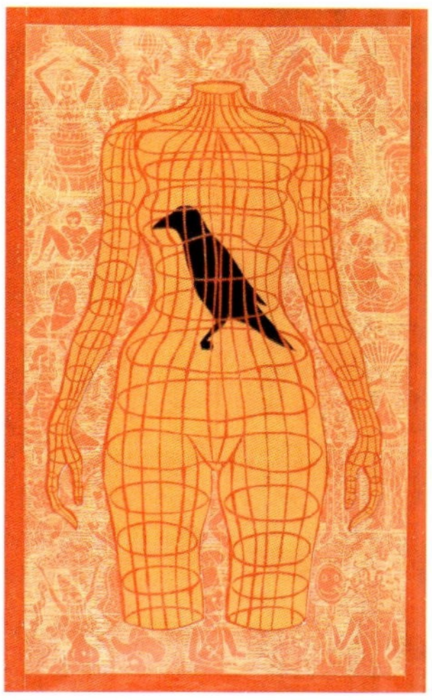

47.
THE COAL MINE, edition 6/15
1996
Four color woodcut
62 x 37 inches
Printed on White Thai Mulberry paper, edition of 15, plus 5 AP, 2 PP, 2 WP, 1 BAT, 1 Archive impression
Bud Shark assisted by Matthew Christie and Evan Colbert
Shark's Ink., Lyons, Colorado
Collection of the Jordan Schnitzer Family Foundation
1999.34

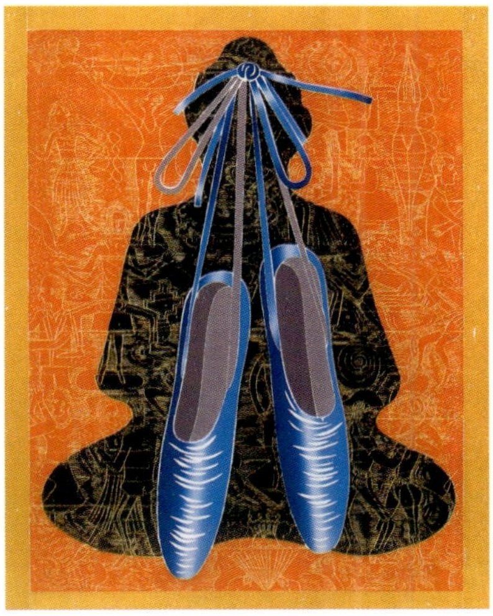

48.
THE DANCING SHOES, edition 6/15
1996
Seven-color woodcut
50 x 37 inches
Printed on White Thai Mulberry paper, edition of 10, plus 2 AP, 2 TP
Bud Shark assisted by Matthew Christie
Shark's Ink., Lyons, Colorado
Collection of Jordan D. Schnitzer
2002.24

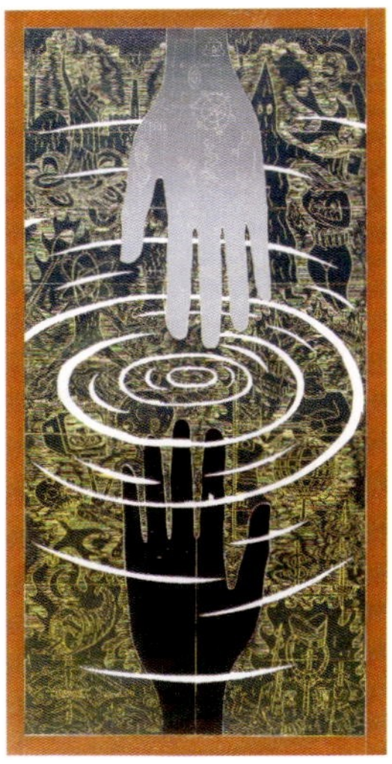

49.
THE EMPTY HAND, edition 8/15
1996
Sixteen-color woodcut
72 x 37 inches
Printed on White Thai Mulberry paper, edition of 15, plus 5 AP, 2 PP, 2 WP, 1 BAT, 2 TP, 1 Archive impression
Bud Shark assisted by Matthew Christie
Shark's Ink., Lyons, Colorado
Collection of the Jordan Schnitzer Family Foundation
1999.35

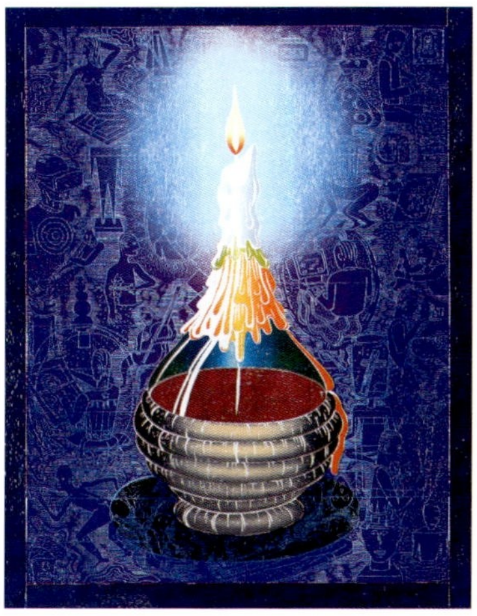

50.
THE ETERNAL FLAME, edition 6/15
1996
Fifteen-color woodcut
50 x 37 inches
Printed on White Thai Mulberry paper, edition of 15, plus 5 AP, 3 WP, 2 PP, 2 TP
Bud Shark assisted by Matthew Christie
Shark's Ink., Lyons, Colorado
Collection of Jordan D. Schnitzer
510

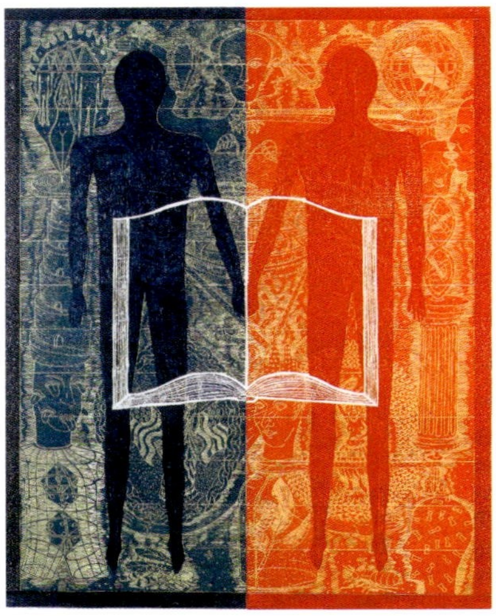

51.
FACT AND FICTION, edition 9/15
1997
Eight-color woodcut
74 x 58 inches
Printed on two sheets of Sekishu handmade paper, edition of 15, plus 5 AP, 2 PP, 2 WP, 1 TP, 1 BAT, 1 Archive impression
Bud Shark assisted by Matthew Christie and Evan Colbert
Shark's Ink., Lyons, Colorado
Collection of Jordan D. Schnitzer
1998.54

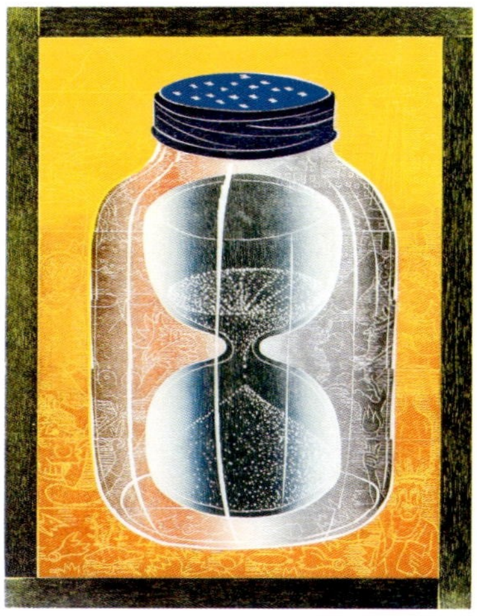

52.
THE GLASS FURNACE, edition AP 4/4
1997
Fifteen-color woodcut
23¾ x 18 inches
Edition of 14, plus 4 AP, 2 PP, 19 TP
Mathew D. Jackson
Pilchuck Glass School
Collection of Jordan D. Schnitzer
588

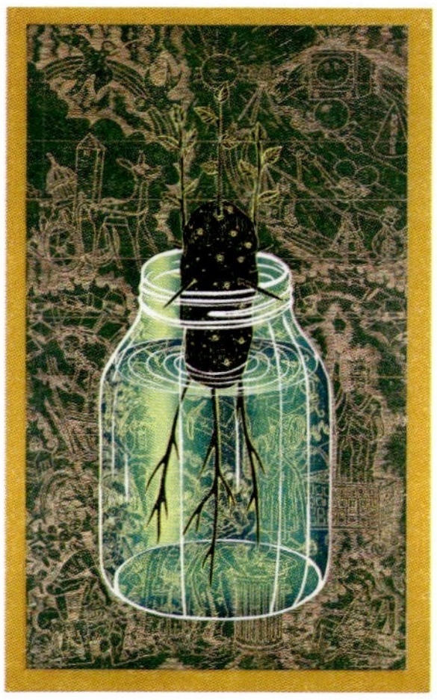

53.
ARGOSY, edition 10/15
1998 (signed 1999)
Eight-color woodcut
62½ x 37 inches
Printed on White Thai Mulberry paper, edition of 15, plus 5 AP, 3 workshop proofs, 2 PP, 1 TP, 1 Archive impression
Bud Shark assisted by Matthew Christie
Shark's Ink., Lyons, Colorado
Collection of the Jordan Schnitzer Family Foundation
1999.32

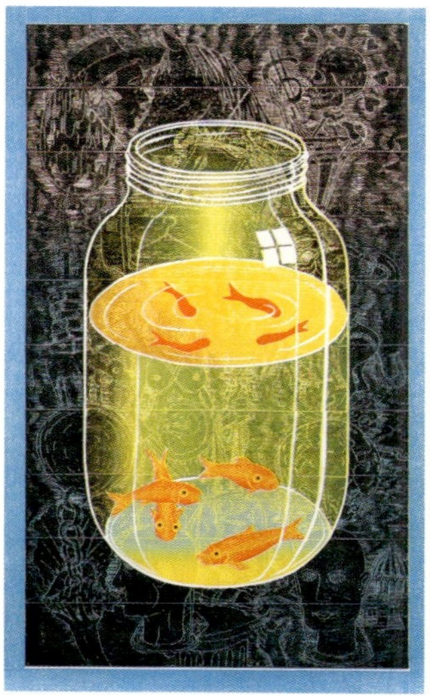

55.
THE DEEP END, edition 9/15
2000
Thirteen-color woodcut and chine-collé
62 x 37 inches
Printed on White Thai Mulberry paper, edition of 15, plus 5 AP, 3 WP, 2 PP, 1 TP, 2 Patron's impressions, 1 Archive impression
Bud Shark assisted by Matthew Christie
Shark's Ink., Lyons, Colorado
Collection of the Jordan Schnitzer Family Foundation
2000.88

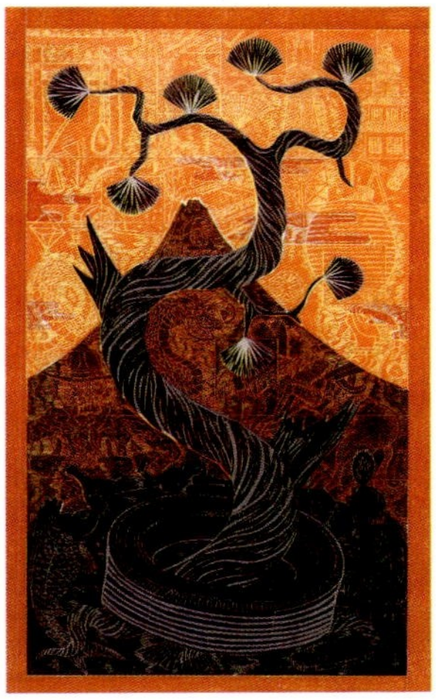

54.
HEART MOUNTAIN, WYOMING, edition 6/15
2000
Seven-color woodcut
62 x 37 inches
Printed on White Thai Mulberry paper, edition of 15, plus 5 AP, 2 WP, 2 PP, 1 TP, 2 Patron's impressions, 1 Archive impression
Bud Shark assisted by Matthew Christie and Evan Colbert
Shark's Ink., Lyons, Colorado
Collection of the Jordan Schnitzer Family Foundation
2000.87

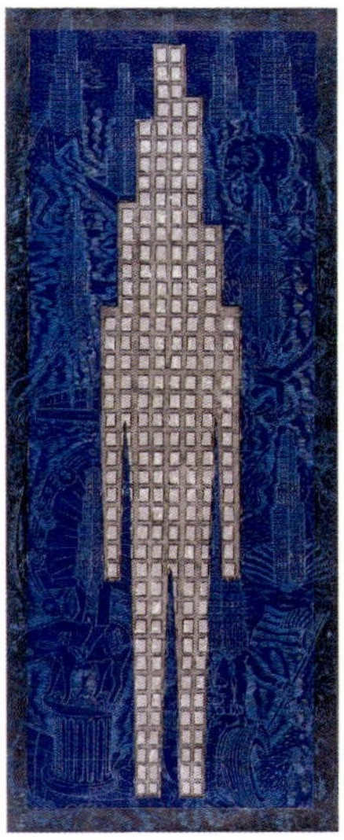

56.
SKYLINE, edition 4/15
2000–2002
Four color woodcut
92 x 37 inches
Printed on White Thai Mulberry paper, edition of 15, plus 5 AP, 3 WP, 2 PP, 1 TP, 2 Patron's impressions, 1 Archive impression
Bud Shark and Evan Colbert
Shark's Ink., Lyons, Colorado
Collection of Jordan D. Schnitzer
2002.63

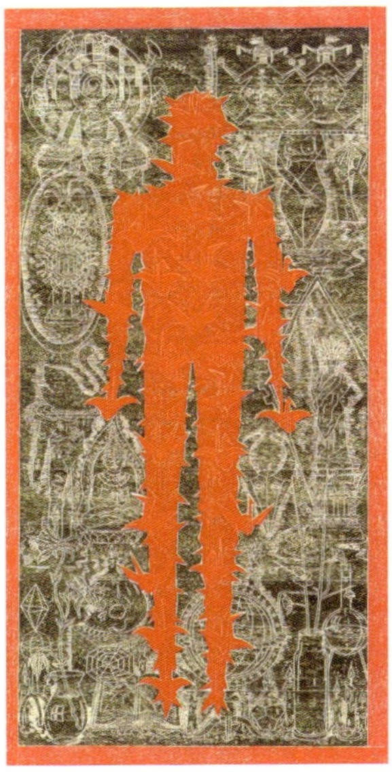

57.
A THOUSAND CRANES
2001
Six-color woodcut
73 x 38 inches
Printed on Okuwara Natural, edition of 10, plus 3 AP, 1 TP, 1 PP, 3 Landfall Press impressions
Jack Lemon, Tom Reed, Steve Campbell, and Barb Labus
Landfall Press, Inc., Chicago, Illinois

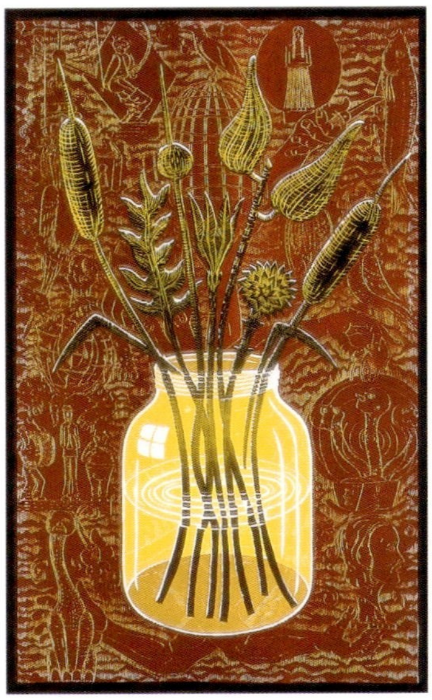

59.
THE WINTER BOUQUET
2001
Five-color woodcut
62 x 37 inches
Printed on handmade paper, edition of 16, plus 3 TP, 1 AP, 1 PP
Hiroki Morinue assisted by Sara Hudson
Anderson Ranch Arts Center, Snowmass Village, Colorado

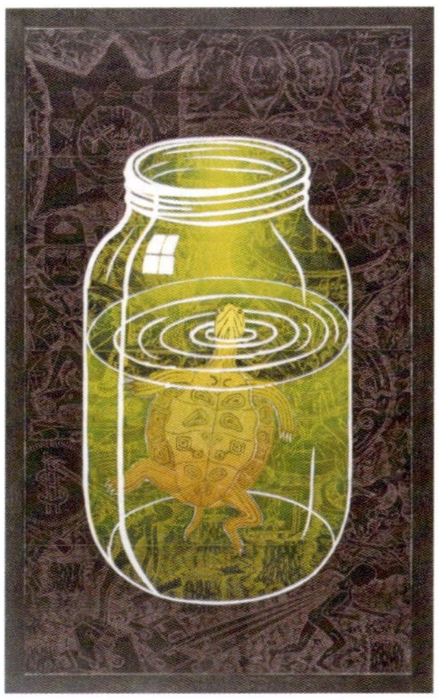

58.
CRYSTAL LAKE, edition 6/15
2001
Twelve-color woodcut
62 x 37 inches
Printed on White Thai Mulberry paper, edition of 15, plus 5 AP, 2 PP, 2 WP, 1 Archive impression
Bud Shark assisted by Matthew Christie
Shark's Ink., Lyons, Colorado
Collection of Jordan D. Schnitzer
2002.25

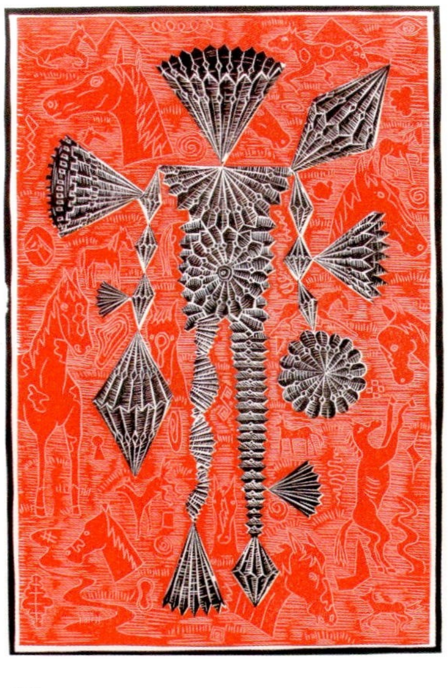

60.
MAN WITH HORSES
2002
Five-color woodcut
28½ x 18½ inches
Printed on Coventry 100% rag paper, edition of 120, plus 20 AP, 5 PP, 5 presentation proofs, 5 TP
Charles E. Matson
Madison Print Club, Madison, Wisconsin

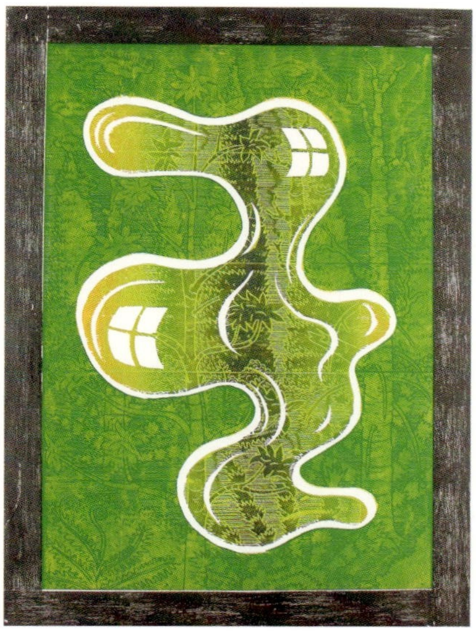

61.
PILCHUCK GLASS
2002
Three color woodcut
30 x 22 inches
Printed on handmade paper, edition of 8, plus 2 TP, 1 AP
Terry Chastain
Pilchuck Glass School, Stanwood, Washington

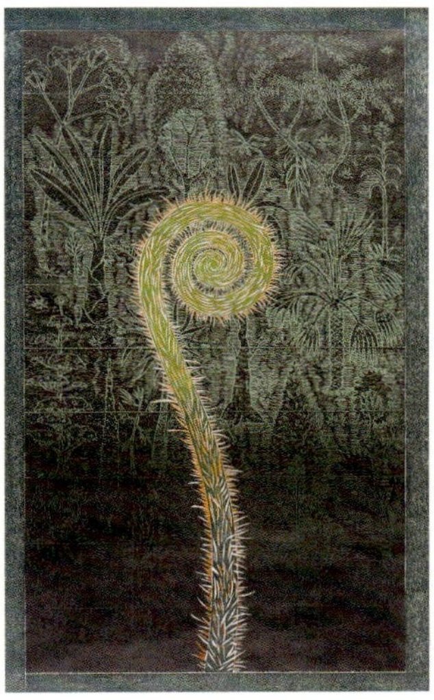

62.
BOTANICA, edition 10/15
2003
Nine-color woodcut
62 x 37 inches
Printed on White Thai Mulberry paper, edition of 15, plus 5 AP, 2 workshop proofs, 2 PP, 1 TP, 2 Patron's impressions, 1 BAT, 1 Archive impression
Bud Shark assisted by Evan Colbert
Shark's Ink., Lyons, Colorado
Collection of Jordan D. Schnitzer
2003.42

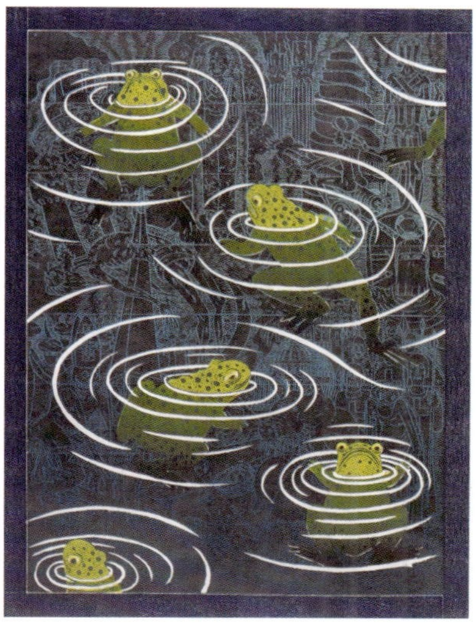

63.
THE REFLECTING POOL, edition 4/10
2004
Fourteen-color woodcut
50 x 37 inches
Printed on White Thai Mulberry paper, edition of 10, plus 4 AP 2 WP, 2 PP, 2 Patron's impressions, 1 BAT, 1 Archive impression
Bud Shark assisted by Evan Colbert
Shark's Ink., Lyons, Colorado
Collection of the Jordan Schnitzer Family Foundation
2004.7

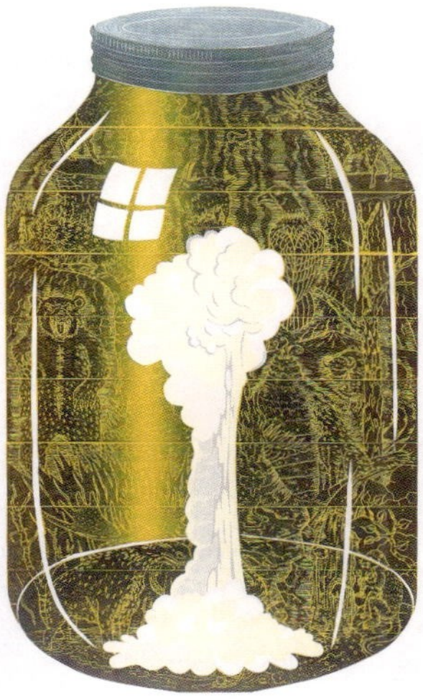

64.
THE PRESERVE, edition 6/15
2005
Eleven-color woodcut
62 x 37 inches
Printed on White Thai Mulberry paper, edition of 15, plus 5 AP, 3 WP, 2 PP, 1 TP, 2 Patron's impressions, 1 Archive impression
Bud Shark assisted by Evan Colbert
Shark's Ink., Lyons, Colorado
Collection of Jordan D. Schnitzer
2005.103

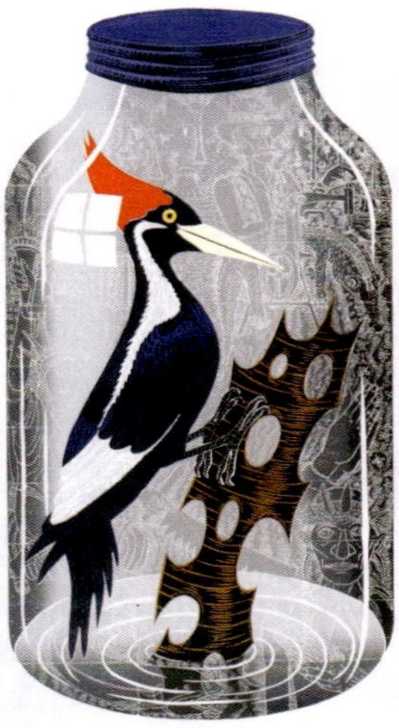

65.
THE SINGER TRACT, edition 6/15
2005
Eleven-color woodcut with pochoir
67¾ x 37 inches
Printed on White Thai Mulberry paper, edition of 15, plus 5 AP, 2 WP, 2 PP, 2 TP, 2 Patron's impressions, 1 Archive impression
Bud Shark assisted by Evan Colbert
Shark's Ink., Lyons, Colorado
Collection of Jordan D. Schnitzer
2005.167

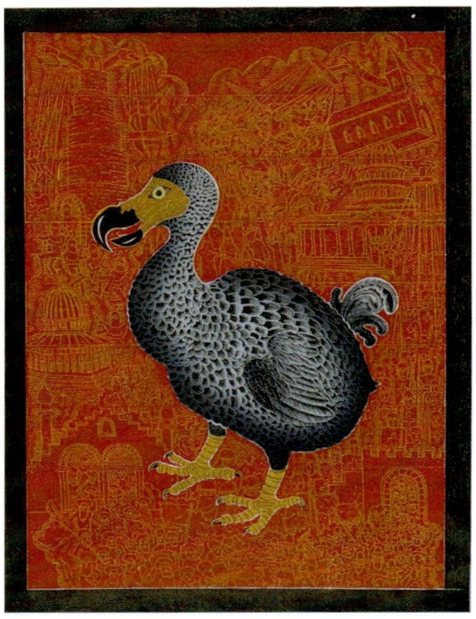

66.
PHOENIX RISING, edition 1/10
2006
Seven-color woodcut with pochoir
50 x 37 inches
Printed on White Thai Mulberry paper, edition of 10, plus 4 AP, 2 WP, 2 PP, 2 TP, 2 Patron's impressions, 1 Archive impression
Bud Shark assisted by Evan Colbert
Shark's Ink., Lyons, Colorado
Collection of Jordan D. Schnitzer
2006.431

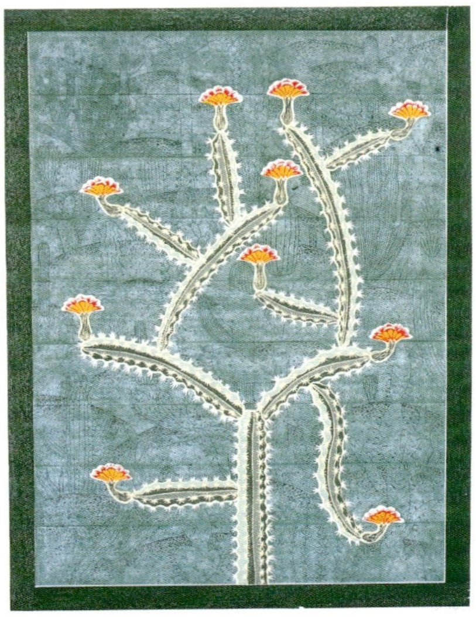

67.
NEEDLES, edition 8/15
2007
Seven-color woodcut
50 x 37 inches
Printed on unbleached Thai Mulberry paper, edition of 15, plus 5 AP, 3 WP, 2 PP, 3 TP, 2 Patron's impressions, 1 BAT, 1 Archive impression
Bud Shark assisted by Evan Colbert
Shark's Ink., Lyons, Colorado
Collection of Jordan D. Schnitzer
2007.296

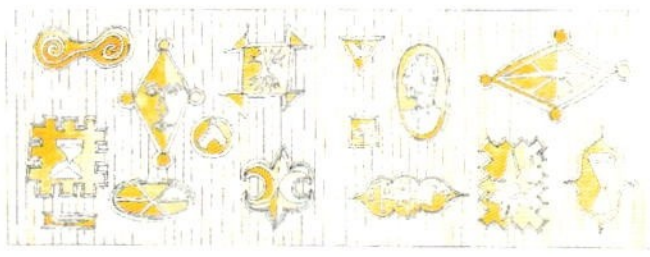

68.
PILCHUCK LEFT TO RIGHT
2007
Sandblasted glass block
22 x 30 inches
Printed on Rives BFK, hand tinted with gouache, edition of 10, plus 1 AP, 1 PP, 1 presentation proof
Kelvin Mason, with tinting by John Buck and Dawn Ahlert
Pilchuck Glass School, Stanwood, Washington

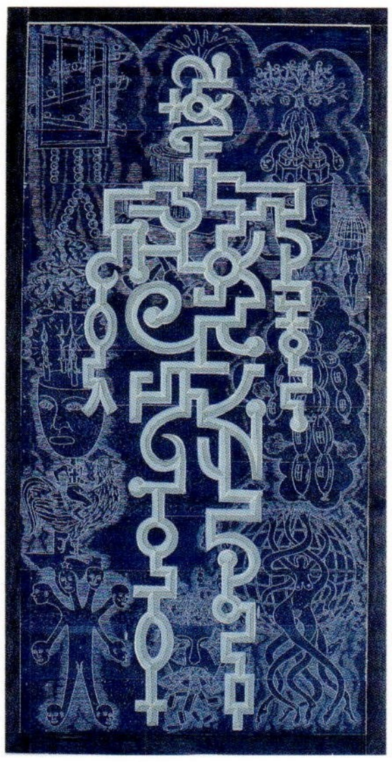

69.
THE NIGHT PRISM, edition 4/20
2007
Four color woodcut
74 ½ x 37 inches
Printed on White Thai Mulberry paper, edition of 20, plus 5 AP, 3 workshop proofs, 2 PP, 3 TP, 2 Patron's impressions, 1 BAT, 1 Archive impression
Shark's Ink., Lyons, Colorado
Collection of Jordan D. Schnitzer
2008.3

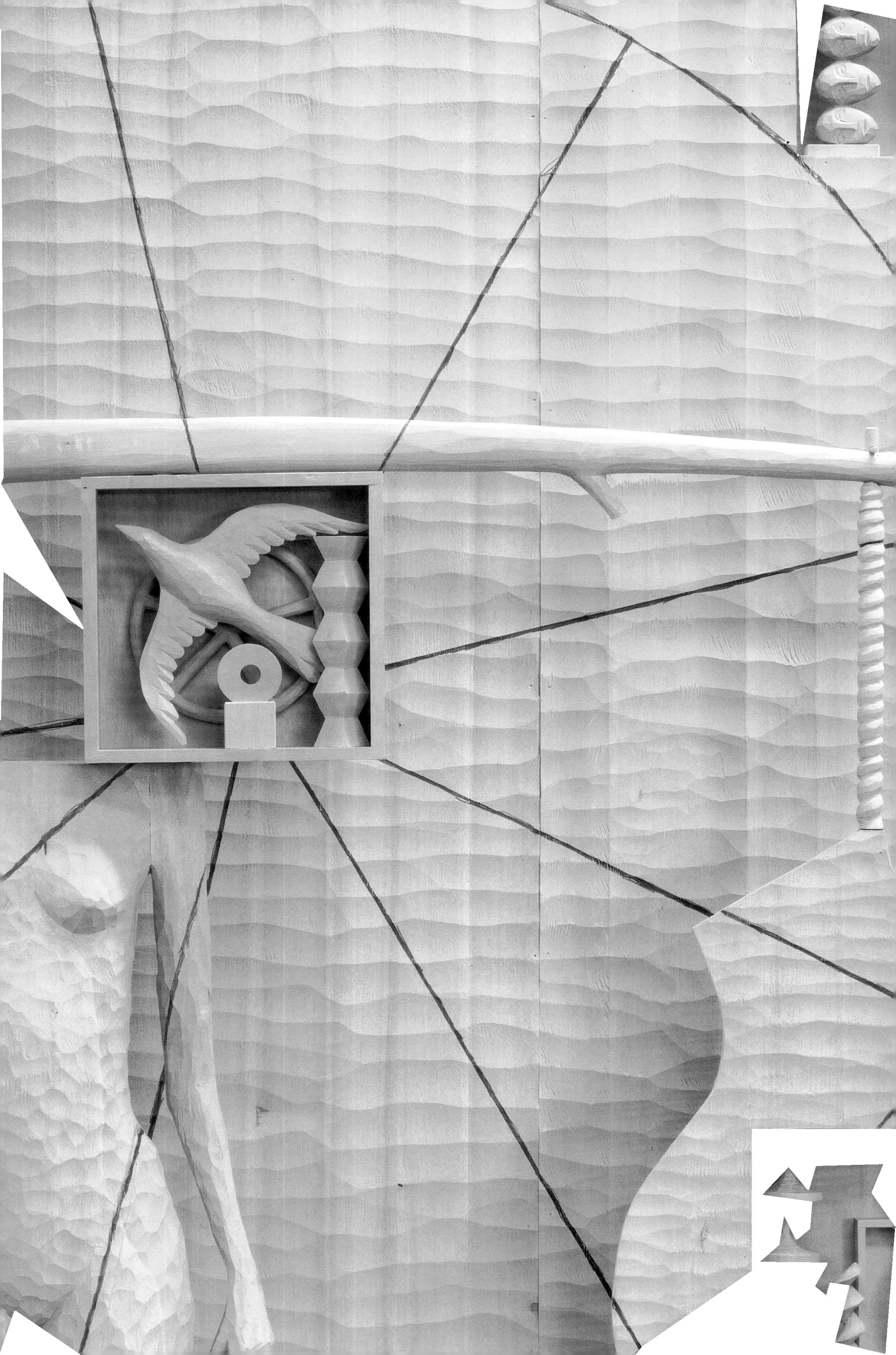

About the Collector

When I first saw John's work I was instantly taken by the brilliant complexity of his themes and techniques, working with wood blocks. His work creates an enchanting state of wonder for me.
—Jordan Schnitzer

Jordan Schnitzer grew up in Portland, Oregon, graduated from the University of Oregon, and in 1976 earned his doctorate degree from the Northwestern School of Law, Lewis & Clark College. Today he is President and CEO of his family's business, Harsch Investment Properties, the largest privately held real estate investment and management company in the Pacific Northwest. He is also President of the Jordan Schnitzer Family Foundation.

His passionate commitment to the arts and support for community have grown over five decades. "I had the wonderful privilege of being exposed to the world of business through my father, Harold Schnitzer," he says, "who helped me learn and love our real estate business. And it was my mother, Arlene Schnitzer, who introduced me to the world of art and from whom I learned how important art and culture are in our lives and our communities." He began collecting art of all mediums at an early age, first selecting works by Pacific Northwest contemporary artists and later expanding to add other major American artists; today he has brought together work by more than 550 artists. He is best known for his interest in works on paper and in this area his personal and family foundation collections now hold more than 5,000 prints.

The first exhibition from his personal collection at the University of Oregon in Eugene, Oregon, in 1995 was an epiphany for him. He walked into the gallery alone and for the first time saw pieces from his collection on the wall. Soon, people of all ages began to arrive and to engage with the works. "I realized at that very moment how important it might be if I were to create a collection of art that could be shared with the public."

From that singular experience a vision evolved, reflecting a profound shift of purpose from private collector to steward of artworks, marked by a wish to share the collection with audiences young and old. At the same time he understood that shrinking budgets increasingly made it difficult for small- and mid-sized museums to collect or even to borrow works of stature.

He is particularly concerned with bringing contemporary art to underserved audiences, especially audiences in smaller cities.

To that end, Jordan Schnitzer developed an outreach program that includes loaning works from the two collections to museums nationwide, as well as helping to fund educational programs—including curriculum based on exhibitions' themes and content—tailored to community needs. In time, as the collections grew, more museums and curators began to inquire about showing them. In the last seven years alone over twenty exhibitions have been organized out of the collection by curators throughout the country, and works have been loaned to an additional twenty-five national and international exhibitions. Many hundreds of thousands of visitors have had the opportunity to enjoy and study works in the collections in more than seventy-five museums. New traveling exhibitions showcasing five prominent American artists are in the works as of this writing.

At its heart, the impulse to look at and live with the works of artists of our time, the imaginative innovators of the twentieth and twenty-first centuries, grew from Jordan Schnitzer's desire to heighten his own sense of participation in and close observance of art in his daily life. This passion has engendered a significant and deep resource of artwork others can experience directly for themselves. And in all this, his personal response has also been transformed beyond gathering works of art. As an art curator once said, "Most people collect to own. Jordan collects to share." This exhibition and its accompanying book offer rich evidence of his passion and the wisdom of his decision.

Artist's Dedication and Acknowledgments

This book is dedicated to my friend Roy De Forest, *The Great Dingo.*

I would like to thank Jordan Schnitzer for his continued interest and support of my artwork and my career. Jordan is a true patron of the arts and this book would never have happened without his contribution and enthusiasm. I also thank Jordan's staff, Kandis Brewer Nunn and Catherine Malone, for their help with facilitating this book and the accompanying exhibition. Thank you to Greg Kucera who was also instrumental in the logistics of this project.

Thank you Ben Mitchell, our orchestrator, for your curatorial expertise and your efforts to coordinate and curate this book and the exhibition associated with it. I want to thank Jack Lemon of Landfall Press for giving me the opportunity to make some of my first editions. I wish to thank Bud Shark who has worked with me continuously since 1983 creating the majority of my prints. Our creative relationship has developed into a collaborative team where I create the problems and Bud solves them. I would like to thank John Yau and Eleanor Heartney for traveling all the way to my studio in Montana to experience my work in the environment from where it comes. It's an honor to have their insights included in this book.

For over twenty-five years my friend and colleague Guy Klaas has assisted me in building my work from the basics of assembly to the most complex of structures. I wish to give special thanks to Guy for all these years of dedication and support for my artwork and my family.

Thank you to Diana Fuller and Dorothy Goldeen for exhibiting my work early in my career. I would also like to thank Roberta Lieberman for her "sharp eye." Thanks to Carlo Lamagna for my first New York show, and my current galleries: Greg Kucera Gallery, Seattle; Zolla/Lieberman Gallery, Chicago; Imago Galleries, Palm Desert; DC Moore Gallery, New York; Robischon Gallery, Denver; David Floria Gallery, Aspen; Anne Reed Gallery, Ketchum; and Gallery Paule Anglim, San Francisco.

My family deserves a big thank you for being the core of my inspiration. Thank you to my wife, Deborah Butterfield, who is the mother of my two sons Wilder and Hunter, for holding my hand and bandaging it too. I thank my grandfather and father, Emil and Woodrow Buck, and my brothers Mike and Gene for teaching me how to carve.

Thank you Dawn Ahlert for all you do. And finally, I'd like to express thanks to my employees and support staff who allow me to concentrate on my art.

JOHN BUCK
Bozeman, Montana

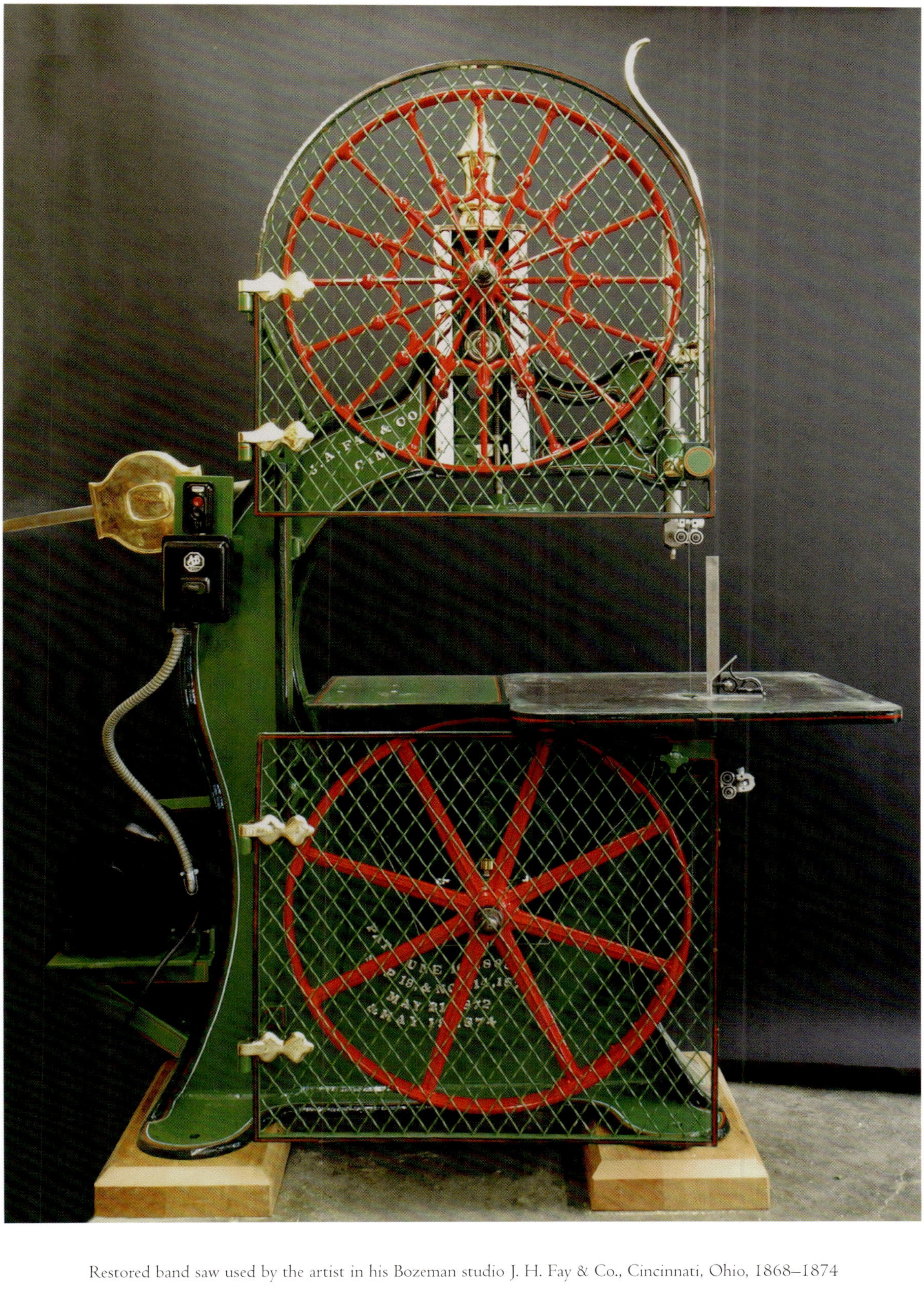

Restored band saw used by the artist in his Bozeman studio J. H. Fay & Co., Cincinnati, Ohio, 1868–1874

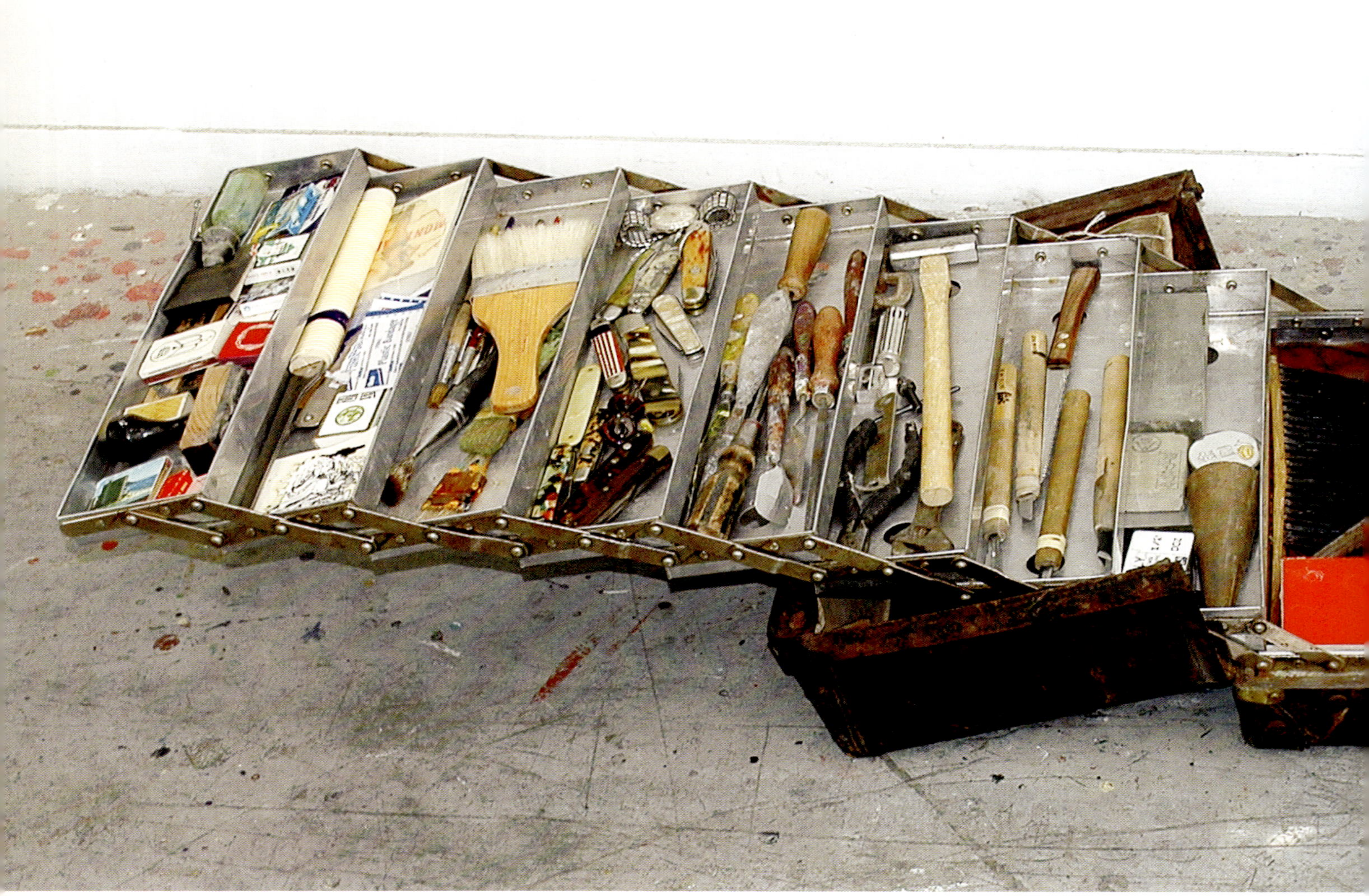

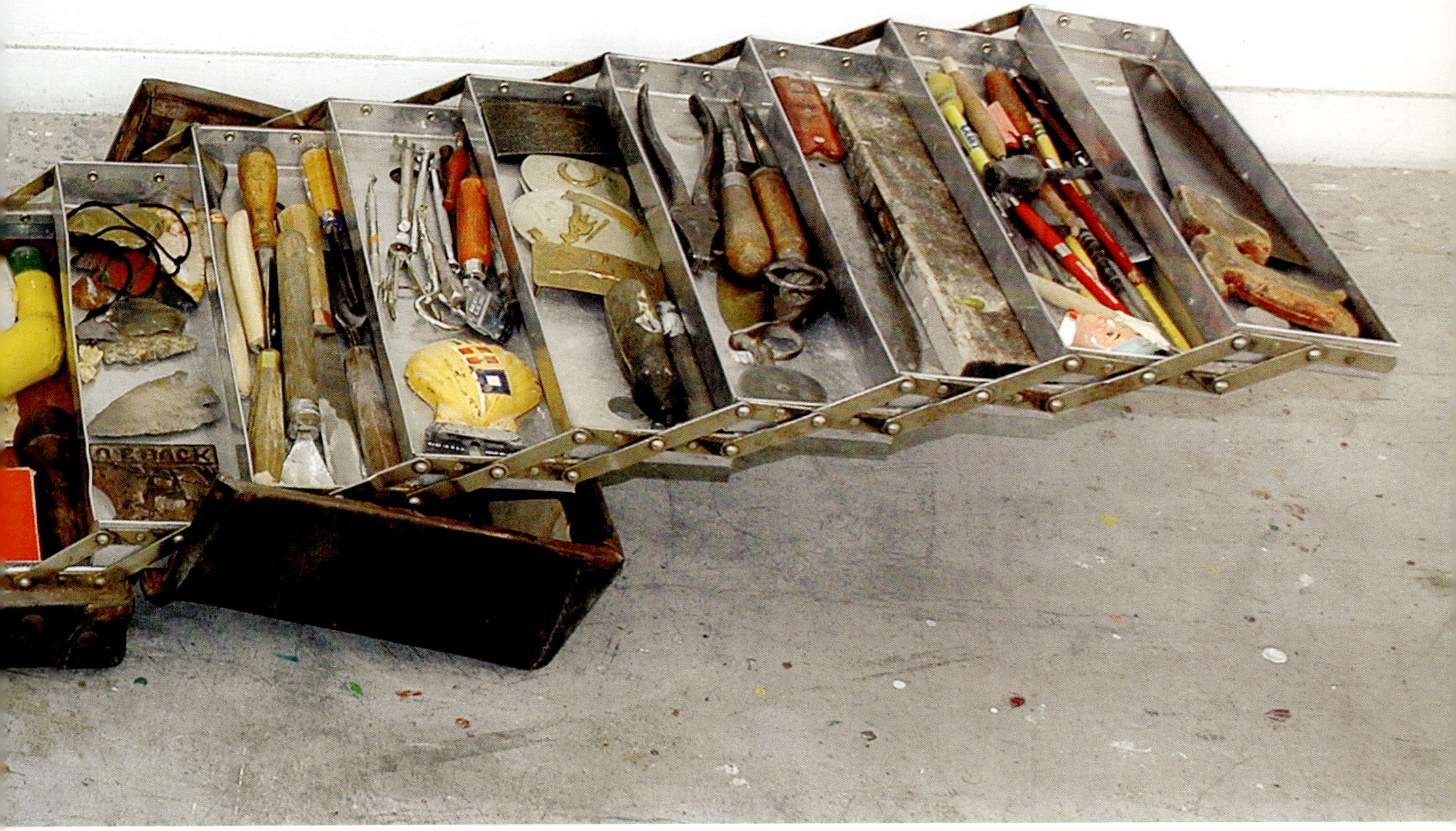

Antique tool case with a selection of the artist's tools

THIS EXHIBITION AND PUBLICATION WERE MADE POSSIBLE BY A MAJOR GRANT FROM THE JORDAN SCHNITZER FAMILY FOUNDATION.

ADDITIONAL SUPPORT PROVIDED BY:

The Spokesman-Review (Spokane)

Scot and Sue Bradley
DC Moore Gallery, New York
Gallery Paule Anglim, San Francisco
Greg Kucera Gallery, Seattle
Imago Gallery, Palm Desert
Robischon Gallery, Denver
Zolla/Lieberman Gallery, Chicago

The museum's programs are supported by the Washington State Arts Commission and the National Endowment for the Arts

WASHINGTON STATE ARTS COMMISSION

NATIONAL ENDOWMENT FOR THE ARTS

Photographer credits

Dawn Ahlert: Frontispiece; 9; 10; 22; 25; 26; 90; 93; 115; 116; 132 no. 60; 133 no. 61; 134 nos. 67, 68;141; 142–143.

Anderson Ranch Arts Center: 121 no. 14; 132 no. 59.

Experimental Workshop. San Francisco: 119 no. 7.

Rob Outlaw: 118 no. 2;119 nos. 6, 8; 120 no. 11; 121 nos. 13, 15; 122 nos. 18, 19; 123 nos. 22, 23; 124 no. 25; 125 no. 31; 127 no. 37; 130 nos. 50, 51, 52; 131 nos. 53, 55; 132 no. 57, 61; 89.

Barbara Stark: 112.

Strode Photographic, LLC, Portland, Oregon: Front cover; 6; 14; 15; 17; 18; 21; 24; 28; 30; 31; 33; 35; 38; 43; 44–47; 49–53; 55–57; 59; 61; 63; 64; 67; 69–71; 73–75; 77; 79; 80–85; 87; 89; 91; 93; 118 nos. 3, 4; 119 no. 5; 120 nos. 9–12; 122 nos. 17, 20; 123 nos. 21, 24; 124 nos. 26–28; 125 nos. 29, 30, 32; 126 nos. 33–36; 127 nos. 38–40; 128 nos. 41–44; 129 nos. 45–48; 130 no. 49; 131 nos. 54, 56;132 no. 58; 133 nos. 62–64; 134 nos. 65, 66; 135 no. 69; back cover.

Sun Valley Center for the Arts & Humanities: 121 No. 16.